THE
MORNIN
BREAK

THE MORNING BREAKS

The Trial of Angela Davis

Bettina Aptheker

SECOND EDITION

Cornell University Press
Ithaca and London

First published 1999 by Cornell University Press
First printing, Cornell Paperbacks, 1999

Printed in the United States of America

Library of Congress Cataloging-in-Publication Data

Aptheker, Bettina.
    The morning breaks : the trial of Angela Davis / Bettina Aptheker.
—2nd ed.
    p.   cm.
    ISBN-13: 978-0-8014-8597-8 (pbk. : alk. paper)
    1. Davis, Angela Yvonne, 1944—Trials, litigation, etc.   2. Trials
(Conspiracy)—California—San Jose.   I. Title.
KF224.D3A68 1999
345.73'02523—dc21   98-52220

Cornell University Press strives to use environmentally responsible
suppliers and materials to the fullest extent possible in the publishing
of its books. Such materials include vegetable-based, low-VOC inks
and acid-free papers that are recycled, totally chlorine-free, or partly
composed of nonwood fibers. For further information, visit our website
at www.cornellpress.cornell.edu.

Paperback printing   10 9 8 7 6 5 4 3 2

This book is dedicated to my mother
Fay P. Aptheker (1905–1999)
To her strength, her integrity,
and her wonderful laughter

I dedicate this new edition
in loving memory to

Kendra Alexander
Franklin Alexander
Victoria Mercado
and
Mary M. Timothy

CONTENTS

PREFACE TO THE FIRST EDITION

This book is a personal account of my experiences in the movement to free Angela Davis. I have tried to present an historically accurate record of the events leading up to her trial, and of the struggle to save her life.

The book is based upon my personal recollections and notes, as well as the files of the National United Committee to Free Angela Davis, and the transcripts of the proceedings and appeals in the trials of James McClain, Ruchell Magee, Fleeta Drumgo, John Clutchette, George Lester Jackson and Angela Davis. News stories by Mark Allen, Juan Lopez, Ellis Goldberg and Robert Kaufman in the *People's World* and the *Daily World* between August 1970 and June 1972 were also extremely helpful.

For those who may be interested in further research or information on the *Davis* case, the files of the National United Committee to Free Angela Davis have been preserved in the archives of the Main Library at Stanford University in Palo Alto, California. This collection includes tens of thousands of letters received by the Committee and Ms. Davis from people throughout the world. The complete transcript of the Davis trial, including all appeals and legal memoranda, have been preserved in the Meiklejohn Civil Liberties Library in Berkeley, California.

I am deeply indebted to a great many people who read this manuscript in whole or in part, and offered invaluable suggestions and criticisms; and to members of the staff of the National United

Committee to Free Angela Davis, and to comrades and friends and members of my family—all of whom offered their time and energy in recalling events and their impressions of them, and in providing me with much background material. Without their help, encouragement and support this book could not have been written.

My appreciation then, to: John Abt, Franklin Alexander, Kendra Alexander, Anthony Amsterdam, Fay P. Aptheker, Herbert Aptheker, Robert A. Baker, Archie Brown, Margaret Burnham, Angela Y. Davis, Ellis Goldberg, Fania Davis Jordan, Jack Kurzweil, Albert J. Lima, Helen Lima, Susana Magdaleno, Victoria Mercado, Charlene Mitchell, David Newman, Gary Schuller, Jessica L. Treuhaft, Gloria Trevino, Jean Stein, Margaret Wilkinson and Henry Winston.

I wish to express a special word of gratitude to Mary M. Timothy. As foreperson of the jury that acquitted Angela Davis, and ultimately as colleague and friend, she has provided me with a wholly unique and steady source of insight, enthusiasm and encouragement.

INTRODUCTION TO THE
CORNELL PAPERBACKS EDITION

A ngela Davis was brought to trial in 1972 in San Jose, California, on charges of murder, kidnapping, and conspiracy. Davis, placed on the FBI's "Ten Most Wanted" list and designated "armed and dangerous," had been arrested in New York City on October 13, 1970. President Richard M. Nixon congratulated the FBI on its "capture of the dangerous terrorist, Angela Davis," a sentiment echoed by Ronald Reagan, then governor of California, and by an editorial in the *New York Times* (October 16, 1970). Images of a handcuffed Davis appeared on the covers of *Newsweek* and other leading journals. News media vied to give maximum coverage to her case. Davis, an African American Communist, faced the death penalty at the time of her arrest. She had been a lecturer in the philosophy department at UCLA and was a doctoral candidate in philosophy at the University of California, San Diego.

The Black community was virtually unanimous in its support of Angela Davis. Her arrest came only a year and a half after the assassination of Dr. Martin Luther King, Jr., and in the wake of ghetto uprisings that had seen hundreds of African American people wounded and killed. Likewise, campus civil rights and antiwar protests had resulted in the wounding and killing of scores of students from Jackson State University in Mississippi to UC Berkeley. The Ohio National Guard had shot and killed students at Kent State University in May 1970, only five months before Davis's arrest.

At the time of her arrest Angela Davis was a member of the Che-Lumumba Club of the U.S. Communist Party in Los Angeles. This was an all-Black collective named in memory of Che Guevara, a hero of the Cuban Revolution, and Patrice Lumumba, the leader of the Congolese National Liberation Movement. Davis was also closely associated with the Los Angeles chapter of the Black Panther Party (BPP).

The Davis trial unfolded as state and federal authorities coordinated a nationwide assault against the Black Panther Party. They raided BPP offices, confiscated papers, and destroyed equipment. Police agents infiltrated the BPP itself. Many individuals fell victim to this intrigue. Those killed included Fred Hampton, Mark Clark, Bobby Hutton, and Jon Huggins. Among those wounded by police and imprisoned were Assata Shakur and Huey P. Newton, cofounder of the BPP. Others stood trial in the media spotlight. Ericka Huggins was tried for murder in New Haven, Connecticut, and acquitted. Bobby Seale, also a cofounder of the BPP, was tried for conspiracy in Chicago for his participation in protests at the 1968 Democratic National Convention. When he protested the proceedings, Seale was bound and gagged in the courtroom. He was acquitted along with his seven (white) codefendants. A subsequent congressional investigation determined that the Chicago police themselves had rioted and been responsible for countless injuries, including the beating of Dan Rather, a leading CBS reporter.

Geronimo Pratt, a BPP member and Vietnam veteran, was tried for murder in Los Angeles and was convicted. Pratt was released in 1997 after twenty-seven years in prison when his attorneys presented new, incontrovertible evidence of his innocence. The Los Angeles Police Department and the FBI, they contended, had been aware of this evidence at the time of Pratt's arrest and had suppressed it. A year after his release, Pratt sued the FBI and LAPD for false arrest. Mumia Abu-Jamal, a journalist who covered the Panthers' activities in Philadelphia and served as their minister of information, remains on death row, convicted of killing a white police officer. Appeals are pending. His book, *Death Blossoms,* is exemplary of writings by political prisoners.

Angela Davis was a founding member of the Soledad Brothers Defense Committee. The Soledad Brothers were three Black prisoners accused of killing a guard at Soledad Prison, near Salinas, California, in January 1970. George Jackson, Fleeta Drumgo, and John Clutchette were activists in a movement for prisoners' rights. Angela Davis knew the families of all the accused men. She was particularly close to George Jackson's family and knew his younger brother, Jonathan. She had attended pretrial hearings of the Soledad Brothers, and was widely and publicly identified with their defense. She had corresponded with George Jackson. Sometime in the spring of 1970 she and George had become personally committed to each other.

THESE ARE the specific events that led to the prosecution of Angela Davis. On August 7, 1970, Jonathan Jackson, an African American high school student who was 17 years old, took over a courtroom in Marin County, California. He was heavily armed. A trial was in progress. The defendant in that trial was James McClain, a San Quentin prisoner accused of attempting to assault a guard. Ruchell Magee, another San Quentin prisoner, was on the witness stand testifying for McClain, who was acting as his own counsel. A third prisoner, William Christmas, was waiting to testify. The judge was Harold Haley; the prosecutor was Gary Thomas, who was Judge Haley's son-in-law. All the prisoners were Black. The judge, the prosecutor, and the jurors were white.

Jonathan Jackson armed Magee, McClain, and Christmas. They took five hostages: the judge, the prosecutor, and three women jurors. A procession of armed prisoners and hostages left the courtroom and made its way out of the building and to a van parked in an adjoining lot. Everyone climbed inside. Jonathan Jackson was driving. He stopped at a roadblock hastily erected by sheriff's deputies. As the van stopped, San Quentin prison guards opened fire. Jackson, McClain, and Christmas were killed. Judge Haley was killed. Ruchell Magee was wounded, along with the prosecutor and one of the jurors. At the Davis trial it was established that the San Quentin guards (and Gary Thomas, the prosecutor) had killed and wounded everyone. Jonathan Jackson was the younger brother of the Soledad Brother George Jackson. Several of the guns used by Jonathan were legally registered to Angela Davis.

To understand the Davis case is to understand the labyrinth

of events that led up to August 7. In this book I attempt to lay out the sequence as clearly as possible. The book's "Prologue" moves from UCLA to Soledad to San Quentin as the elements of the story unfold. The book documents the routine harassment, beatings, and killings of Black prisoners. It puts into context the decision of Black activists, including Angela Davis and the Che-Lumumba Club, to arm themselves. Angela herself was the recipient of numerous death threats.

The book tells the story of the worldwide movement for Angela's freedom and the struggle to win her release on bail. The last section details the trial itself, from the selection of the jury to the collapse of the prosecution's case and the very limited "pinpoint" rebuttal mounted by the defense. For this new edition I have also included an "Afterword" to account for the principals in the case since the trial.

The Davis trial commenced on February 28, 1972; it lasted just over three months. The prosecution presented 104 witnesses and introduced 203 items in evidence. The defense presented twelve witnesses in two and a half days. On June 4, 1972, 597 days after the arrest of Angela Davis and after thirteen hours of deliberation spread over three days, the jury returned a verdict of not guilty on all counts.

ANGELA AND I have been friends since high school. A year before her arrest I was involved in efforts to reverse a decision by the University of California Board of Regents to fire her from her teaching position at UCLA. When she was arrested I joined her defense committee. I, too, was a member of the U.S. Communist Party. I had been one of the leaders of the 1964 Free Speech Movement at the University of California, Berkeley, where I was a student. I had been very active in both the movement against the war in Vietnam and the civil rights movement. When the attacks began against the Black Panther Party, many of us stood outside the Panthers' national headquarters in Oakland. We believed that as white people we might serve as a protective shield to prevent further violence.

At the time of the trial I was married to Jack Kurzweil, who was an assistant professor of electrical engineering at San Jose State

University. We had a son, Joshua. He was three years old when Angela was arrested. Our family lived in San Jose, where Angela's trial was eventually to take place. Our home became an informal headquarters for Angela and her attorneys, friends, and family. Fania Davis, Angela's sister, and her infant daughter, Eisa, lived with us. Just as the Davis case erupted, my husband was given a terminal year at the university. He was fired because of our political affiliations and activities. The *Kurzweil* case was won in federal court, and Jack was awarded tenure the summer before Angela's trial began. Our attorney, Doris Brin Walker, was also one of the trial lawyers in the *Davis* case.

A member of the staff of the National United Committee to Free Angela Davis (NUCFAD), I was appointed by the court, at Angela's request, as one of five "legal investigators" for the defense. In this capacity, I was allowed to meet with Angela in jail unencumbered by specified visiting hours or by attorneys. I worked on many aspects of the case. Angela and I also coedited a book, *If They Come in the Morning: Voices of Resistance*. Each of us contributed essays analyzing the U.S. prison system as an agency of political repression. We documented the cases of many political prisoners, and included letters, poetry, and essays they had written. The first paperback edition of our book sold 400,000 copies in the United States and was widely translated and published abroad. I attended every day of the trial and participated in the debates about our legal and political strategies. I wrote this book in the year after Angela's acquittal. The story poured out of me. While I felt enormous gratitude for Angela's freedom, I was also overwhelmed by grief and rage at the system that had imprisoned her and taken the lives of so many.

I MUST MAKE one significant correction. The book gives the impression that the Communist Party was unanimous in its support of Angela Davis. That is not true. I did not write about the controversy at the time because I believed I needed to protect the Party from its critics on both the left and the right. Here is a brief account of what happened.

Although the Communist Party provided Angela with counsel at the time of her arrest, its National Committee, meeting in

New York in March 1971, was sharply divided. (The National Committee consisted of 120 people elected at the Party's national convention. I had been elected to it in 1966. We set national policy.) Most of the comrades had never heard of the Soledad Brothers and knew nothing about the prison struggles. They were deeply suspicious of the Black Panther Party, and most categorically rejected its policy of armed self-defense. They believed that Jonathan Jackson was a terrorist (or, in leftist jargon, an "adventurist") and that any defense of Angela required a repudiation of his actions. Although muffled in their dissent, a few comrades wanted the Party to dissociate itself completely from Angela, and among them some (privately) advocated her expulsion.

Comrades from the Che-Lumumba Club and others of us familiar with the issues spoke again and again at the National Committee meeting, laying out the facts of the case, explaining the Soledad Brothers' defense, Angela's involvement, Jonathan's frustration, and his commitment to his brother and to the movement among Black prisoners. We urged a middle course for Angela's defense, neither advocating nor condemning Jonathan's action, but insisting that it was understandable in the context of his life. All of us, including Angela, believed we would jeopardize her defense if we simply condemned Jonathan. We felt that we must distinguish our understandings from those of the prosecution, which saw Jon simply as a terrorist.

We also tried to show that "terrorism" is historically constituted, and is also a matter of class and racial positioning. For example, we said, one would hardly condemn the slave revolts of Denmark Vesey and Nat Turner, among hundreds of others, as terrorist, although that is precisely what the slaveholders felt them to be. Later, as if to prove our point, Ruchell Magee, the surviving San Quentin prisoner of the August 7 carnage, requested that the judge read the Thirteenth Amendment to the U.S. Constitution (abolishing slavery) to the jury at the end of his trial. His motion was denied. But Magee felt himself to be a slave, falsely imprisoned, deprived of his constitutional rights. He claimed the right to *take* his freedom. At his trial, several months after Angela's, eleven of the twelve jurors agreed with him.

Millions of words were flung about during our National Committee meeting. Unfortunately, the issue under debate was posed as a tactical choice between "individual acts of terrorism" and "the building of a mass movement." A few of us tried to point out that the hundreds who came to pay their respects to Jonathan Jackson at his funeral *were* a mass movement. We certainly wanted to organize one to win Angela's freedom.

In the end, these issues were never resolved within the Communist Party. As the case proceeded, our comrades put aside their differences and worked with undiminished intensity for Angela's freedom. In court we presented our case in accord with Angela's wishes and with our understanding of the realities that had informed Jonathan's life. This is especially evident in Angela's opening statement to the jury, in our cross-examination of key prosecution witnesses (e.g., the San Quentin guards), and in our closing argument.

MORE THAN twenty-five years have passed since Angela's trial. A few thoughts in retrospect seem appropriate. What struck me most forcibly as I recalled this debate about terrorism at the National Committee meeting was the extent to which the revolutionary rhetoric of the times equated manhood with guns and armed struggle. None of us saw this. Now it seems to me simply a mirror image of white male projections of manhood, and a very distorted view of masculinity. This view, however, has been widely promulgated by the (white-controlled) mass media and is especially evident in many Hollywood films. In contemporary times this view of masculinity has contributed in no small measure to the escalation of gang violence.

In the late 1960s and 1970s we women on the left and in the Communist Party also equated our own liberation with armed insurrection. Posters picturing Vietnamese, Cuban, Algerian, and Chinese women carrying rifles or in guerrilla uniforms adorned the walls of our homes and offices. We believed that the national liberation and socialist revolutions would, by definition, result in "women's equality." Even our understanding of equality was extremely limited. We saw it in masculinist terms, women orbiting their men in the struggle. Men determined the policies and strategies, and women implemented them "equally" with men. We accepted the patriarchal vision of a manhood of the oppressed vested with weaponry. We strove to prove our equality with it by ourselves bearing arms. This vestment so blinded us that we did not see that the nuclear arms race, which we so vigorously opposed, was simply another manifestation of the same process. We did not then understand the parallels between the militarism of patriarchy on a global scale and as it was enacted locally.

We had little understanding of our own history as women, of our own forms of resistance: to racism, patriarchy, colonialism, war. Such resistance had always been rooted in the dailiness of our lives, in our struggles for survival, for dignity, and for the future of our children. We had as yet no vision of the autonomy necessary for our movement to define a specifically women's liberation, to contest men's continuing violence against women, our degradation and subordination.

My book on the trial ends with an allusion to socialism as the end of oppression. (I meant racial oppression.) In 1973 that was what I believed. By 1981 I had left the Communist Party. I was committed to a different understanding of women's liberation than the slogans of "equality" advanced by the Party. I was also living openly as a lesbian with my partner, Kate Miller, and our three children. Although little was said to me personally, many in the Communist Party, and especially those in the highest echelons of its national leadership, responded to the gay and lesbian movements with conservative, profamily, homophobic rhetoric. By 1989, socialism itself had collapsed in the Soviet Union and Eastern Europe. It soon became apparent that European socialism had not healed the wounds caused by racial, ethnic, and anti-Semitic hatreds. By 1990, the U.S. Communist Party, too, had splintered.

A SECOND ERROR in my original text is more technical, but it is significant. In revoking the death penalty in February 1972, and thus paving the way for Angela Davis's release on bail, the California State Supreme Court did *not* hold it to be cruel and unusual punishment (as I claimed). Rather, the court held that in the penalty phase of the trial in the *particular* case before it, the jury had not been given any standard by which to determine its verdict. These were much narrower grounds for appeal. The Supreme Court decision did end executions in the state for several years, but California has since reinstated the death penalty.

As I REREAD this book on the trial and recalled the details of racist violence in the prisons and in society, I was appalled. Very little has changed. Yes, there is a larger and growing middle and even upper class among people of color. Yes, affirmative action had some success. There is, however, a vast underbelly of suffering in the inner cities, in the barrios and rural backwaters, on Indian reservations, and in the prisons. There is a haunting continuity between the killings and persecutions of the 1960s and 1970s and the realities of racial violence as we approach the millennium.

The police beating of Rodney King in Los Angeles in 1991 was not an aberration. Such assaults happen in ghettos and barrios across the country every day. The aberration was that an alert and courageous citizen filmed it. That is the only reason the officers were brought to trial. It is almost unbelievable that Rodney King, face down on the ground and begging for mercy, was still perceived as a threat by an all-white jury viewing the video. In that first trial, the officers were exonerated. Of course, the ghetto exploded in its aftermath. Only after a second, federal trial was some semblance of justice achieved.

The Cabinet and other appointments made by Bill Clinton (regardless of what else we may wish to say about him) were the most integrated by race and gender in the history of this country. A Republican-controlled Congress went after almost every person of color on charges of "corruption," many of them so minor as to be ludicrous. They attacked the African American attorney Lani Guinier, who was proposed to head the Civil Rights Division of the Justice Department, because she would have actually enforced affirmative action. And they forced the resignation of the surgeon general, Joycelyn Elders, an African American physician, because she talked openly about sex.

These congressional politics reflect the racism at every other level of government. The reversal of affirmative action in California and elsewhere, the effort to barricade the Mexican border, the attacks on bilingual education and on undocumented immigrants (even preventing pregnant women in California from receiving prenatal care), the dismantling of the welfare system, the failure to honor the sovereignty of Native Americans, and the cutbacks in funding for health and education on the reservations, all evidence a pervasive racism. The decisions are couched in the cultured and reasoned language of suited legislators and public officials. The damage done to human beings, and especially to women and children, is incalculable.

ACCORDING TO Troy Duster, a sociology professor at UC Berkeley, African Americans constituted 7.5 percent of California's population in 1997 and 38 percent of its prison population. In 1984, there were eleven state prisons in California. By 1997, sixteen new prisons had been built, and eight more are slated for completion by 2002. By 1997, fifteen thousand people, most of them men of color, had been sentenced to life imprisonment in California under the "three-strike" law, which mandates a life sentence upon conviction for a third felony. The state with the next highest number of prisoners sentenced to life under a similar provision is Washington, with 63. Even given the differences in population between California and Washington, the California figure is very distressing. On the national level, one in three Black males between the ages of 20 and 29 is under the control of the criminal justice system. One in fifteen is incarcerated. Ninety-four percent of the crack offenders in federal courts are African American. These are the conditions twenty-eight years after Jonathan Jackson entered the courtroom in Marin County and Ruchell Magee acted to take his freedom. We do not have a domestic policy in the United States. We have a domestic war.

As long as white people, in their majority, see racism as either a minor inconvenience or the figment of a colored imagination, we are all complicit in its worst excesses. In this sense, too, we were all responsible for Jonathan Jackson's actions, and we are responsible for the revolts and uprisings that continue to erupt. Those of us who are white know that if we lived under these same conditions, and if our families had lived under them for generations, we too would rise up. Until these conditions are changed, until white people in overwhelming numbers join with people of color to rise up against racism, this terrible suffering cannot be ended, and these wounds cannot be healed.

WINNING THE FREEDOM of Angela Davis was a singular achievement. Three conditions were decisive: the intervention of world public opinion; the unanimity of the Black community, achieved because of the still persisting strength of the 1960s civil rights movement; and the organizational coherence of the U.S. Communist Party. In the wake of the worldwide movement to free Angela, millions of people were made aware of prison conditions in the United States. Public concern affected the outcome of additional trials, including those of the Soledad Brothers and Ruchell Magee. On June 29, 1972, three weeks after Angela's acquittal, fifteen thousand people gathered at Madison Square Garden in New York City to celebrate. The audience was mostly Black and mostly young. Nina Simone's voice filled the Garden, invoking the freedom songs of the decade. Angela's appearance climaxed the evening. As she came onto the stage, the entire audience rose in tribute.

IT IS MY HOPE that this book may in some small measure help a new generation to learn of this history. I hope, too, that it may contribute to a better understanding of the realities of racism as it has affected our criminal justice system, our prisons, and women's lives. Racism continues to inflict untold suffering. Please act to bring about peacefulness and healing in whatever ways you think are best.

I THANK Cornell University Press and its editor-in-chief, Frances Benson, for issuing this second edition of *The Morning Breaks,* and my colleagues Victoria Byerly, France Winddance Twine, and Joy James for their most excellent support and advice. My gratitude to Carol Champion and Paul Stubbs at Special Collections, McHenry Library, University of California, Santa Cruz, for their archival expertise and assistance; Don Harris, senior photographer with the photo lab of the University of California, Santa Cruz, for his marvelous assistance in preparing photographs for this second edition; and Betsy Wootten, Faculty Services, Kresge College, University of California, Santa Cruz, for her professional assistance in preparing this manuscript for publication. I thank my partner, Kate Miller, for her many helpful suggestions as I wrote the Introduction and Afterword, and for her generous and loving support over twenty years. I thank Angela Davis for her assistance in preparing this second edition of *The Morning Breaks* for publication, and for the gift of our lifelong friendship.

BETTINA APTHEKER

Santa Cruz, California

DRAMATIS PERSONAE

Angela Y. Davis	*A political prisoner*
John Abt	*General counsel, Communist Party, U.S.A.*
Franklin Alexander	*Co-chairperson, National United Committee to Free Angela Davis (NUCFAD)*
Kendra Alexander	*Member, national staff, NUCFAD*
Stephanie Allan	*Press director, NUCFAD*
Richard E. Arnason	*The judge*
Robert A. Baker	*Member, national staff, NUCFAD*
Rodney Barnett	*Member, national staff, NUCFAD*
Leo Branton, Jr.	*Defense counsel*
Margaret Burnham	*Defense counsel*
William Christmas	*A political prisoner, San Quentin Prison. Killed by guards, August 7, 1970*
Ben Davis	*Angela's brother*
Frank B. Davis	*Angela's father*
Reginald Davis	*Angela's brother*
Sallye Davis	*Angela's mother*
Albert Harris	*The prosecutor*

George Lester Jackson   *A political prisoner. Assassinated by guards at San Quentin Prison, August 21,1971.*

Georgia Jackson   *Mother of George and Jonathan Jackson. Member, Soledad Brothers Defense Committee (SBDC)*

Jonathan Jackson   *Brother of George Jackson. Member, SBDC. Killed by guards, August 7, 1970*

Fania Davis Jordan   *Co-chairperson, NUCFAD; and sister to Angela*

Albert J. Lima   *Chairman, Communist Party, Northern California*

Ruchell Magee   *A political prisoner, San Quentin Prison, A survivor of August 7, 1970*

James McClain   *A political prisoner, San Quentin Prison. Killed by guards, August 7, 1970*

Victoria Mercado   *Member, national staff, NUCFAD*

Charlene Mitchell   *Executive secretary, NUCFAD*

Howard Moore, Jr.   *Defense counsel*

Sheldon Otis   *Defense counsel*

The Soledad Brothers   *George Jackson, Fleeta Drumgo and John Clutchette, political prisoners, Soledad Prison*

Doris Brin Walker   *Defense counsel*

Inez Williams   *Chairperson, Friends of the San Quentin Adjustment Center Committee; mother of Soledad Brother Fleeta Drumgo*

Henry Winston   *National chairman, Communist Party, U.S.A.*

PROLOGUE

1

Margaret Burnham and I grew up together in Brooklyn, New York. We went to different high schools, but we saw each other on various week-ends and holidays. Margaret was a fine musician. She played the violin. She went to a special high school in Manhattan called Music & Art. We spent several summers at the same children's camp in Vermont. Our parents were good friends.

We were about fifteen years old when we got together with a few other young people, including Margaret's best friend, Angela Davis, and formed a socialist club called *Advance*. Angela was from Birmingham, Alabama. She had come to New York to attend high school on a scholarship provided by the American Friends Service Committee. Our club met once or twice a month in the basement of my parents' home.

Our primary activity in those days was picketing the Woolworth's Department Store in downtown Brooklyn in solidarity with southern students. The sit-ins had just begun. It was two years after the first March on Washington for Integration and four years since Rosa Parks had refused to move to the back of the bus in Montgomery, Alabama.

Angela and Margaret and I split-up a few years later to go to college. Margaret went south to Tougaloo College in Mississippi, Angela went north to Brandeis University in Massachussetts, and I came west to attend the University of California at Berkeley.

I saw Angela again nine years later—in October 1969. We were both twenty-five years old. I was an assisting editor at the *People's World*, a weekly Communist newspaper published in San Francisco. Angela was a former professor. She had just been fired from her teaching position in the philosophy department at the University of California at Los Angeles (UCLA) by the Board of Regents, because of her (publicly affirmed) membership in the Communist Party.

I came to Los Angeles to do an interview with Angela for the *People's World*. I had experience as a writer, but Angela was the first person I had ever been asked to interview. I wasn't sure I would do a good job. I remember telling her that. She laughed and told me not to worry. She hadn't had many interviews, she said, and wasn't sure she'd do such a good job either. I began with a few questions. She took it from there.

Angela talked about her activities in the Che-Lumumba Club, a club in Los Angeles of the Communist Party of the U.S. to which she belonged. She stressed the widespread support she had received from all sections of the Black community, and from students and faculty on the campus since being fired.

The philosophy department, Angela explained, had been initially divided over whether or not to hire her. The logicians and positivists didn't see the desirability of retaining a scholar of Marxist persuasion. The dialecticians and Hegelians did. Ultimately only a bare majority within the department voted to offer her the two year contract. However, when the regents intervened, the philosophers determined to set aside their differences, and all within the department had resolved to fight the dismissal.

Among the students, Angela said, there was nearly universal opposition to the regent's action. Two thousand had come to hear her first lecture on Frederick Douglass.

Angela explained her current status. The regents' action would not take effect immediately. She had appealed their decision and appropriate academic bodies had still to consider her appeal. A substantial movement was gathering strength to assure that a proper decision reversing the regental edict would be made.

ABOUT a week after the interview I received a telephone call from Kendra Alexander. Kendra was one of Angela's closest friends, and a founding member of the Che-Lumumba Club. Her husband, Franklin, was chairman of the club. They were to lead the fight for Angela's freedom a year later.

A campus-wide congress was being organized, Kendra explained, to protest Angela's dismissal. It was set for October 17th, 1969. Kendra asked if I could come to Los Angeles to participate in it. They particularly wanted me to talk about the functioning and composition of the university's Board of Regents.

I readily agreed. Having been involved in years of student struggles at Berkeley the regents were an old adversary. I knew a lot about the financial and political intrigues of the wealthy, white, primarily Protestant men who dominated the board.

The main rally took place at noon that Friday afternoon. It was not as well-attended as Kendra and other organizers of the day's events had hoped it would be, but people were enthusiastic and later gatherings with smaller groups of students and professors allowed for detailed discussion of strategy and tactics.

Angela meanwhile was closeted in a secret hearing, the purpose of which was to determine whether or not her Communist affiliation tainted her academic competence. The proceeding involved select members of UCLA's administration and faculty, plus several lawyers who served as counsel to the Board of Regents.

At three o'clock that afternoon Kendra and I rendezvoused with Angela in the ladies' lounge near the hearing room. A fifteen minute recess had been called.

Angela told us that the regents' counsel had put in evidence certain articles by a man named Sidney Hook to set forth the theoretical foundation for their position.

Angela asked me to tell her about Sidney Hook.

Briefly I told her what I knew of the Hook thesis: A Communist, by virtue of the fact that he was a member of the Party, held allegiance to a foreign power. He endorsed Party doctrine and Marxist dogma with unchallenged loyalty. A Communist was by definition incapable of critical analysis and independent judgment, and was therefore professionally incompetent.

Angela said that was precisely the position advanced by the regents' counsel. In this instance, she went on, their presentation was deeply racist, spiked with allusions to various stereotypes of the Black woman.

The recess was ending. Angela had to return to the hearing room. As we walked down the corridor we suddenly found ourselves face to face with one of the regents' counsel. His name was Sparrow. I hadn't seen him in four years—not since the trial in which he had helped to convict me and several hundred other students on criminal charges for sitting-in at the university's administration building during the Berkeley Free Speech Movement. Sparrow recognized me right away. He paled, looked over at Angela and then back at me, pondering what terrible plot we could have hatched in the ladies' lounge.

ULTIMATELY the appropriate academic and administrative bodies at UCLA did render a decision, in favor of Angela Davis. The regents ignored their recommendations and fired Angela anyway. She took her case to court and quickly won another favorable decision, based upon Supreme Court rulings which held that the government may not fire a person solely for membership in the Communist Party. Angela was reinstated.

The academic controversy simmered through the Spring of 1970. The governor made periodic denunciations. The regents were unhappy, but legally their hands were tied. Angela continued to teach. Then, on June 19th, 1970, the Board of Regents fired Angela Davis again (by voting not to renew her contract). The board held that her speeches on behalf of the Soledad Brothers—three Black inmates charged with murder in the death of a guard at Soledad Prison—had been inflammatory and constituted a breach of professional ethics.

2

On Tuesday morning January 13th, 1970, all the inmates on the first floor of "O" wing, a maximum security section of Soledad Prison, were ordered into the recreation yard. It was the first time in several months that the men in "O" wing had been allowed out. Thirteen inmates went to a caged area known as the Sally Port. They were stripped and searched. Guards let them out into the yard.

The Black prisoners were ordered to the far end of the yard, near the handball court. The white prisoners remained toward the center of the yard. Officer O. G. Miller was in the guard tower thirteen feet above the men. He was an expert marksman. He had a rifle.

A group of white prisoners attacked the Black prisoners. A fist fight ensued. Officer Miller opened fire. There was no warning shot. His first three shots hit three Black inmates.

W. L. Nolen and Cleveland Edwards died in the yard. Alvin Miller died a couple of hours later in the prison hospital. The guard's fourth shot wounded a white prisoner in the groin.

Three days later the Monterey County Grand Jury was convened. No Black prisoners at all were permitted to testify, not even those who had survived the morning's recreation. The grand jury exonerated Officer Miller. The killing of Nolen, Edwards and Alvin Miller was ruled justifiable homicide.

The prisoners heard the report of the grand jury's finding on the prison radio. Thirty minutes later, a white guard, John V. Mills, was found dying in "Y" wing, a maximum security section of Soledad Prison. He had been beaten and thrown from a third floor tier thirty feet to the television room below.

The prison authorities conducted the investigation of Mills' death. All 137 inmates in "Y" wing were locked in their cells for a month. Several suspects were put in solitary confinement. The grand jury was reconvened.

On February 14th, 1970 the grand jury indicted three Black prisoners—Fleeta Drumgo, George Lester Jackson and John W. Clutchette—for first degree murder.

I heard about the three young men in Soledad shortly after the murder indictment was returned, from friends in the San Jose community who had previously organized a Committee for Defense of Political Prisoners.

News of the indictment, and the earlier killings, reached a member of the Committee whose son was in Soledad. She contacted others in the group. They took some initial steps to help start a defense movement.

Soledad Prison is situated just outside of Salinas, a town in California's agricultural heartland. It is known as the "lettuce capital of the world." San Jose, fifty miles to the north, is the nearest big city.

The first meetings in San Jose of what was eventually to become a statewide Soledad Brothers Defense Committee, were held at the home of Emma Gelders Sterne. Emma was the author of more than a score of children's books. She was also a Communist.

Fleeta Drumgo, George Jackson and John Clutchette were brought before Judge Gordon Campbell in the Monterey County Superior Court in Salinas for arraignment and trial.

The men were delivered to the courthouse by prison guards in a specially marked van. They were chained together. Each time they were scheduled to appear in court a white mob hissed and shouted obscenities and hurled lighted cigarettes at them.

FLEETA Drumgo was twenty-three years old. Police arrested him the first time when he was thirteen. Half of his life had already been spent in "correction centers" and jails. He had been in Soledad three years. He was serving an indeterminate six month to fifteen year sentence for second degree burglary.

John W. Clutchette was twenty-four years old. He had first come to the attention of the police when he was fourteen. John finished high school. After high school he went to work as a mechanic in an aircraft company.

John was arrested in 1966. The police said he stole a television set. John explained he had bought the set from someone else. He hadn't known it was stolen. A public defender advised John to plead guilty. He said John had a prior record. A serious defense was not possible.

John did what the public defender told him to do. He was given an indeterminate sentence for second degree burglary: six months to fifteen years.

George Lester Jackson was twenty-eight years old. He had lived with his parents and three brothers and sisters in Pasadena, California. At fifteen he took a joy ride in the family car. He had an accident. The car hit the side of the neighborhood grocery store. George's father paid the damages. The storekeeper didn't file any charges. The police arrested George for driving without a license. He was sent to a prison reformatory.

George got out. He was not yet eighteen years old. He made a down payment on a motorbike. The bike had been stolen. George didn't know. He was arrested. His mother went to court with him. She had the receipt for the purchase of the bike in her hand. The judge sent George back to prison reformatory for theft.

George got out. He was eighteen years old. He bought an old car. He took someone he knew for a ride. His acquaintance asked George to stop at a gas station. George stopped. The fellow got out, went inside the station, held up the attendant (for $70.00), came out and told George to "get going."

George Jackson was arrested. He was charged with armed robbery. The Jacksons hired a lawyer to defend their son. The lawyer didn't want to prepare a defense. He said with George's prior record a defense would be hopeless.

The white attendant at the gas station was willing to testify that George had not held him up. The fellow who robbed the gas station and was eventually caught was willing to testify that George had had no part in it. The lawyer didn't want to prepare a defense.

George was convicted. He was given an indeterminate sentence for second degree robbery: one year to life.

When the guard was killed at Soledad George Jackson had been in the state penitentiary for ten years. According to California law he faced a mandatory death sentence if he was convicted of murder in the death of the guard because he was already serving a life sentence.

THE SOLEDAD Brothers were arraigned. They pleaded not guilty. The judge wanted to proceed with the trial. He was impatient with pleas of innocence. A few progressive-minded lawyers were hastily assembled. They demanded time to prepare an adequate defense. Inez Williams, Georgia Jackson and Doris Maxwell, the mothers of Fleeta, George and John respectively, stood up in the courtroom and protested the proceedings. Supporters, still few in number, picketed the courthouse. The judge was forced to grant a continuance. It was the opening wedge.

One of John Clutchette's high school friends was Kendra Alexander. Kendra had learned of the situation in Soledad as it was breaking. The Che-Lumumba Club quickly resolved to launch a campaign to save the Soledad Brothers from a Legal Lynching. Their cause symbolized the oppression of a people.

Less than a week after the indictment was returned the club organized its first demonstration on behalf of the Soledad Brothers, and Angela Davis called her first press conference to explain the case.

ANGELA said: "The situation in Soledad is part of a continuous pattern in the Black community. Three Black men who are unarmed, who are not attempting to escape, are killed, and this is called justifiable homicide . . . One white guard is killed and this is immediately called murder . . . Three Black men who are known for their attempt within the prison to organize the inmates towards some form of united struggle against the real causes of our oppression, those three Black men are then singled out, and indicted for murder . . ."

Angela announced that a demonstration would be held the following day at the state building in Los Angeles. A series of demands were to be presented to the Adult Authority and the California Department of Corrections. She said: "We are calling for basic structural changes within the prison system and we are also attempting to build a movement directed towards the liberation of political prisoners . . ."

A reporter asked Ms. Davis if she was optimistic or pessimistic about the possibilities of securing justice for the Soledad Brothers.

Angela said: "I don't think optimism and pessimism are

categories with which one works in a movement. We see what has to be done and we see what we have to do in order to accomplish our goals, and this is the way in which we work."

Angela Davis became the co-chairperson of the Soledad Brothers Defense Committee in southern California. As a public figure she was in a position to focus attention on the case. She committed herself to the struggle.

Wherever she was invited to speak Angela talked about the Soledad Brothers. She mentioned them at every press conference, even when the conference was held to explain the status of her case at UCLA.

Angela noticed that the press often excised her comments about the case in their reports. She consciously restructured her statements. Every paragraph contained at least one and usually more references to the Soledad Brothers. The press couldn't report what she had said unless they also mentioned the case.

Angela gave assistance in the organization of new defense committees. Groups were formed in San Diego, San Jose, San Francisco. She urged maximum attendance at the pre-trial hearings in Salinas. By May 1970 the courtroom was packed with supporters.

The Brothers were still brought to the courthouse in chains. But the mob didn't gather anymore. Only supporters came. They waited anxiously for a glimpse of the Brothers. Now the guards transported them from Soledad in an unmarked vehicle and hustled them inside through a back door.

Judge Campbell told the predominantly Black spectators in his courtroom to "conduct themselves properly and not sit as if they were in a pool hall or at a barbecue table." He appealed to California State Senator Donald Grunsky to introduce legislation in Sacramento to make it unlawful for people to picket his courthouse in support of the Soledad Brothers.

(On September 18th, 1970 the legislature did pass Section 169 of the California Penal Code which said: "Any person who pickets or parades in or near a building which houses a court of this state with the intent to interfere with, obstruct, or impede the administration of justice, or with the intent to influence any judge, juror, witness or officer of the court in the discharge of his duty shall be guilty of a misdemeanor." The law was to be invoked eighteen months later in an effort to cripple support for Angela Davis.)

Lawyers for the Soledad Brothers challenged Judge Campbell for bias. He retired precipitously from the case without a hearing. A new presiding judge was appointed. His name was Anthony Brazil.

The defense moved for a change of venue. The lawyers said the Brothers couldn't get a fair trial in Salinas. Judge Brazil denied the motion. The public outcry grew more intense. The judge reversed himself. He ordered the trial moved to San Francisco.

Early in June 1970 California State Senator Mervyn Dymally, a Black legislator from Los Angeles, toured Soledad Prison, accompanied by Fay Stender, one of the Soledad Brothers' lawyers.

Senator Dymally had intended to submit questionnaires to the inmates in maximum security. Ray Procunier, director of the California Department of Corrections, said he couldn't do that. Procunier took the senator through the prison. Procunier's presence precluded any possibility of Dymally talking privately with the prisoners. None of them were about to say anything substantive with Procunier standing there.

Dymally and other members of the Black Caucus in the California Legislature decided to pursue an independent investigation of Soledad. They interviewed the families of the inmates. They read hundreds of letters from scores of prisoners. Their Report of the Black Caucus on Soledad Prison gave the Soledad Brothers Defense Committee a new degree of legitimacy and respect. The report confirmed the committee's accounts of the atrocities committed at the prison. The defense already enjoyed a solid base of support in the Black community. Its support extended now into other areas. Dymally got personally involved in the work of the committee. People like Jane Fonda and Marlon Brando associated themselves with the defense.

By the middle of June 1970, when Angela was fired for the second time from the university, she was leading an impressive movement to save the Soledad Brothers.

Fleeta Drumgo, John Clutchette and George Jackson were impressive men.

John sent a letter to a friend. He detailed the realities of prison life. He concluded: "We are, like the people outside of the prison walls . . . forced . . . into . . . resisting . . . force!"

Fleeta sent a message to the Soledad Brothers Defense Committee: "On behalf of all of us in maximum, please don't reject or forget us, because this allows the monster to brutalize, murder and treat us inhumanly. We are of you, we love you and struggle with you . . ."

George was the most prolific writer of the Brothers. His letters to family, friends and lawyers were to be published in October 1970 by the largest paperback publisher in the United States. The book, though containing solely private correspondence, was universal in its appeal. With its publication the cause of the Soledad Brothers reached tens of thousands of people.

Despite shackles, chains around the waist and under the crotch and handcuffed wrists chained to the waist, each Brother always managed a clenched fist salute on entering the courtroom.

IN THE Spring of 1970 George Jackson and Angela Davis began to write to each other. Their letters were passionately political —argumentative, probative, incisive. Angela got to know the Jackson family, stayed at their home. She got to know more about George. Her letters grew more intense. Her feeling for George deepened.

George's feeling for Angela changed also. On May 8th, 1970 he requested visiting privileges for her. The request was denied—for "administrative reasons," the authorites said. On the printed application form, next to the word *Relationship,* George had written, "I have known this person *for life* . . ." He had underlined the last two words.

Sometime that spring or summer or fall they fell in love with each other.

ON JULY 8th, 1970 Fleeta Drumgo, John Clutchette and George Jackson were transferred from Soledad Prison to San Quentin prison. San Quentin was the state penitentiary closest to San Francisco. Their trial had been set to begin on September 21st, 1970. It didn't actually begin until November of the following year.

3

Fred Billingslea was twenty-four years old. He was Black. He was an inmate at San Quentin prison. His cell was in "B" section. The men in "B" section knew he was very sick. They tried to take care of him as best they could. They repeatedly urged the authorities to secure his transfer to a hospital. The authorities refused. Fred Billingslea died in San Quentin. The authorities said he died of smoke inhalation. This is the story of how he died as told in an affidavit prepared by the men in "B" section:

Approximately 11 p.m. on the date of February 25, 1970 in San Quentin State Prison, Tamal, California, inmate Fred Billingslea, a known emotionally-ill person started a fire within his cell in "B" section, said fire and smoke grew so intense that it was necessary to remove Billingslea from his cell to prevent him from hanging himself.

Approximately four correctional officers proceeded to the 4th floor of "B" section and informed Billingslea that he must come out of his cell. However, Billingslea failed to come out, stating that he was scared of being beaten by the officers.

Whereupon the officers shot through a large amount of tear gas into the cell with Billingslea therein and then proceeded to have the *door locked so that Billingslea could not come out.*

To be sure the tear gas was in the amount that would be used to control about 1,000 persons.

After approximately one hour the officers opened said cell door and rushed in to remove Mr. Billingslea. The officers went in the said cell beating or fighting and removed Mr. Billingslea.

There the attack upon inmate Billingslea continued from the 4th floor to the first floor, where he was taken into another cell.

When Mr. Billingslea went to the first floor cell he was *alive and very active*. The officers stayed in that cell with him approximately 10 to 20 minutes. When they came out of the cell, Fred Billingslea was dead.

David Johnson, a Black prisoner in "B" section signed the affidavit. He filed a civil complaint in the United States District Court against San Quentin Warden Louis S. Nelson, and Associate Warden James W. Park and known and unknown agents of Nelson and Park. The complaint charged that prison authorities were trying to prevent evidence and witnesses from reaching Billingslea's mother. The court summarily denied a hearing and returned the complaint, stating that it had not been properly drawn.

Other Black prisoners in "B" section—including Ruchell Magee, William Christmas, James McClain, Jeffrey Gaulden and Fred Pendleton—prepared new affidavits. They tried to obtain legal help. Several wrote directly to Mrs. Billingslea. The Billingslea family retained a lawyer to investigate their son's death.

On May 18th, 1970 inmate Fred Pendleton was stopped by guards in a corridor in "B" section. He was returning to his cell with a cup of hot coffee. The guards searched him. They were looking for a list of names of other inmates who had signed affidavits in the Billingslea murder.

Fred Pendleton didn't have a list. A guard shoved him. The hot coffee spilled, scalding Pendelton's arm. "Move nigger," the guard shouted. Three minutes later, Pendleton recounted in still another affidavit, he was "rat-packed" in his cell—jumped and beaten by a gang of guards.

Also in May 1970 guards came to the cell of Jeffrey Gaulden. He was ordered to strip. He asked why. The guards sprayed him full in the face with a can of mace. They yelled: "Strip. Strip."

Gaulden stripped. The guards told him to crawl out of his cell. They dragged him down the hall. They put him in a strip cell. They beat him senseless. They left him there.

In June 1970 James McClain was brought to trial for assaulting a guard at San Quentin. McClain was alleged to have stabbed at a guard with a kitchen knife. The guard's name was Freitas. He sustained no wounds.

The incident was supposed to have occurred on Monday morning, March 2nd, at 7:45, five days after Billingslea's death.

McClain was supposed to have lunged at the guard with this knife, missed him, run through the kitchen, thrust the knife into the bottom of a 55 gallon drum of waste vegetables and escaped. McClain was apprehended inside the prison more than an hour later. He was nowhere near the kitchen when he was apprehended. Officer Frietas did not know McClain. He positively identified him as his would-be assailant.

The trial was held in the Marin County Superior Court. The prosecutor was Gary Thomas, the assistant district attorney for Marin County. The presiding judge was Harold Haley. Mr. Thomas was married to Judge Haley's niece. James McClain defended himself.

The trial ended when an all-white jury failed to agree on a verdict. A mistrial was declared. Judge Haley ordered a new trial.

McClain's second trial began on Monday, August 3rd, 1970. Thomas prosecuted, Haley presided and McClain defended himself. By Friday morning, August 7th, a jury had been selected and Thomas had completed the prosecution's case. McClain was just beginning his defense. All of his witnesses were fellow-prisoners. Ruchell Magee and William Christmas had been brought from San Quentin to the Marin County Superior Court. At 10:45 that Friday morning Ruchell Magee was on the witness stand . . .

JONATHAN Peter Jackson was five years old when his older brother, George, was sent to prison reformatory the first time. When Jonathan was eight years old George was sent to the state penitentiary.

Jonathan lived in Pasadena with his mother and father and two sisters. His father worked two jobs most of the time. As often as possible the family went to see George. Jonathan attended Blair High School in Pasadena. He turned seventeen in May 1970. He graduated from high school in June.

Jonathan was one of the editors of the student newspaper at Blair High School. It was called *Iskra*. That had been the name of the clandestine paper published by Lenin in 1902. Iskra means spark.

Three months before his graduation Jonathan published an article under the headline: "Racist Educational Structure Attacked." He wrote:

I am the only Black in my English, U.S. History and Algebra II classes, and one of three in my chemistry class . . . I am constantly being bombarded with such questions as: "Where did you learn that?" and "Where did you get all this culture?" All of the above questions come with the standard incredulous look. These people cannot believe that a ghetto progeny could know something that they did not. All over the country, these upper and middle class whites are watching in stunned horror as their balloon of white superiority rapidly deflates with a black spear in its exact center . . .

The last issue of *Iskra* for the Spring semester was dated June 18th, 1970. Page four was called the George Jackson Memorial Page. Jonathan excoriated the prison system and the awful violence done to Black people. He explained the things that had happened to George in ten years of imprisonment, and he talked about the new charges and the prospect of yet another trial. At the end Jon wrote: "They couldn't get George one way so they are now trying to crucify him for a murder that he did not commit. If he's bound up tight, I'll hold back the night and there won't be no light for days . . ."

Jonathan Jackson actively participated in the work of the Soledad Brothers Defense Committee. He attended almost all of the pre-trial hearings in Salinas. George was concerned about Jonathan. He wrote to Angela on May 21st, 1970: "Jon is a young brother and he is just a little withdrawn, but he is intelligent and loyal . . . He is at that dangerous age when confusion sets in and sends brothers either to the undertaker or to prison. He is a little better off than I was and than most brothers his age. He learns fast and can distinguish the real from the apparent, provided someone takes the time to present it . . . He is a loyal and beautiful black man-child. I love him . . ."

Although the situation at San Quentin surrounding the killing of Billingslea was not publicly known, Jonathan Jackson learned about it. It is likely he heard about it through some of the letters sent by the men in "B" section to relatives and friends, describing the officially-sanctioned terror against all who had witnessed the killing, and pleading for help.

For Jonathan it must have appeared as an agonizing repetition of the Soledad pattern, epitomizing the mindless brutality of the system. Jonathan resolved to act. He would dare to rescue the men in "B" section. In this way he would reveal to the world the dimensions of George's ordeal.

RUCHELL Magee continued his testimony, in a virtually empty courtroom, save for the jury and the official court personnel. Jonathan Jackson entered the courtroom quietly. He took a seat in the spectators section. A few minutes later he stood up, held a pistol firmly in his hands and said: "All right, gentlemen. This is it. I'm taking over now."

Jonathan died in a hail of bullets an hour later. James McClain, William Christmas and the judge also died. Ruchell Magee and the prosecutor were severely wounded. A juror was shot in the arm.

Jonathan had never fired a shot. Neither had McClain, Christmas or Magee to whom Jonathan had given guns. Four San Quentin guards and the prosecutor had done all the shooting.

Moments after the shooting had ended prosecutor Gary Thomas told Marin County District Attorney Bruce Bales he had grabbed McClain's gun and fired until it was emptied of bullets. "I got three of them," Thomas said, "and I hope I killed them . . ."

San Quentin guard John Wesley Matthews told investigators it was he who had opened fire on the escaping prisoners. He said he let loose with a 30-30 Winchester rifle. He said he was certain his first two shots had hit Jackson and McClain respectively.

John Wesley Matthews had been one of the guards to beat Fred Billingslea to death in February.

Ruchell Magee survived the shooting on August 7th. He was taken to Marin General Hospital. A bullet was removed from his abdomen. Three days later he was shipped back to his cell in the San Quentin Adjustment Center.

RUCHELL Magee was born and raised in the rural community of Franklin, Louisiana. Ruchell lived with his mother and his step-father. His step-father, Merley Magee, was a railroad worker.

Ruchell was sixteen years old at the time of his first arrest. He was alleged to have committed an "aggravated *attempted* rape" of a white woman. He was convicted. The judge waived the legal requisites of a juvenile proceeding. At the time of sentencing Ruchell had just turned seventeen.

Ruchell Magee was sent to the Louisiana State Penitentiary in Angola. He was sentenced to twelve years. He served six years and eight months. He was paroled. The authorities set, as the principle condition of his release, his immediate departure from the state of Louisiana.

Ruchell left Louisiana. His parents arranged for him to live with his aunt and uncle in Los Angeles. He was twenty-two years old. Ruchell lived in Los Angeles for six months.

Ruchell got into an argument. The argument was over ten dollars. A man in a car with him said that Ruchell had stolen ten dollars from him. The car rolled during the altercation. Technically, Ruchell had kidnapped his adversary. A kidnapping is legally defined as moving someone forcibly from one spot to another.

Ruchell was arrested. He was charged with kidnapping (committed during a robbery). There was a trial. A judge appointed a lawyer to handle Ruchell's defense. Ruchell wanted to plead not guilty. The lawyer pleaded him guilty. Ruchell objected. He was bound, gagged and beaten. He was convicted of kidnapping. He was sentenced to life imprisonment. He was sent to San Quentin.

Ruchell taught himself to read. The United States Constitution was his primary text. He taught himself law. He asked for the transcript of his first trial. It was sent. He discovered the transcript had been doctored. He filed petitions. He demanded a new trial. He said his first trial had been unconstitutional. He cited numerous errors. He focused on the point that in his first trial a lawyer had entered a false plea over his strenuous objections. He maintained that under the law only the accused can enter a plea.

Two years later, Ruchell's conviction was overturned. It was overturned on a technicality, rather than on the substantive issue of his appeal. A second trial was ordered.

There was a second trial. The charge was the same. The same judge presided. The judge appointed a new lawyer to handle Ruchell's defense. Ruchell wanted to plead not guilty. The new lawyer pleaded him not guilty by reason of insanity. Ruchell screamed. He was bound, gagged and beaten. A jury found him guilty. He was sentenced to life imprisonment without the possibility of parole. He was sent back to San Quentin. He demanded the transcript of his second trial. He started filing new appeals.

By the summer of 1970 Ruchell Magee had been in San Quentin seven years. He was thirty-one years old.

WITHIN moments of Judge Haley's death all flags in Marin Conty had been lowered to half mast. Judicial colleagues, friends and neighbors gathered in front of his home on Peacock Drive in the white, predominantly upper middle class suburban community of San Rafael. Judge E. Warren McGuire paced back and forth in front of the Haley residence, his hands clasped behind his back, his head bowed: "I just don't understand it," he said.

Harold Haley had been born and raised in San Rafael. The townsfolk considered him one of their most distinguished native sons. He had served in the district attorney's office for fifteen years before his gubernatorial appointment in the mid-1950's to the municipal and ultimately superior court bench. He had been a Republican his whole life. Seven hundred people attended his funeral.

ON SEPTEMBER 4th, 1970, Ruchell Magee was indicted by the Marin County Grand Jury for aggravated kidnapping and first degree murder in the death of Judge Harold Haley. Four days later he was arraigned before Judge E. Warren McGuire. The arraignment was held at San Quentin in a makeshift courtroom within the prison . . .

4

D etailed, graphic accounts of the action on August 7th at the Marin Civic Center in San Rafael lit up television screens that same night, and were spread across the front-page of every California newspaper by the next morning.

A news photographer for the San Rafael *Independent Journal* had arrived on the scene just minutes after the abortive escape had begun. He had the entire drama on film.

Reporters tripped over each other to interview the scores of deputy sheriffs, highway patrolmen and county employees who had witnessed some portion of the day's events.

California Governor Ronald Reagan offered his condolences ". . . to the families of the innocent victims of this vicious attack." The governor said he had instructed the Department of Justice in Sacramento to begin an immediate investigation.

The following morning the San Francisco *Chronicle* reported that the escape plan had been backed by an arsenal of automatic weapons and plenty of ammunition.

"What triggered this massive blood-letting," the story said, "was a carefully planned courtroom escape in which the unidentified accomplice played a major role . . ."

There was no further mention of the unidentified accomplice.

The story concluded: "Police said Jackson . . . visited his brother, George (Karate) Jackson, one of the so-called Soledad Brothers at San Quentin early this week. They did not know whether George Jackson and the inmates involved yesterday knew each other . . ."

Two days later—on August 9th—the associate warden at San Quentin, James W. Park, called a news conference to announce that he was beginning a full-scale investigation to determine whether or not the incident at the Marin Civic Center was, in fact, part of some "wild plot to free the so-called Soledad Brothers," George Jackson, Fleeta Drumgo and John Clutchette.

Park confirmed that George Jackson had had two visits at San Quentin with his younger brother, Jonathan, earlier that week. He said officials were still trying to ascertain whether or not George Jackson had known any of the inmates involved in the escape.

Park said he wanted something else made clear. He thought his men, and in particular Officer John Matthews, had acted properly in opening fire. He said he had since learned that Marin County Sheriff Montanos had apparently given orders not to shoot. Park said his men never heard those instructions. In the absence of any, they acted in accord with established prison policy to prevent a break, "hostages or no hostages."

The associate warden's announcement of an investigation into the August 7th events as some bizarre plot to free the Soledad Brothers lent credence to a news-photographer's assertion that he had heard one of the rebel prisoners shout "Free the Soledad Brothers by 12:30!" Nobody else reported hearing this. The initial reports of the event did not mention it. Public officials, nevertheless, latched on to the warden's suggestion of a plot to free the Soledad Brothers.

Later that same afternoon, August 9th, San Francisco Sheriff Matthew Carberry held a press conference. He announced that in view of the attack on the Marin County Hall of Justice, apparently intended to force the release of the Soledad Brothers, "extreme precautions" would be instituted for their trial.

Sheriff Carberry said the prisoners would be kept at San Quentin for maximum security, and flown via army helicopter to the San Francisco Hall of Justice for their court appearances.

The next day the Presiding Judge of the San Francisco Superior Court Carl H. Allen, called a press conference to announce that in light of the attack on the Marin County Hall of Justice to free the Soledad Brothers, he was proposing that their trial be held in San Quentin prison altogether.

For days the media was filled with speculative comments from San Quentin authorities, Marin County and Sacramento officials, alleging the connection between the abortive escape and the Soledad Brothers.

The facts surrounding Fred Billingslea's death were ignored. The brutalization of the prisoners in "B" section who had witnessed the killing, was denied. The idea that Magee, Christmas and McClain might have wished to take their freedom rather than endure further suffering at the hands of San Quentin guards was never even contemplated by the commercial media.

In the public mind the August 7th events had become inextricably tied to some bizarre plot to free the Soledad Brothers. State officials now intended to launch their attack against the Soledad Defense Committee, the Black Liberation Movement and the Communist Party. Their first target was Angela Davis.

At 6:50 p.m. on Friday, August 14th a warrant was issued for the arrest of Angela Yvonne Davis. She was charged with aggravated kidnapping and first degree murder in the death of Judge Harold Haley.

The authorities were in a hurry to obtain the warrant for her arrest. They didn't go through the formality of a grand jury proceeding.

The warrant was issued by Marin County Superior Court Judge Peter Allen Smith. The judge issued the warrant solely on the basis of an affidavit filed by the Marin District Attorney Bruce Bales. The affidavit alleged that three of the guns used in the abortive escape were registered in the name of Angela Davis.

The warrant charged Angela Davis as a principal in the crimes of murder and kidnapping, although the Bales affidavit had not alleged her presence at the scene of the crime. The law under which such a warrant could be issued was Section 31 of the California Penal Code, which provided, in part: "All persons concerned in the commission of a crime, whether it be a felony or misdemeanor, and whether they directly commit the act constituting the offense, or aid and abet it in its commission, or, not being present, have advised and encouraged its commission . . . are principals in any crime so committed. . . ."

Section 31 of the Penal Code had been passed by the California State Legislature in 1872. It had seldom been invoked. Its constitutionality was questionable because it abolished the distinction between an accessory before the commission of a crime, and a principal partaking in the commission of a crime.

By charging Angela as a principal in the capital crimes of murder and kidnapping, a massive hunt for her could be initiated by state and federal authorities, with seemingly legitimate motives.

Hours after the murder-kidnap warrant was issued, heavily-armed members of the San Francisco tactical squad raided the San Francisco headquarters of the Soledad Brothers Defense Committee, ostensibly in search of Angela Davis. They tore through the office, terrorizing its occupants. They arrested Fania Davis Jordan, Angela's sister. They handcuffed her and hauled her off to police headquarters. They questioned her for several hours. They had no warrant for her arrest. No charges were filed against her. She was released.

At about the time the tactical squad was mounting its assault in San Francisco, a commentator on a Los Angeles television station, KNXT, reported that Angela Davis had obtained a passport and was heading for the Canadian border.

Early on the morning of August 15th the Federal Bureau of Investigation issued a warrant for the arrest of Angela Yvonne Davis for interstate flight to avoid prosecution for murder and kidnapping.

On the 18th of August FBI director, J. Edgar Hoover, placed Angela Davis on his list of "Ten Most Wanted" criminals. A wanted poster was printed and copies were circulated throughout the country. It said: "Angela Davis is wanted on kidnapping and murder charges growing out of an abduction and shooting in Marin County, California, on August 7, 1970. She has allegedly purchased several guns in the past. Consider armed and dangerous."

A few days later two FBI agents came to my house in San Jose. One of the agents said: "Now that Angela Davis is involved in a kidnapping, we're sure you'll want to cooperate with us . . ." He paused for a moment.

"Where is Angela Davis?", he asked.

I said: "I don't have anything to say to you."

The agent said: "You'd better tell us what you know. Where is Angela?"

I said: "I don't have anything to say to you."

The agent said: "You'd better cooperate with us. We can put you away for a long time for harboring a fugitive."

I said: "Don't you threaten me."

The agent said: "When we get her we'd better not find out you knew where she was. If we do, we'll come back and get you . . ."

I said: "Go to hell."

They left.

PEOPLE across the country had similar experiences. Wild rumors circulated through the press. One report said Angela was in Birmingham. Birmingham police claimed to have missed capturing her by minutes.

Another report placed Angela enroute to Paris. Another said she was still in Los Angeles. Still another said she had been spotted in Toronto . . .

A veritable reign of terror descended upon every Black community in the country. Young women, especially if they happened to be light complected and happened to wear their hair in an Afro style, were most vulnerable to the dragnet. Literally hundreds were detained, searched and questioned.

Members of the Che-Lumumba Club bore the brunt of the attack. People were summoned to investigative hearings, their homes were searched, employers and friends were questioned. On Tuesday night, August 18th, police surrounded the home of Kendra and Franklin Alexander and sealed off the street on which they lived. Police occupied the neighborhood for more than three hours before dispersing. There were no warrants, no arrests and no explanations.

The Alabama Chapter of the American Civil Liberties Union protested the police raids in Birmingham. The authorities, the ACLU statement said, were using the search for Angela Davis as an excuse to invade the Black community at will.

The Los Angeles *Sentinel,* the largest Black community newspaper in Southern California decried what it called the crucifixion of Angela Davis by the white-run media. The Los Angeles *Free Press* denounced ". . . the parody of due process which has characterized the handling of the Soledad Brothers case . . .", and now threatens the life of Angela Davis. The *People's World* in San Francisco issued an appeal for "the righteous defense of Angela Davis," in a lead editorial on September 5th.

In New York City the Political Committee of the Communist Party of the United States issued a statement on August 29th deploring "the goading realities of a bestial prison system," which had led to the tragedy at the San Rafael courthouse, and denounced the massive FBI and police hunt for Angela Davis. Noting its rejection of individual acts of escape, such as the San Rafael effort, as an untenable method of political struggle, the Party warned people in the movement to nevertheless, ". . . be vigilant against reaction's efforts to exploit the tragedy," by undertaking "diversionary assaults upon the Communist Party."

On September 29th, 1970, Ruchell Magee made another prison/court appearance before Judge McGuire. Magee told the judge that San Quentin authorities were trying to force him to implicate Angela Davis in the August 7th events. He said: "I have been threatened because I will not lie on Angela Davis. . . . I don't care what the power structure does to me, I will not lie about Miss Davis."

The judge refused to consider any motion relating to Ruchell Magee's allegations.

A few days later another San Quentin prisoner, Leo Robles, presented an affidavit to Judge McGuire stating that the prosecution in the Magee case had made overtures to him to approach Magee "as one convict to another, to convince him that he would be granted immunity from prosecution and better living conditions while in prison if he would testify against Angela Davis . . ."

Judge McGuire again refused a hearing on the matter. The judge said: "Similar accusations have been made by Mr. Magee . . . and are false."

Angela was arrested by special agents of the FBI on October 13th, 1970 in New York City.

President Richard M. Nixon appeared on national television for ceremonies attendant to the passage of his new crime bill. The President took the occasion to congratulate FBI Director J. Edgar Hoover for the capture of the dangerous terrorist, Angela Davis.

The *New York Times* also congratulated the FBI for its "brilliant investigative effort" in apprehending Angela Davis, in an editorial on October 16th, 1970. The *Times* despaired of Ms. Davis' supporters who were already seeking "to politicize her case, and deflect attention from the specifics of the charges against her."

CALIFORNIA authorities quickly moved to obtain Angela's extradition from New York.

Angela resisted extradition. John Abt, general counsel for the Communist Party, and Margaret Burnham, Angela's childhood friend and now a lawyer serving as co-counsel in Angela's defense, were prepared to argue the case all the way to the United States Supreme Court.

The warrant for Angela's arrest—based as it was simply upon the affidavit of the Marin County District Attorney Bruce Bales—was hopelessly defective. With Angela resisting extradition the California authorities were forced to convene an emergency session of the Marin County Grand Jury.

The grand jury met on November 10th. It returned an indictment the same day. Now Angela Davis and Ruchell Magee were indicted in a joint charge for first degree murder, kidnapping and a new third count: conspiracy.

The new indictment was sent to New York. New York Governor Nelson Rockefeller signed the order of extradition at once.

John Abt and Margaret Burnham appealed the extradition order. They went through the New York Supreme Court, the New York Appellate Division, the New York Court of Appeals, the United States District Court and the United States Court of Appeals in thirteen working days.

Abt noted wryly that it was ". . . the fastest Cook's tour of the appellate courts I have ever been given in 45 years of practice."

A final appeal to stay extradition pending a hearing before the United States Supreme Court was presented on the 14th working day, to Justice Harlan. He received the appeal at 10 a.m. Monday morning, December 21st. He denied the stay just after 12 noon the same day.

At 3 a.m. on Tuesday, December 22nd, 1970, Angela was awakened by officials at the New York Women's House of Detention. She was informed her attorneys wished to see her. Still in her night clothes she went downstairs. Instead of her attorneys she was confronted by two policemen and two policewomen.

Angela demanded to call her lawyers. She was ordered to strip. She refused. The four officers slammed her to the floor, handcuffed her with her hands behind her back, and threw her into a police car.

Angela was driven to an air force base in New Jersey. A National Guard plane sat on the runway. It was surrounded by soldiers with fixed bayonets. She was put on the plane. She was now in the custody of the Marin County Sheriff's Department. The plane landed at Hamilton Air Force Base in Marin County eleven hours later. The runway was lined with soldiers. She was escorted into a waiting car. She was driven to the Marin County jail. She was booked for murder, kidnapping and conspiracy. There was no bail.

On January 5th, 1971 Angela Davis appeared with her co-defendant Ruchell Magee, in the Marin County Superior Court. The presiding judge was E. Warren McGuire. Angela read a statement to the court over the strenuous objections of the Assistant Attorney General Albert Harris.

Angela said:

> . . . I now declare publicly before the court, before the people of this country that I am innocent of all charges which have been leveled against me by the State of California. I am innocent and therefore maintain that my presence in this courtroom is unrelated to any criminal act.
>
> I stand before this court as a target of a political frameup which far from pointing to my culpability implicates the State of California as an agent of political repression . . .

THE FIGHT FOR BAIL

The morning after Angela Davis' arrest in New York City, Franklin Alexander, the chairman of the Che-Lumumba Club of the Communist Party, held a press conference in Los Angeles, California.

Franklin said: "The Che Lumumba Club of the Communist Party of Southern California, is the organizational choice of Angela Davis and the collective to which she belongs. We are completely and without reservation committed to lead in building the largest, broadest, most all encompassing movement this country has ever seen to free our comrade . . . The hounds have captured her physically and made her a political prisoner. With the people we will set her free again . . ."

Days later four hundred people gathered in a Black church in south central Los Angeles and founded the National United Committee to Free Angela Davis and All Political Prisoners (NUCFAD). Franklin Alexander and Fania Davis Jordan, Angela's sister, were elected national co-coordinators.

In the first weeks of activity posters, buttons, bumper stickers, leaflets were printed and distributed in the tens of thousands. Volume one, number one of NUCFAD's "Free Angela" newsletter appeared on November 13th, 1970, exactly one month after Angela's arrest.

Angela's first two lectures to her philosophy class at UCLA on Frederick Douglass were published by the committee, with a joint *introduction signed by thirty colleagues at the University. They wrote: "We take pride in presenting these lectures by a distinguished colleague and friend. May they everywhere contribute to the defeat of oppression."*

Support of Angela Davis did not have to be generated. It had to be organized. In the weeks following her incarceration virtually every Black newspaper in the United States—The New York Amsterdam News, The Chicago Defender, The Los Angeles Sentinel, The San Francisco Sun-Reporter, The Pittsburgh Courier, Muhammed Speaks and scores more demanded her unconditional release. At the very least they urged a fair trial and her release on bail.

Black writers in New York formed a committee called Black People in Defense of Angela Davis. They issued a statement appealing to all Black people to unite to save Angela's life. The statement was signed by Nikki Giovanni, Chester Higgins, Jr., Sonia Sanchez, Maya Angelou, Toni Cade, Barbara Crosby and a half dozen other people.

James Baldwin penned his own, "Open Letter to My Sister Angela," from Europe. It was published first in the New Statesman in London. Then it appeared in the New York Review of Books.

Popular recording artist Aretha Franklin called a press conference to announce that she would post Angela's bail, no matter what the amount. "I've been locked up," she said, "for disturbing the peace . . . and I know you've got to disturb the peace when you can't get no peace . . . ."

A committee of Black Women for the Freedom of Angela Davis toured nearly every church in Harlem on a Sunday, four weeks after Angela's arrest. The women obtained the signatures of 4,000 people on that day alone, for an appeal to New York Governor Nelson Rockefeller, to stop Angela's extradition.

Before the end of October, 1970, Franklin and Kendra Alexander and Fania Jordan were in New York. They joined with Angela's co-counsel Margaret Burnham and John Abt, and Charlene Mitchell, co-chairperson of the Black Liberation Commission of the Communist Party, and Jose Stevens of the New York Committee to Free Angela Davis, and began a systematic tour of eastern, southern and mid-western cities. They organized "Free Angela" committees, solicited national sponsorship for the committee, raised money, urged that protests be sent to the New York governor demanding that the order of extradition be rescinded.

In Europe, Africa, Asia and Latin America movements for Angela's freedom emerged. In Western Europe the Communist Parties took the initiative in forging movements of such breadth as to dwarf all similar efforts in anyone's memory. In the Socialist countries solidarity with Angela Davis was the watchword. Letters by the tens of thousands—especially from the people of the German Democratic Republic with their special knowledge of the fascist oppression and resistance to it—flooded the Marin County jail. Massive public meetings for Angela were held at industrial enterprises, collective farms and offices throughout the Soviet Union, in the Ukraine, Byelorussia, Uzbekistan and Georgia. Thousands, attending a protest meeting in Moscow convened by the Soviet Peace Committee, sent a telegram to Angela. "For millions of persons throughout the world," their message said, "your name has become a symbol of the honour and conscience of today's America." In the Congo, Tanzania, Guinea, and in the liberated areas of Mozambique, Angola, and Guinea-Bissau the struggle for Angela's freedom became part of the movements for national liberation. Freedom for Angela Davis became symbolic of anti-imperialist sentiment everywhere in the world.

Months after Angela's freedom had been won, Henry Winston, national chairman of the Communist Party, USA, was to write that the world movement for her liberation "was on a scale surpassing the mobilization against the Reichstag fire frame-up" trial of Georgi Dimitrov through which the Nazis in Hitler Germany had intended to launch the anti-Communist pogroms. "Angela Davis," Winston continued, "was freed by the intervention of world public opinion."

By February 1971—five months after Angela's arrest—there were two hundred local committees in the United States, and sixty-seven in foreign countries, all affiliated with the National United Committee to Free Angela Davis. After Angela's extradition to Marin County, California NUCAD moved its national headquarters from Los Angeles to San Francisco.

WE ORGANIZED our first meeting of the Angela Davis Defense Com-

mittee in San Jose, California on December 1st, 1970. It was held at the home of Emma Sterne. On March 5th, 1971 we had our first public meeting for Angela at the Roosevelt Junior High School Auditorium in San Jose. Eight hundred people came.

When NUCFAD moved its headquarters to San Francisco, I joined the national staff. In March 1971 I became one of Angela's legal investigators. Kendra, Franklin, Fania and Charlene Mitchell were also investigators. In that capacity the five of us were given permission by court order to visit with Angela any day of the week, unaccompanied by a lawyer, from 8 a.m. to 4 p.m. We worked together with Angela to plan our political and legal defense.

The National Committee of the Communist Party convened in New York City on March 13th and 14th, 1971. We assessed the campaign for Angela's freedom and projected further activities. We focused on ways to enhance the scope of the campaign. We knew ultimately we would have to embrace every potential source of support no matter how remote it might seem.

The national committee established a special sub-committee, consisting of those comrades in California who were directly involved in the defense. Kendra and Franklin Alexander and myself were among its initial members. As chairman of the Party in Northern California, Mickie Lima was asked to assume responsibility for the work of the sub-committee, and he served as its chairman. In the course of what was to be a two-year battle to save Angela's life Mickie became a source of inspiration to all of us. I have never met anybody before or since who could remain as calm, steady and determined as Mickie in the face of seemingly insurmountable obstacles.

Henry Winston, national chairman of the Communist Party, was asked to devote his attention to the case, even as he remained in New York. He was to be responsible for organizing the work of the Party in the defense effort. Gus Hall, general secretary of the Party, in collaboration with James Jackson, its international secretary, took responsibility for informing the international socialist and revolutionary movement of the case and its importance.

The sub-committee afforded us the collective we needed to thrash out the details of the legal and political defense. It provided us with a necessary liaison between our comrades on the scene in Califor-

nia, and those in the national center. It allowed for the fullest coordination of the Party's organizational efforts in Angela's behalf.

Through the winter of '70 and the spring of '71 a national campaign was initiated for Angela's release on bail. Local defense committees were consolidated, their base of support extended. Petitions urging Angela's release on bail were circulated. Public meetings, demonstrations and rallies were held. The Communist Party took the initiative in all of these activities, in city after city, across the country.

One hundred people huddled in a blinding snow storm beneath a statue of Sojourner Truth in Kennedy Square in Detroit, Michigan on December 16th, 1970 to protest the incarceration of Angela Davis. Fania Jordan spoke: "We stand before the monument of Sojourner Truth, a Black woman liberation fighter . . . She was on the slaveowners' most wanted list, just like Angela Davis, another freedom fighter, was on the FBI's most wanted list . . ." Later that same night 500 people gathered at the Central Methodist Church in Detroit to hear U.S. Congressman John Conyers, Michigan State Senator Coleman A. Young and Michigan State Representative Jackie Vaughn, demand Angela's freedom.

Two thousand students and faculty at UCLA celebrated Angela's birthday on January 26th, 1971, with the resolve to continue the struggle for her freedom.

A thousand people gathered in the Tabernacle Baptist Church on Chicago's southside on February 8th, to demand her release on bail.

Fifteen hundred, predominantly white, high school and college students urged a fair trial for Angela Davis at a public meeting in St. Louis, Missouri, on February 25th.

Four thousand people surrounded the Marin County Hall of Justice itself, in San Rafael, California, on March 16th, in the first major action organized by our national defense committee in the San Francisco Bay Area.

Fifteen hundred Chicano, Black and Anglo residents of San Antonio, Texas, gathered at La Villita Assembly Hall on May 23rd despite efforts by the local sherriff's department to force cancellation of the meeting, demanding the freedom of Angela Davis.

Support for Angela extended well beyond the organizational structure of the National United Committee. This was especially true among workers, who used their union affiliations to develop rank and file defense movements.

There was substantial support from steel workers in Birmingham, Alabama; glass workers in Nashville, Tennessee; garment workers in New York; auto workers in Lordstown, Ohio and Ecore, Michigan; copper miners in the Southwest; Chicano and Filipino workers in California; and hospital workers, public school teachers, and state, county and municipal employees, across the country.

A significant breakthrough in the labor movement came on April 22nd, 1971, when the Nineteenth Biennial Convention of the International Longshoremen and Warehousemen's Union (ILWU) passed a resolution by an overwhelming majority, ". . . to support Angela Davis and to see that she receives a fair trial and is released on bail pending trial." Black and Communist members of the ILWU had fought together to assure passage of the resolution. The ILWU was the first international union to take a stand for Angela Davis.

Other organizations urged Angela's release on bail: The NAACP, the Urban League, the Young Women's Christian Association (YWCA), the American Civil Liberties Union, the American Philosophical Association's Eastern Division. The Council on Church and Race Relations of the National United Presbyterian Church voted to give Angela Davis a Legal Aid Grant in the amount of $10,000, in March 1971. The council based its decision on: "Angela Davis' right to a fair trial without regard to her political affiliations and ideological beliefs."

Margaret Burnham remained as a defense counsel following Angela's extradition. She moved, with her family, to San Francisco. Howard Moore, Jr., a lawyer from Atlanta, Georgia, became co-counsel. Howard had defended Georgia State Representative Julian Bond, and SNCC leaders H. Rap Brown and Stokely Carmichael, as well as many other civil rights activists.

Howard Moore had visited Angela while she was still at the Women's House of Detention in New York. His visit had been intended as a gesture of solidarity. Angela asked him to join the defense team. He agreed. Shortly after her extradition, Howard Moore moved, with his family, to Berkeley, California.

Other attorneys, including Sheldon Otis, Michael Tigar, Dennis

Roberts, Allan Brotsky, and representatives from the National Conference of Black Lawyers, the American Civil Liberties Union, and the National Lawyers Guild assisted in the preparations of numerous pre-trial motions over an eighteen month period.

On February 5th, 1971 our attorneys filed a series of motions, and memoranda of points and authority in support of the motions, to set aside the indictment against Angela Y. Davis.

We challenged the method of selection of the Marin County Grand Jury, and the legality of its proceedings.

We argued that pre-trial publicity had been exhaustive and highly prejudicial, precluding any possibility of a fair trial.

We moved for dismissal of all charges under Section 995 of the California Penal Code which provides that an indictment must be based upon reasonable and probable cause. Our brief said: "The motion seeks dismissal of the indictment because it is not founded upon relevant evidence which establishes probable cause, but upon irrelevant evidence which even if true, admissible and given all the weight which the most exuberant prosecutor could claim for it, establishes no more than a set of innocent acts . . ."

On February 21st, 1971, Assistant Attorney General Albert Harris, the prosecutor in the Davis case, told reporters he intended to "use every bit of evidence we can find between now and the time of the trial . . .", to convict Angela Davis. Harris said the prosecution had already amassed over 500 photographic and evidentiary exhibits, and had a list of more than 200 potential witnesses.

RUCHELL Magee conceived and implemented his own pre-trial strategy in accord with the dictates of his case. Ruchell had first of all to seek judicial recognition that he had been falsely imprisoned in the state penitentiary for almost eight years by state authorities. By establishing the illegality of his original conviction, Ruchell could show just cause for his participation in the August 7th events.

Five different judges presided in the Davis-Magee case in the first five months of pre-trial hearings. Either Angela or Ruchell presented causal and/or peremptory challenges against all of them. Finally, the California Judicial Counsel appointed Richard E. Arnason as the presiding judge in the case. Arnason was a superior court judge from nearby Contra Costa County.

Every judge in the case had tried to saddle Ruchell with one or another public defender or court-appointed attorney. Ruchell rejected all legal assistance, insisted upon his right to act as his own lawyer and doggedly pursued his pre-trial strategy.

Ruchell Magee's first pre-trial objective was to win a "petition of removal" of his case from the state court to federal court. His petition sought relief in federal court, on grounds that the California state courts had systematically violated his constitutional rights. Had Ruchell succeeded in this effort he would have cut directly to the core of the legal issues in his case, and won a stunning moral victory.

Judge Arnason insisted that Ruchell Magee could not petition for removal of his case to the federal courts unless Angela Davis, as his co-defendant, joined in the removal petition.

Angela Davis told the judge that she and Ruchell Magee were "bound together by the indictment and bound together in other ways. We are both Black, we were born into a racist society, and we are bound together because we have refused to acquiesce in racism. Each time Magee's rights are trampled upon I am also not receiving the benefits of justice. Each time his rights are negated and denied, my rights are negated and denied . . ."

Angela said for these reasons, she would join Ruchell Magee in his petition for removal.

The state proceedings were automatically suspended. A hearing was set on the removal petition in federal district court in San Francisco. Angela and Ruchell were brought to the federal court. Both were bound in chains. Judge Conti presided. He denied the motion without a formal hearing. The judge said the motion was "frivolous."

The case went back to the state court. Pre-trial hearings on the Davis motions were to resume. Ruchell Magee resolved to pursue his pre-trial strategy as well. The two legal strategies, each fulfilling the requisite needs of each individual, were nevertheless divergent. A legal severance of the two cases seemed a necessity. Ruchell and Angela jointly presented the motion for severance. It was granted.

LESS *than two weeks after Angela's arrival at the Marin County jail, our attorneys had filed papers to have her admitted to bail. A hearing on that issue had been set for March 15th. The motion was not actually argued until the first week in June, 1971. Judge Arnason said he would render a decision on June 15th.*

We presented the court with petitions bearing the signatures of 35,000 people in the United States urging Angela's release on bail. Last minute appeals for bail were sent to the judge by Coretta Scott King, Reverend Ralph Abernathy, Congresswoman Bella Abzug.

The Marin County Probation Department issued its bail report prepared at the request of Judge Arnason. The Chief Probation Officer James B. Soetaert, recommended Angela's release on bail.

On June 15th, 1971 Judge Richard Arnason denied bail.

The judge said Ms. Davis was certainly the type of person to be released on bail. She had no prior criminal record. She could be gainfully employed. She had a place to live. But under Section 1270 of the California Penal Code, he said, he lacked the legal authority to free her pending trial.

Section 1270 held that all persons criminally charged were entitled to bail, except in capital offenses where the presumption of guilt was great, or the evidence thereof overwhelming.

Angela's release on bail was fundamental to restoring the presumption of innocence in her case. The judge's decision reinforced the presumption of Angela's guilt. It was a crushing blow.

We had worked at a frantic pace for eight months, assembled an impressive array of political forces. We had been so sure of a victory in June. Instead we had been unceremoniously and brutally repulsed. Emotionally drained, physically exhausted, the defense collapsed.

During the Summer of '71 I went to Europe, largely in connection with defense efforts. I returned to the San Francisco Bay area in mid-August. The defense was in legal and political disarray. We were still reeling from the June decision. But, the worst was yet to come.

1

Friday, August 20, 1971. I arrived in San Francisco about 8 o'clock that night. I had brought Margaret Burnham's six year old son with me on the plane, back from a summer with her family in New York. Margaret met us at the airport.

It is an hour's drive to San Jose, and, although Margaret lived in San Francisco, she offered to drive me home. I was grateful for the ride. She asked about Europe and I asked about Angela. Abroad support was growing. It had been a rough summer at home. "Par for the course," she had said. It was Margaret's favorite expression.

I found the house dank and cheerless after two months of non-use. I wanted Margaret to stay, but she was anxious to be on her way. I dumped my bags in the dining room, retraced my steps to the front hall, flipping on the lights, scooping up enormous stacks of mail. I settled in the kitchen with the mail.

I read all the letters, most of the newspapers, unpacked, waited impatiently for morning. I hadn't seen Angela in seven and a half weeks.

Saturday, August 21, 1971. There was no point in leaving for the Marin County jail before seven in the morning. They wouldn't let me in before eight. I was restless. At six I went out and had some breakfast at a diner a few blocks from the house. It was crowded with tired truckers. I left an hour later, bought some gas and drove to San Rafael.

It was a beautiful day, sunfilled, clear, crisp. There was no traffic and I sped along the freeway at a more than respectable clip, windows rolled down, the wind reviving me after no sleep.

The Marin Civic Center was deserted as it always was on a Saturday. I parked by the lake, in the park across the street from the jail. The ducks were just beginning to stir. I walked toward the entrance, familiarity flooding back.

"Haven't seen you in a long time . . ." The deputy at the front desk, chatty and in good humor remains anonymous now as then, the blurred image of his face, the smartly pressed khaki uniform. There was no hassle; the searching routine.

I waited only a few minutes in the cubed visiting booth. Angela came in. She was burdened with books and papers. She looked like a professor entering a seminar, except for the childish prison garb hanging shapelessly on her thin frame. Her eyes were warm in welcome. We reached out in natural affection through the steel grating.

At 2:30 in the afternoon Howard Moore tapped on the window of the visiting booth and clenched his fist in greeting. He had brought a young attorney, Barbara Ratcliffe, with him to see Angela.

Angela was escorted back to her cell, and the three of us, Howard, Barbara and I, joined her there.

Barbara was dark, tall, slender, graceful. Her delicate, softly defined features blended easily in a relaxed, almost mischievous smile. She was meeting Angela for the first time. Her awkward expressions of admiration were received with shy embarrassment. Angela kidded gently, and we all relaxed. The legal issues were vigorously pursued.

Barbara knew a lot about the law governing illegal search and seizure. Angela had been the victim of a number of apparently unauthorized searches conducted by various government agencies. One such search was made of her car upon her return from Mexico in July 1970. The constitutionality of the search was in question, and Barbara now efficiently and thoroughly reviewed the factual details with Angela.

At precisely 4 pm the deputies opened the door to the cell and announced that Barbara and I would be required to leave. This was not unusual. Only attorneys-of-record could stay later. We were led out into the inner corridor of the jail. We walked towards the exit, intending to take the elevator we always used in the outer corridor. A deputy blocked our path. He directed us back down the inner corridor and ordered us into an elevator normally reserved for transporting prisoners. He accompanied us for the ride down. Something was wrong.

We stepped out of the elevator. We were in the police garage. It was barricaded shut. The guard shifted the electronic gears on the barricade. The gate opened. We walked outside and into a glaring sunlight.

There was frantic activity all around us. Dozens of deputies, highway patrolmen, rifles, shotguns, were now in full view. Afraid to move, we hugged the concrete embankment protruding from the building.

Aside from the police careening through the parking lot, the area was deserted. We asked what the fuss was all about. Nobody would tell us anything. We watched and waited.

A few minutes passed. A Black family driving an old, beat-up, green Chevy, pulled up and stopped under the archway at the entrance to the jail. In the back seat of the car we could see a couple of little girls playing with each other. A young woman was sitting next to them. An older woman was in the front seat. The driver got out and walked around the rear of the car and approached the deputy standing at the door.

The man walked casually, gestured easily toward the jail.

"Is that the jail?" he asked the deputy.

The deputy jerked his head affirmatively.

"Is Angela Davis in there?", the man asked.

The deputy jerked his head again.

"Just wanted to see the place," the man said. "Just wanted to see it."

He stepped back and surveyed the fortress. Then he smiled as if to dispel the tension, and walked back to his car and got in and drove off.

The deputy hurried into the street with a piece of paper and a pencil and wrote down the license number of the old beat-up green Chevy and put it out over the police radio.

Howard came down a few minutes later, informing us that he had been ordered to leave the jail for "security reasons." Incensed, he had demanded some explanation as Ms. Davis' counsel. He was warned, in no uncertain terms, to leave the area. We left.

I was just outside of San Jose when CBS broadcast its first bulletin from San Quentin. It said simply that there had been an attempted escape, that an unknown number of prisoners were involved, including one of the Soledad Brothers, and that six men had been killed. I knew then that George Jackson was dead. The news continued on into the night.

At approximately 3 pm the authorities said that George Jackson had been shot to death by guards in the prison yard at San Quentin while attempting to escape. "A bullet," it was reported later, "entered the lower part of his back and passed upward along the right side of body and exited through his brain . . ."

That Saturday afternoon Georgia Jackson had rushed to San Quentin to learn of her son's fate. A guard at the gate said: "Last year we killed one of your sons. Today we killed another. If you aren't careful, you'll have no sons left."

Georgia Jackson said to the guard: "I have sons throughout the world wherever people are fighting for freedom."

I REMEMBER once Angela had shown me a photograph of George Jackson. He was 15 years old when it was taken. He was sitting on the beach, hunched over, head down, knees pulled up to his chest, hands hung limply over them, feet dug into the sand. . .

There was no time to grieve. There were political estimates to be made, decisions to be implemented. Our staff worked around the clock. Regardless of what the final details would reveal about his death, we believed that George Jackson had been assassinated. It was an awful provocation. The chilling reports by prison officials alleging the murder of guards and the mutiliation of their bodies could allow for massive police reprisals in the ghettos and prisons across the state.

We feared for the lives of Ruchell Magee, John Clutchette, Fleeta Drumgo, Hugo Pinell, Larry Spain, Luis Talamantez, a dozen other brothers. Repression inside the San Quentin Adjustment Center would be savage.

Franklin Alexander, national co-chairman of our committee, had a way about him in a crisis. His face was taut with fatigue and shock, but his energy was unlimited and contagious. He commanded, debated, listened, acted.

We called our committees around the country and wired others throughout the world. Stop the terror! Investigate the murder! Free Angela on bail!

We organized a twenty-four hour a day picketline manned by hundreds around the gates of San Quentin. We urged a congressional investigation and brought Congressman Ronald Dellums, California Assemblyman Willie Brown and prominent San Francisco physician and publisher Carleton Goodlett, to the gates of the prison. Our massive presence assured their admission.

We issued statements, fought with the media to give accurate coverage, demanded (successfully) that the families and attorneys of the survivors of the August 21st carnage be allowed visiting rights.

The prisoners inside the adjustment center continued to struggle. Black prisoner Larry Justice sent a message out with his lawyer: "We need the support of the people . . . If we don't get that we're dead men."

MONDAY, August 23rd. Attorneys for the two surviving Soledad Brothers, John Clutchette and Fleeta Drumgo, arrived at the San Francisco Hall of Justice for a previously scheduled pre-trial hearing. San Quentin authorities failed to bring the Brothers to court. The prosecution didn't come either. Neither did the judge. The lawyers scurried around the building demanding to know if their clients were still alive. The hearing was re-scheduled for the next morning.

Tuesday, August 24th. The hall of justice was ringed with security. Police carried automatic weapons, even 'tommy guns.' A helicopter flew the prisoners from San Quentin to the courthouse, landing on its roof. Men and women wishing to attend the hearing—and there were hundreds—went through elaborate search procedures, once, twice, three times. Most did not get into the courtroom. Women were forced to undress, lifting bras and dropping their pants. Inside the courtroom a plexiglass shield had been erected, separating the spectators from defendants and counsel.

John and Fleeta entered the courtroom, heavily shackled. Both walked with obvious difficulty. They attempted, through their lawyers, to present a petition to the court. It was on behalf of twenty-six prisoners in the adjustment center. The petition was handwritten, on the back of a large greeting card. It was a motion for a restraining order against San Quentin officials. It began:

> We the undersigned, each being held incommunicado, because of suffering from both wounds and internal injuries inflicted upon our persons by known and unknown agents of Warden Louis S. Nelson, petition the court . . .

The petition charged that the men had been forced to lie nude on the ground outside the adjustment center from 4 p.m. to 10 p.m. on Saturday, August 21st, and that they had been beaten individually with blackjacks, clubs and guns. "Allan Mancino was begging to have his handcuffs loosened," the petition said. "A guard stepped forward and told the man to keep quiet and shot part of his leg off." Mancino, the petition charged, had not received medical attention for more than an hour after he was shot.

The petition stated that the prisoners are "now being threatened constantly" and "are sure that Warden Louis Nelson will continue the beatings and threats."

The judge refused to hear the motion. After court the lawyers released copies of the petiton to the press. Our protests at San Quentin continued.

Two days later John and Fleeta were again brought to court, draped in chains. The Hall of Justice was ringed with security. Court convened. Defense attorneys charged that both men had been severely beaten by prison guards on Tuesday afternoon and night, and all day on Wednesday in reprisal for bringing the prisoners' petition to court. The lawyers sought a restraining order against San Quentin officials. The judge refused to hear the motion. Shaking violently, Fleeta Drumgo screamed, "Kill me now, man, you're going to kill me anyway." Both men struggled with their manacled arms, and finally stripped off their shirts exposing the welts and burns and lacerations.

A defense attorney rose to argue yet another motion for a restraining order, beginning, "Your honor . . ." Doris Maxwell, John's mother, had had enough. Leaping to her feet, her face knotted in anguish, she sobbed and shouted, "What's honor, you're no honor!"

On signal from the judge two deputies seized Ms. Maxwell. She collapsed as two brothers sought to rescue her. Again the judge motioned from the bench and the San Francisco Tactical Squad invaded the packed courtroom. For four minutes it became a screaming bedlam. It was cleared of spectators. There was blood on the floor, on some of the seats, and in spots on the wall.

ANGELA sat in front of the typewriter in her cell thirty-six hours after George's death. It was very crowded with staff and lawyers. The place was littered with cigarettes, and dozens of pieces of paper, many of them containing half-completed sentences, random words and thoughts—drafts of the public statement she was now completing.

She had not slept at all since Howard had brought her the news of George's death. Overwhelmed with grief, her face ashen in shock, her eyes wet with unending tears, comprehending the magnitude of the loss with infinitely greater intensity than any of us, she could still write. Her head bent over the machine, fingers fiercely attacking the keys.

She ripped the last page from the carriage and flung the statement together with George's *Letters From Prison* onto the table in front of us. There were four carbons and the original:

> An enemy bullet has once again brought grief and sadness to Black people and to all who oppose racism and injustice and who love and fight for freedom. On Saturday, August 21, a San Quentin guard's sniper bullet executed George Jackson and wiped out the last modicum of freedom with which he had persevered and resisted so fiercely for eleven years . . .

> His impact on the community was and continues to be boundless. George's example of courage in the face of the spectre of summary execution; his insights honed in the torment of seven years of solitary confinement; his perseverance in the face of overwhelming odds will continue to be a source of inspiration to all our sisters and brothers inside prison walls and outside . . .

In detail she explained the meaning of his life and work, retaught the lessons of prison, argued the roots of the oppression afflicting all people of color. At the end she wrote: "With his example before me, my tears and grief are rage at the system responsible for his murder. He wrote his epitaph when he said:

> Hurl me into the next existence, the descent into hell won't turn me. I'll crawl back to dog his trail forever. They won't defeat my revenge,

never, never. I'm part of a righteous people who anger slowly, but rage undammed. We'll gather at his door in such a number that the rumbling of our feet will make the earth tremble.

2

Emma Gelders Sterne belonged to a very special breed of white woman, like the southern abolitionists Sarah and Angelina Grimké in another era. Emma was born in Birmingham, Alabama before the turn of the century. She was raised in Birmingham.

Emma broke with the racist foundations of southern society. She embraced all that was progressive and liberating.

Emma was a writer. She wrote stories for children. Her stories are about the lives of women and men who devoted themselves to the liberation movement. Her best known work is *The Long Black Schooner*, the story of the slave uprising aboard the *Amistad* in 1839. Her biographies of Mary McLeod Bethune and Benito Juarez are well-known. Her study of twelve southern white people who, from the 18th century to the present, opposed slavery and racial oppression, is a particularly unique contribution. It is called *They Took Their Stand*. Her last published work is a splendid biography of W.E.B. Du Bois.

At the age of 74 Emma, and folk-singer Joan Baez led a sit-in demonstration at the Army Induction Center in Oakland, California to protest the war in Vietnam. Emma was carried off to jail smiling triumphantly, her frail arm upraised, her fingers formed in a glorious "V." She served ten days in the Santa Rita Rehabilitation Center.

Emma was tiny; energetic; her face wrinkled, hair perfectly white, eyes clear blue, humor delicious, spirit undaunted, her capacity for work undiminished. She lived in San Jose in an old comfortable home, in the stately and conservative community of

Willow Glen. Her garden behind the house was renowned among all friends and acquaintances. Emma was forever walking through it, compulsively plucking the weeds while others strained to keep up with her.

Emma wrote the very first pamphlet about the Soledad Brothers. She wasn't credited as the author. It was published by the defense committee. Emma learned of George and John and Fleeta just after the murder charges were handed down by the Monterey County Grand Jury in February 1970. She met with their families. She talked to the lawyers. She journeyed a hundred miles in a day to attend court in Salinas, where the first pre-trial hearings were held. Her pamphlet was a clear, reasoned, compassionate appeal for justice. It ended this way:

> The thousands of Black youth trapped in the prison system through poverty and racial prejudice stand before us in the persons of Fleeta Drumgo, John Clutchette and George Jackson. The wasted lives, the brutal inhumanity inherent in the prison system is here on trial. These men are being routed to the gas chamber for refusing to bow down, for trying to save their identities and self-respect. Their lives are in jeopardy for who they are, not for what they have done.

Emma had understood the significance of the drama about to unfold. Thousands of people read her pamphlet and many joined the movement Angela came to lead.

Emma became seriously ill in July 1971. She was still hospitalized in San Jose on August 21, when news of the atrocity at San Quentin reached her. Enraged, sickened, she just couldn't eat any more. Family and friends—we went to see her. She could not be comforted. She had no act of defiance left. Eight days later, on August 29, 1971, at the age of 77 she died.

A month later on a grassy knoll bedecked with flowers, under a bright sun, in Willow Glen park, a couple of hundred people gathered to pay tribute to Emma Gelders Sterne. She would have loved the memorial.

In her top bureau drawer where some people keep their jewels, Emma kept her worn and dog-eared volume of Walt Whitman's *Leaves of Grass*. Selections from it were read and those who had known her—the children's librarian at the San Jose Public Library, fellow members of the Women's International League for Peace and Freedom, her comrades in the Communist Party,

community activists, Chicano and Black—paid tribute. At the end
Bertolt Brecht's poem *To Posterity*, one of Emma's favorites, was
read:

> Indeed, I live in the dark ages!
> A guileless word is an absurdity.
> A smooth forehead betokens a hard heart.
> He who laughs
> Has not yet heard
> The terrible tidings . . .

A few months later when the site of Angela's trial was shifted to
San Jose, Margaret Burnham moved into Emma's old house.
When Angela finally got out on bail she lived there too. We often
gathered after court for drinks in the garden . . .

3

On the day after George Jackson's murder hundreds of inmates at Attica State Prison in upstate New York paid silent
tribute to their slain brother. The Official Report of the New
York State Special Commission on Attica described the scene in
the dining area on the morning of August 22nd:

> Instead of the usual banter and conversation of inmates coming out of
> their cells to line up for the march to breakfast, officers were greeted
> by somber inmates who moved silently out of their cells and lined up
> in rows of twos with a Black man at the head of each row; many of
> them wore black armbands. They marched silently to breakfast where
> they took their usual places around the tables, but did not eat. Inmate
> participation at the morning meal was far from universal, and many
> of those who participated in the fast were unsure of the reason for it.
> By noon, however, all knew they were observing a day of mourning
> and protest over the death of George Jackson. For the young correc-
> tion officers who found themselves in the mess hall with 700 silent,

fasting inmates wearing black armbands, the very silence and the
mood of unreserved hostility was the most threatening and frighten-
ing experience in their memory . . .

The protest was not an isolated event. Prisoners at Attica had
engaged in a series of actions during the preceding months to
protest inhuman conditons and racist provocations. In July 1971
a group of prisoners had drawn up a Manifesto of Demands and
sent it to the commissioner of prisons and the governor of the
state. The Manifesto was patterned after one drawn by the men at
Folsom Prison in California the previous November. The Attica
Manifesto began:

> We the imprisoned men of Attica prison, want an end to the injustice
> suffered by all prisoners, regardless of race, creed or color. The prep-
> aration and content of this document has been constructed under the
> unified efforts of all races and social segments of this prison . . . Attica
> prison is one of the most classic institutions of authoritative inhuman-
> ity upon men . . . The programs which we are submitted to under the
> facade of rehabilitation, is relative to the ancient stupidity of pouring
> water on a drowning man, inasmuch as we are treated for our hos-
> tilities by our program administrators with their hostility as medica-
> tion . . .

There were 27 "moderate" demands, in the actual words of the
Special Commission, "including a commitment to peaceful
change." The Manifesto set forth what the prisoners believed to
be their basic constitutional and human rights.

In August, Herbert X. Blyden, who was to play a leading role in
the September uprising, wrote to New York State Senator John
Dunne. Referring to the prisoners' demands, Blyden said: "We
have been trying to apprise the public and the news media of
conditions for sometime, to no avail. Your assistance in these
serious matters is urgently needed."

The protest on August 22nd, honoring the memory of George
Jackson, served as the focal point for the gathering of oppositional forces within the prison. On this day the men had, according to the Special Commission, ". . . demonstrated their ability and
their willingness to act en masse and there was now some talk
about organizing a prisonwide sitdown strike."

The official response to the prisoners' Manifesto, to their letters and appeals, was negligible, relative to the urgency of the situation. The uprising began on Thursday, September 9th. It was spontaneous. It was triggered by an incident in the yard the day before, not unlike thousands of prison altercations that had happened previously, and would come again. But on this particular day the prison erupted. Twelve hundred men took control of cell block D and held 38 guards as hostages. Out of the initial chaos, emerged a prisoner-elected leadership, and a series of demands patterned after those appearing in the Manifesto.

Saturday, September 11. Two days after the insurrection had begun, I was sitting with Angela in the cell in Marin County. We were following every detail over the radio. The twelve hundred men were still holding cell block D. While the majority of the men were Black and Brown, many white prisoners were to be found in the rebel camp. A group of observers had been called to the prison by the rebels, and were meeting with them. In this way the prisoners had hoped to reach a settlement with prison authorities.

AMONG those on the Observers Committee were some well-known personalities, most sympathetic to the prisoners: New York State Assemblyman Arthur Eve, *New York Times* columnist Tom Wicker, attorney William Kunstler, Black Panther Party Chairman Bobby Seale, New York State Representative Herman Badillo, the owner and publisher of the *Amsterdam News*, Clarence Jones.

Angela and I pored through all available newspapers for information on what was happening. I had gone to Carrol & Bishops in San Jose, a store which specializes in selling out-of-town papers, and picked up the *New York Times, Washington Post, Los Angeles Times.* We kept the radio turned on and listened for every bulletin.

We listened especially for any break in the negotiations. It seemed to us that the very fact that negotiations were in progress was encouraging. Most uprisings were unceremoniously suppressed. The Attica uprising was different. There were too many prisoners involved, and the unity of Black with Brown with white, appeared unshakable. Outside support was growing.

Sunday, September 12th. Negotiations at Attica continued on and off all day. Our vigil in the cell continued. The Observers

Committee fought valiantly to stall for time, to prevent a military assault to retake the prison. At 11 o'clock Sunday morning the Observers Committee issued an appeal. It went out for immediate broadcast. We heard it a few hours later in California:

> The committee of observers in Attica prison is now convinced a massacre of prisoners and guards may take place in this institution. For the sake of our common humanity, we call on every person who hears these words to implore the Governor of this state to come to Attica to consult with the observer committee, so we can spend time and not lives in an attempt to resolve the issues before us. Send the following telegram immediately to Governor Nelson Rockefeller in New York City, "Please go to Attica Prison to meet with the observer committee."

Monday, September 13th. The governor did not go to Attica. The invasion was on. The massacre was over in New York by the time I got in to see Angela at 8 o'clock in the morning, California time. We strained to catch every detail over the radio. The sound faded intermittently because the radio waves didn't easily penetrate the concrete and steel behind which we were locked. The frenzied voices of the reporters sounded as an echo of the chaos and terror around them.

Seventeen hundred National Guardsmen, state troopers and sheriffs' deputies, under a heavy blanket of tear gas, stormed the prison and took it, just after dawn. The once anonymous brothers inside Attica had become our closest comrades. We listened for news of the fate of those whose names and faces we had come to know. We remembered especially Brother L. D. Barclay, tall and slender, sensitive, studious face, with steel-framed glasses. He was dead.

A prisoner, transferred to Attica a few months earlier, who died in the massacre, had written a letter to a friend, "Attica, formerly the hunting grounds of the Seneca tribe of the Iroquois Nation . . . is now my home . . ."

Converging images of Indians and inmates . . . The Attica prisoners were promised food and clothing and medical care and no reprisals if they would surrender their hostages and themselves. They had refused surrender. The shooting was over. The survivors were herded into the prison yard. They were made to crawl on their stomachs. They were forced to strip. They were paraded naked before television cameras, assorted newsmen and military personnel. They were lined up to be run through tunnels back to their cells. They were repeatedly clubbed and kicked by police and guards.

Forty-three men died in the massacre, thirty-four of whom were prisoners. Well over 200 were wounded. Many of the wounded inmates were left lying among the dead and dying in the yard. Others were put on stretchers—row upon row of stretchers. All were left unattended for hours in the yard. The hostages who died (there were nine) were shot to death by police in the initial assault.

Later, a guard—one of the hostages—was interviewed on television. He said he, and others, were alive because when the invasion began the prisoners threw themselves over him and the other hostages to protect them.

Tom Wicker had reported truly: "The racial harmony that prevailed among the prisoners—it was absolutely astonishing. The prison yard was the first place I have ever seen where there was no racism."

That's right. That's why the prisoners were shot.

TIME magazine featured Attica in the September 27th issue —smart, slick reportage, informing the public of its "bitter lessons." An "unknown prisoner," it was reported, had written a poem. It was found on a scrap of paper among the ruins—the shredded document now dramatically reproduced in the pages of *Time*. The editors—refined, discriminating, charitable—judged its literary merits. It was, they said, ". . . crude but touching in its would-be heroic style . . ." Only the first stanza appeared in *Time*'s reproduction. It was painstakingly printed in black ink.

> If we must die—let it not be like hogs,
> hunted and penned in an unglorious spot.
> while round us, bark the mad and hungry dogs,
> making their mock at our accursed lot.

Time was inundated with letters informing the editors of the poem's origins. They had in fact published the first lines of Claude McKay's classic *If We Must Die*. Claude McKay, who wrote hundreds of poems and a half dozen novels, a leading figure in the Harlem Renaissance. The irony! During World War II Winston

Churchill had read this very poem before the House of Commons:

If we must die, let it not be like hogs
Hunted and penned in an inglorious spot,
While round us bark the mad and hungry dogs,
Making their mock at our accursed lot.
If we must die, O let us nobly die,
So that our precious blood may not be shed
In vain; then even the monsters we defy
Shall be contrained to honor us though dead!
O kinsmen! we must meet the common foe!
Though far outnumbered let us show us brave,
And for their thousand blows deal one deathblow!
What though before us lies the open grave?
Like men we'll face the murderous, cowardly pack,
Pressed to the wall, dying but fighting back!

("If We Must Die" is from *Selected Poems of Claude McKay* copyright 1953 by Twayne Publishers.)

4

It was three days after the Attica massacre. I'd been out at the jail most of the day. One of our lawyers—Sheldon Otis—asked me to drop by his home in Berkeley on my way back to San Jose. He said he had something urgent to discuss with me.

I arrived at Sheldon's house about 5:30 in the afternoon. There weren't many preliminaries. His distress was apparent. We went into his study. It was overflowing with paper, all of it relating to the *Davis* case. He leaned back in one of those big, brown swivel chairs, and I sank comfortably into a butterfly seat. He shoved a stack of papers into my hands and told me to "read that." There were a total of 18 pages, typed, single-spaced. This was a xeroxed copy. On each page in the lower right-hand corner, was a number. On the first page the number was hand-written in large black figures, "873." On the second page the number was stamped, upside down, "000874." On the third page, "000875" appeared, right side up, and so on. I knew from the numbers that this was something we had obtained from the prosecution, perhaps something they intended to use as evidence against Angela.

They had released copies to us in accord with the court's discovery order.

I started to read the first page: "I'm totally intoxicated, overflowing with you, wanting you more than ever before . . ." I felt the flush of tension pass through my body. It was a diary. The first entry was July 8, 1971. The last entry was August 5th. It was something Angela had written to George, or at least for him.

Angela and George had met together on July 8th. It was their first and only encounter. Judge Arnason had issued a court order permitting a meeting between them, and John Clutchette, Fleeta Drumgo, Ruchell Magee and all our respective attorneys. With the prosecution alleging that the purpose of the August 7th events had been to free the Soledad Brothers, and with George's name appearing repeatedly throughout the grand jury indictment against Angela and Ruchell, the meeting was essential to trial preparations.

The conference had gone on for eight hours. It had taken place in the men's mess hall at the Marin County jail. "A place," Angela said, "that's colder (both figuratively and literally) than the work cell or any other place in this jail . . . Throughout the entire session there was a small army of leering pigs standing behind the glass in the kitchen—all this and George was chained and shackled, as was Ruchell . . ."

I continued reading the diary, my eyes skimming the pages: "I'm totally intoxicated, overflowing with you, wanting you more than ever before. An hour and a half since the last embrace. You're in your cell and I'm in mine . . . if you knew what a hard time I'm having typing out these few words—my mind wanders into other worlds full of you, my chin in my hand, reality-fantasies lure me away from this machine . . . though time seemed short, eight hours but a moment . . . it was a moment containing a happy, loving eternity . . . Love you . . . with love even more unbounded . . ."

I stopped. I handed the diary back to Sheldon. I didn't want to read any more. He handed it back to me. He said the attorney general had it. They'd searched George's cell within hours of his death and found it among his legal papers. It was now part of the prosecution's case against Angela. Presumably, Sheldon then explained, they intended to shift some of the overtly political emphasis of their case to portray Angela's love for George as motivation for murder. Sheldon said he thought I should finish reading it.

I went back to it and through it. It was tender, awkward, sublime, anguished. I finished it. I had nothing to say. I went home.

ON OCTOBER 1st, 1971 the Marin County Grand Jury formally accused George Lester Jackson of murder in the death of a guard at San Quentin on the day he died. The grand jury also returned first degree murder indictments in the deaths of three guards and two inmates, against six survivors of the August Massacre: Hugo Pinell, John Larry Spain, Luis Talamantez, David Johnson, Willie Tate, and Soledad Brother Fleeta Drumgo.

David Johnson and Willie Tate had been among the first prisoners in San Quentin's Adjustment Center to file affidavits detailing the killing of Fred Billingslea by prison guards eighteen months before.

Three days after the indictments were returned, the San Quentin Six, shackled and collared, were led into the Marin County Superior Court on a chain/leash and arraigned.

1. Jonathan Jackson and Angela Davis at a rally in support of the Soledad Brothers, spring 1970. (UPI photo, by permission of UPI)

2. Angela Davis and Victoria Mercado entering the courtroom in San Jose, March 1972. (Bettina Aptheker Archive, Special Collections, McHenry Library, University of California, Santa Cruz)

3. The Soledad Brothers George Jackson and Fleeta Drumgo en route to court. (From a Soledad Brothers Defense Committee pamphlet, in Bettina Aptheker Archive, Special Collections, McHenry Library, University of California, Santa Cruz)

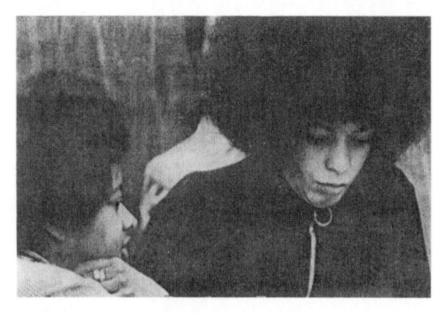

4. Attorney Margaret Burnham and Angela Davis consulting in a Marin County courtroom, September 1971. (UPI photo, by permission of UPI)

5. Press Conference in San Jose, February 23, 1972, just after Angela Davis's release on bail. Front row, left.to right: attorney Howard Moore, Fania Davis, Angela Davis, attorney Doris Brin Walker. Behind Ms. Davis is Franklin Alexander. (From a newsletter of the National United Committee to Free Angela Davis, in Bettina Aptheker Archive, Special Collections, McHenry Library, University of California, Santa Cruz)

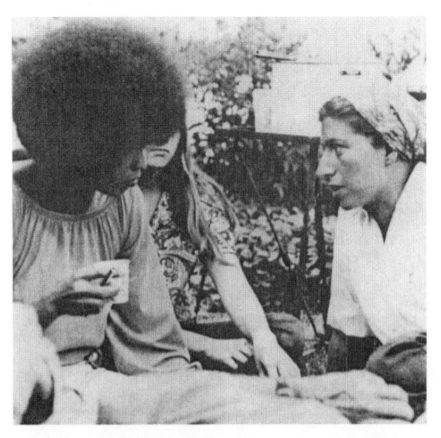

6. Angela Davis and Bettina Aptheker in San Jose, California, August 1972. (Bettina Aptheker Archive, Special Collections, McHenry Library, University of California, Santa Cruz)

7. Charlene Mitchell, executive director of the National United Committee to Free Angela Davis. (From *People's World*, in Bettina Aptheker Archive, Special Collections, McHenry Library, University of California, Santa Cruz)

8. The Soledad Brother John Clutchette. (From a Soledad Brothers Defense Committee pamphlet, in Bettina Aptheker Archive, Special Collections, McHenry Library, University of California, Santa Cruz)

9. The San Quentin prisoner Ruchell Magee, survivor of the August 7 revolt. (From a newsletter of the Ruchell Magee Defense Committee, in Bettina Aptheker Archive, Special Collections, McHenry Library, University of California, Santa Cruz.)

10. Mary Timothy, foreperson of the Angela Davis jury. (Bettina Aptheker Archive, Special Collections, McHenry Library, University of California, Santa Cruz)

11. Mrs. Sallye Davis campaigned vigorously for her daughter's freedom. (From *People's World*, in Bettina Aptheker Archive, Special Collections, McHenry Library, University of California, Santa Cruz)

12. Attorneys Doris Brin Walker and Leo Branton outside the San Jose courtroom the day of Angela Davis's acquittal. (From a newsletter of the National United Committee to Free Angela Davis, in Bettina Aptheker Archive, Special Collections, McHenry Library, University of California, Santa Cruz)

13. Angela Davis with Henry Winston, national chairman of the U.S. Communist Party, after her acquittal. (From *People's World*, in Bettina Aptheker Archive, Special Collections, McHenry Library, University of California, Santa Cruz)

5

Henry Winston, national chairman of the Communist Party, arrived in San Francisco on Tuesday, September 21st. He had come at our request. The trial was scheduled to begin in a week. We were certain there would be a delay, but we didn't expect more than a four to six week respite.

I'D KNOWN Winnie—we all called him Winnie or Winston, nobody ever called him Henry—since childhood. One of my most vivid memories, in fact, is of Winston in a banquet hall, with large chandeliers, in a hotel somewhere in Manhattan. The hall was very crowded, hot and smoky. My mother and father were there. Winnie was sitting at a long table in front of the room. The table was covered with a white cloth. Winnie was sitting towards the middle of the table. There were many other people at the table with him. I don't remember who they were except that at the extreme right end sat W.E.B. Du Bois. He was then 92 years old.

Dr. Du Bois made a speech. When he finished he walked over to Winnie. Winston stood up. The two men embraced.

The occasion was the celebration of Winnie's release from prison. He had served more than six years in a federal penitentiary for "conspiring to advocate the overthrow of the United States Government by force and violence." After worldwide appeals President John Kennedy had commuted his eight-year sentence.

Winnie had been very ill and the prison authorities had denied him proper medical care. He had had a brain tumor. It was finally removed, but it had already severed his optic nerve. And so Winnie stood there in the banquet hall and he couldn't see us, and he couldn't see Du Bois.

When it was quiet Winston made a speech. The only thing I remember him saying was, "They have robbed me of my sight, but I have not lost my vision." And the people around me were standing and cheering and crying.

WE TOOK Winston out to the Marin County jail to meet with Angela on Wednesday and again on Thursday. As with everyone else, the lieutenant made him empty all of his pockets, and put everything onto a counter, and searched him. Winston's cane—a white cane with a red tip—made the metal detector bleep. They looked it over and decided he could keep it. Winnie and Franklin walked arm-in-arm down the corridor towards Angela's cell. We passed through an electronically-controlled steel door, whining open and shut. The matron's keys clattered against another steel object. She opened the door to Angela's cell. Angela got up as we came in. Winnie moved rapidly in the direction of her voice. They hugged each other.

Winston insisted, first of all, upon knowing every detail of Angela's personal situation. He had read the affidavit by her physician, Tolbert Small, filed in conjunction with our bail motions. Dr. Small had stated that the conditions and extended nature of her confinement had "contributed immeasurable, and in some respects irrevocably" to a deterioration in her health—loss of weight, severe headaches, recurring viral infections, a fungus infection which had spread over her entire body after faulty diagnosis by the jail doctor. Most of all, Winston asked Angela about her eyes. Dr. Small had reported that "her vision has been and continues to be impaired." An opthalmologist had just that week completed an examination and stated that "early results indicate that Ms. Davis may have an early chronic glaucoma in each eye." If not promptly and properly treated we knew that this condition could lead to blindness. Winston pressed Angela for every detail. Only reluctantly did she concede any discomfort. She didn't want to talk about herself. Winston persisted. She agreed to heed his suggestions to secure what immediate relief and care might be available. Privately, Winston impressed upon me the urgency of her release on bail.

We turned to the politics of the moment. Winnie had just finished writing an analysis of the Attica rebellion. It was called, "Attica, the Road to Fascism." He handed me a carbon of the article. It was about 15 pages. He asked me to read it it aloud so we could all discuss it. I did. It took about 45 minutes. As I read his own thoughts back to him, Winston would get agitated, hurrying me on, as it were, to get to the point. His assessment of Attica, in terms of the political pressures developing in the country's highest ruling circles, and the potential breadth of oppositional trends among the people, served as the basis for the strategic decisions we were to make about Angela's defense.

It began:

> The men massacred at Attica join the list of those murdered at Jackson State, Kent State, Orangeburg, Chicago, San Quentin . . . In order to justify its murders the U.S. ruling class has to resort to even bigger lies. The "credibility gap" that deepened during the Vietnam war has now become a chasm filled with the bodies of people fighting racism and oppression at home and abroad.

> Behind these . . . massacres can be seen a vast conspiracy against the people's movements for change. And from situation to situation the same characters can be seen—Nixon, Rockefeller, Reagan . . . And in every situation—whether to frame Angela Davis, murder George Jackson or unleash a domestic My Lai at Attica—they use the same lying script: the victims are the guilty ones . . .

He accused the governor and the prison authorities of deliberately sabotaging the negotiations with the Observer Committee at Attica. He unequivocally supported the demands of the prisoners. "Attica," he said, "is the road to fascism, racism, repression. The frameup of political prisoners is the road to Attica. . ."

Recalling the Ludlow Massacre of striking miners in 1913, executed by the governor's father, John D. Rockefeller, in which over 100 men, women and children were shot to death, Winston sought to remind the labor movement that justice was on the side of the Attica insurgents. At the end he called for Nelson Rockefeller's impeachment, for the implementation of the 28 demands already promised the prisoners, for no reprisals against them, and for indemnity to the families of all those slain or wounded at Attica. He also renewed the appeal for Angela's immediate release on bail, and called for the freedom of all political prisoners.

Winston had made the events of the past weeks fall into a political perspective, and not simply the personal traumas that had so shaken each of us. Angela's trial fell into sharp relief. She was a political target, as George had been, as the prisoners at Attica had been, as the people of Vietnam were. Her freedom transcended the fate of a single individual. Her life was bound up with the whole future direction of the country—not in some messianic sense, but in terms of concrete realities of power and politics.

Winston spoke at length about a rally being planned in New York for that coming Saturday, September 25th. Originally the New York "Free Angela" committee had conceived of an action to coincide with what we thought was to have been the opening of the trial. Now it had burgeoned into a potentially massive assembly in response to Attica. Winnie detailed the breadth of organizational endorsement. Over and over again he urged upon us the fight for bail.

Bail. Bail. Bail. It's the link to move the chain. It's the prosecution's strongest link, therefore it's also their weakest link. You can reach the largest number of people with this issue. They don't have to evaluate the evidence against Angela, they don't have to affirm her innocence. All they have to do is affirm her right to a fair trial, affirm her *presumption* of innocence. Release would transform Angela's status. She would no longer be as a caged criminal too dangerous to walk the streets. Release would make possible proper defense preparations, restore her health, inspire greater support.

Winston fervently believed that bail could be won. I don't think any of us believed him, but we did see in his concrete examples and in his appeal, a way to resume the fight. We agreed to launch a new offensive for bail. It was the most important strategic decision we were to make.

6

The contours of the political campaign emerged with striking clarity. By the first week in October our staff had plunged into activity.

We faced monumental problems. We had almost no money. Nobody beyond our own limited circles knew what was happening in the case. Press coverage had been sparse since June, the drudgery of legal wrangling hardly worthy of front-page coverage. The trial was seemingly upon us.

Sheldon Otis, who had done much of the evidentiary work in the pre-trial phase of the case was unable to continue as defense counsel. We needed at least one and possibly two more trial lawyers.

Our bail appeal was already pending before the California State Supreme Court. A decison was expected by the end of October. We had three, four weeks at the most, to pull everything together.

Margaret and Howard notified the court on September 20th that we intended to make two additional pre-trial motions. One would seek the suppression of certain evidence. Another would seek a change of venue, to shift the site of the trial from Marin County to San Francisco. In a brief court appearance on September 27th, Judge Arnason postponed the start of the trial until November 1, and agreed to hear formal arguments on the suppression and change of venue motions commencing October 14th.

Despite the severance of Ruchell Magee's case from Angela's we had resolved to continue with efforts which might aid in his defense. Late in August he requested assistance. There was reason to believe that Marin County officials had filed an incomplete and inaccurate autopsy report on Judge Harold Haley.

Rob Baker of our national staff was released for several weeks from his responsibilities in the Committee's offices in order to research this and related legal issues. Rob worked with Ruchell and with his court-appointed lawyer, Ernest Graves. They succeeded, on September 23rd, in securing a court order to have the judge's body exhumed. The new autopsy revealed important information which was to be utilized by our defense in the cross examination of presecution witnesses and would no doubt be used by Ruchell when his case was finally brought to trial.

By the end of September our staff was in desperate need of reinforcement. While many people generously volunteered their time, there were only five of us working steadily as full-time staff. Rob Baker's main responsibility was to run the national office, and Kendra, Franklin and myself tried to do everything else. Fania had just left for Europe to begin a six-week speaking tour. She was not due to return to the United States before the middle of November. There was no doubt that her trip came at a critical moment. World opinion was significant, and its impact in the coming weeks was to be one of several decisive factors in our fight to win Angela's release on bail. Nevertheless, her departure left only four of us in the national center.

Early in October Charlene Mitchell arrived in San Francisco from New York and joined our beleaguered crew. Charlene had been working with the defense from our New York regional office ever since Angela's arrest. She had been one of the main organizers of the rally in New York's Central Park Mall called in response to Attica. She was co-chairperson of the Black Liberation Commission of the Communist Party. Charlene was to make an immense contribution to our work.

I had first met Charlene when I came to California in 1962 to attend college. She was living in Los Angeles. Common political causes assured our acquaintance. Over the years we had attended countless meetings together.

We became friends in Berlin in June 1969. We were attending a Women's Congress as fraternal delegates from the United States. A group of women from North and South Vietnam were also attending the Congress as fraternal delegates and invited us up to their rooms late one evening.

They greeted us formally, but very warmly. Almost at once our attention was drawn to one of them. She was of the Montagnard people, darker in complexion than her compatriots, and she spoke a distinctive language. Her name was Duana. She said little in the beginning.

Our initial discussions were formal, reserved, focusing on factual accounts of the situation in Vietnam, and the political dimensions of the anti-war movement in the United States.

An hour passed. Duana began to speak. Her words had first to be translated into Vietnamese, then from Vietnamese to German, and finally from German to English. It took two to three minutes before her thoughts reached us. She watched our faces intently for the moment of understanding, so she could go on.

She described the war in the countryside as she had lived it. All formality was gone. In her whole lifetime she had never known peace. "We rebuild our homes and they bomb them again and again and again. These are our villages. Where do they want us to go? Where do they want us to live?"

Duana continued: "I have to fight. I don't want to fight. I don't want to kill your soldiers. They are so young. They are just boys. Why don't they go home? All we want is to be left alone."

The Vietnamese women presented us with gifts, rings and combs made from F-105 fighter bombers shot down over the North, and beautiful scarves made by members of the National Liberation Front in the South.

Clumsily we dug into our own bags and pulled out peace buttons and pinned them onto their black, loosely-fit garments.

We said good-bye and extended our hands. They took our hands in theirs and drew us closer. Duana embraced Charlene. They kissed each other. Out of a common oppression they had forged a special bond of solidarity.

Charlene and I stepped out into the hallway. Arms pressed tightly around each other. We walked down the red-carpeted corridor in silence.

CHARLENE took one look at the inadequate organization of the National United Committee to Free Angela Davis and began to set things right side up. For example, it was not only that our financial situation was precarious, but we hadn't known how to keep proper financial records. During the first year the campaign had, by-and-large, been sustained by small contributions from thousands of people. The money had been deposited regularly and receipts had been sent to each contributor. None of us, however, had any training in accounting. As Franklin said one night at a meeting, the only thing we did know was that when we withdrew money we were supposed to keep a record of the date, the amount and the purpose. We did. Hundreds of pieces of paper were scattered all over the office in folders and desk drawers. It was a bookkeeper's nightmare.

We couldn't launch a proper financial drive approaching individuals and organizations for substantial contributions until we put our own books in order. We had to be able to account for every penny. Charlene worked for three weeks pasting scraps of paper together and recontructed our financial history. Then she taught a couple of volunteers how to keep proper books.

Costs incurred in any criminal prosecution are massive. In one of this magnitude we estimated that total expenses in the next year were going to approach a quarter of a million dollars.

By the end of the summer we had no current literature about the case. We had no money to pay a printer, or even to buy paper and ink for use on a mimeograph machine. There were thousands of unanswered letters in the national office. We had no money for postage. We had accumulated debts running into thousands of dollars.

Our lawyers had not been paid in weeks. Just to work effectively they needed office space and equipment, secretarial assistance. All had families to support.

Our financial bankruptcy reflected a concrete political reality, and it was this that Charlene, and Winston earlier, had brought home to us. We were talking about the case amongst ourselves and our close friends and associates. But that was all. We had to reach out to people on whatever basis they were willing to start listening. There was tremendous sentiment for Angela as evidenced by the mail, the spontaneous actions we heard about. But we weren't organizing that sentiment into a unified, political movement. We had to overhaul our approach to the case and overcome a sectarian syndrome that threatened us with paralysis.

OUR PROBLEM was reinforced by deep racist and anti-communist prejudices among white people in general, and New Left activists in particular. Repeated accusations swept the movement. Angela was being used by the Communist Party. The Party was confiscating defense funds for its own purposes, etc.

Denials from the Party, from Angela, from the committee were ignored. Support from those who should have been most willing to commit themselves to the defense of a political prisoner was often late in coming, or withheld entirely.

Months later, in February 1972, Ed Montgomery, a notorious right-wing columnist for the San Francisco *Examiner* published one of his exclusives charging that the Communist Party was diverting defense funds into its own organizational pockets. Montgomery reported that the star witness to this pilfery was Gerard Connolly, a twenty-two year old *agent provocateur* employed by the FBI to infiltrate the Young Workers Liberation League and the Angela Davis Defense Committee in New York. Connolly had recently testified before the Subversive Activities Control Board and the House Committee on Internal Security on defense activities, Montgomery reported.

As our political approach toward organizing and fund-raising in the committee changed, we achieved greater and greater success, despite these obstacles.

There were many people who might not be willing to assume Angela's innocence, but they were willing to help guarantee her a fair trial. While they might be reluctant to contribute to a political campaign which called for her immediate freedom, they would be willing to contribute toward her legal defense. It was a valid distinction.

After considerable discussion we decided to establish a special fund to be used solely for Angela's legal defense. Charlene, in conjunction with others in New York City, most notably William L. Patterson, took the necessary steps to insure its creation.

Ossie Davis, actor and playwright, agreed to be chairman of the Board of Trustees of the Angela Davis Legal Defense Fund. A number of other well-known personalities agreed to serve as trustees, and Marvel Cooke, long time activist in the liberation movement, agreed to serve as the Fund's executive secretary. Its offices were opened in New York City.

With this accomplished we could consider new approaches to fund raising. I was given the responsibility to initiate some efforts in this direction. I saw people in New York, Los Angeles and elsewhere. The response reaffirmed what we should have remembered all along: people were prepared to help.

Stanley Levison was an attorney in New York. He had been a close associate of Martin King. He was still very much involved in the work of the Southern Christian Leadership Conference (SCLC). After some discussion as to the status of the *Davis* case Stanley agreed to speak with other members of the SCLC Board of Trustees to see what assistance they might render. He called a few days later to inform me that the board had decided to allow the Angela Davis defense to send a fund appeal to their entire national mailing list. It comprised more than 100,000 individuals. We had never before considered such an ambitious project.

Stanley enlisted the help of Moe Foner, public relations director for the Hospital Workers Union, Local 1199. Together they raised enough money to pay for the cost of the mailing. They suggested that the most effective letter could be written by Angela herself. I drafted one version. Stanley drafted another. We gave both to Angela, and she wrote the final appeal:

> I am writing to you from a cell in the Marin County jail . . .
>
> As my trial approaches, the need to insure judicial fairness and bail in order that I may better prepare my defense becomes increasingly urgent. Even if we disagree on some things, we are surely united in our affirmation of principles of due process and equality before the law.
>
> I am charged with three capital offenses—murder, kidnapping and conspiracy. My life is at stake, but as I have repeatedly said, not simply the life of a lone individual, but a life which belongs to Black people and all who are tired of poverty and racism and the unjust imprisonment of tens of thousands . . .

The letter was taken to a printer in New York. He read it and told Stanley he would cut his fee in half. One of the partners in the printing house personally contributed $300 to defray expenses. Stanley spoke with Gloria Steinem, the editor of *MS* magazine, and she readily agreed to serve as the treasurer for this emergency appeal. All money was to go to our legal defense fund.

The response was overwhelming. In the first six weeks we received upwards of $35,000. By December the total had climbed to over $50,000. In fact, the response was so fine that the reactionary columnist William Buckley devoted an entire column, syndicated in newspapers across the country, to a scathing attack on Ms. Steinem for lending her support to such an ignoble cause.

In Los Angeles the response to our appeals was equally gratifying. For more than a year a group of artists and writers had maintained an Artists Committee to Free Angela Davis. During the summer they had held an art auction and raised several thousand dollars for the defense. Robert Klonsky, a veteran of the Abraham Lincoln Brigade during the Spanish Civil War, was one of the organizers of this artists group. Klonsky was also a veteran of countless political battles in the United States. I sought his help during several week-end trips to Los Angeles in October.

We saw dozens of people. We secured several thousand dollars in immediate contributions. More important, we considered the feasibility of a large-scale benefit for Angela where we might be able to raise ten or twenty thousand dollars in one evening. Robert had organized such events before. At the height of the Civil Rights Movement both the SCLC and the Student Non-Violent Coordinating Committee (SNCC) had succeeded with such efforts.

Our national staff met to plan for a benefit in Los Angeles. It would take time and money. We projected the event for January or February 1972. We went to see more people. Maya Angelou, Black writer, poet, actress, dancer, offered us every assistance. Through her we were able to reach other artists. Tim Marshall, a student at San Francisco State College knew many leading musicians. With Tim's and Maya's help we decided to attempt two benefits at the start of the New Year, one in Los Angeles and the other in the San Francisco Bay Area.

The benefits would raise needed funds. They would also be symbolic of popular sentiment. Thousands would gather to hear Sammy Davis, Jr., Aretha Franklin, Roberta Flack, Quincy Jones, and others "In Concert for Angela." In fact, four months later, thousands did gather at the Shrine Auditorium in Los Angeles for this concert which turned into a gala celebration of Angela's release on bail.

The book Angela and I had edited, *If They Come In The Morning*, was published in October. A paperback editon appeared before

Christmas, with a first printing of 400,000. It was a popular, inexpensive edition. We were certain to reach tens of thousands of people who would otherwise have remained uninformed about the issues and facts in Angela's case.

Our committee, as recipient of the royalties for the book, collected a substantial advance from the paperback publisher, which helped to alleviate our financial situation.

Foreign editions were also appearing. The British edition published in September had sold 60,000 by the end of October. Contracts had been signed with publishers in Norway, Sweden, the Netherlands, Denmark, France, Germany, Japan, Mexico, Spain and Greece.

Kendra and Franklin devoted themselves to the initiation of a renewed campaign for bail. Kendra was to be its national coordinator. Franklin was to be on the road, meeting with our committees in different cities, and speaking at any larger assemblies which might be organized.

A new bail petition, to be circulated throughout the country and the world, was prepared. We printed tens of thousands of copies:

TO: The Honorable Judges of the Appellate Courts for the State of California, the Federal Courts and for World Opinion:

WE, THE PEOPLE, DO HEREBY DEMAND THE FREEDOM OF ANGELA Y. DAVIS ON REASONABLE BAIL PENDING TRIAL. Angela Davis was refused bail on June 15, 1971, by Judge Richard E. Arnason, Contra Costa Superior Court Judge, in spite of the completely favorable report from the Marin County Probation Officer recommending bail for Ms. Davis.

California law provides for bail prior to conviction in all cases, including capital charges, and there are recent precedents in California where persons accused of capital crimes are free on bail pending trial. But "purely legal" was the reason given by Judge Arnason for this highly prejudicial decision to deny bail to Ms. Davis who has not been tried, let alone convicted.

We contrast the treatment of Angela Davis to that of Lieutenant William Calley who walks in virtual freedom after being *tried* and *convicted* of the murder of 22 Vietnamese women, men and children. Ms. Davis, a Black woman, a member of the Communist Party, a consistent fighter for the freedom of all political prisoners, is unjustly denied bail.

The people demand to know why Angela Davis has not been granted bail. Continued refusal to grant bail increases our concern as to the possibility of a fair trial for Ms. Davis in the court system of this country.

We submit, finally, that it is the grossest kind of denial of equal protection and due process for Ms. Davis to be held in punitive detention while awaiting trial.

Margaret Burnham took time out from her immediate legal responsibilities and edited a 75-page pamphlet on bail which documented the legal situation and projected the political dimensions of the issue. It contained the text of Howard Moore's argument in court; and an introduction by Margaret Burnham.

It was to be used primarily as an organizing tool for groups wishing to circulate the petition. Virtually any question a prospective signer might ask was answered in the pamphlet. Likewise, we prepared shorter, popular leaflets for mass distribution.

Rob Baker set to work writing the next newsletter of the National United Committee. It was devoted almost entirely to the fight for bail, and to our motion to change the site of Angela's trial from Marin County to San Francisco. It also contained articles on the cases of other political prisoners including the Soledad Brothers, Ruchell Magee, the brothers in the San Quentin Adjustment Center. We printed thousands for distribution to our local committees, all of whom were anxiously awaiting current material.

At the same time Kendra, Charlene, and myself set about to rebuild coalition relations between our committee and other groups and individuals in Los Angeles, the San Francisco Bay Area and nationally. We established working relations with representatives from the California Democratic Council (CDC), the United Farm Workers Organizing Committee, the NAACP, the Urban League, the YWCAs, various church groups, professors and students on dozens of campuses, the International Longshoremen and Warehousemen's Union, the American Federation of Teachers, the American Federation of State, County and Municipal Employees, and so on. We called people together and laid the urgency of the bail campaign before them.

Organizations and unions committed themselves to mobilize their memberships to circulate the petition. They agreed to approach still other churches and unions for support. They agreed to distribute our literature.

Anthony Amsterdam, special counsel in charge of our bail appeal, urged us to obtain "friend of the court" briefs in support of our bail petition, to be presented to the California State Supreme Court.

Frank Wilkinson, a veteran of the battle to abolish the House Un-American Activities Committee, who had himself served a year in prison in 1959 on contempt of Congress charges for refusing to testify before that committee, came to our assistance.

Frank was still a leading civil liberties advocate, and was now chairman of the National Committee Against Repressive Legislation. In that capacity he called upon three leading constitutional scholars, Vern Countryman of the Harvard Law School, Thomas Emerson of the Yale University Law School, and Paul Miller, Dean of the Howard University Law School, to submit an amicus curiae on Angela's behalf.

The American Civil Liberties Union in both northern and southern California likewise prepared an amicus curiae. All were then circulated among law professors, and to organizations for their endorsement. The briefs were filed with the State Supreme Court.

They emphasized the unconstitutionality of pre-trial detention. Both insisted that Angela Davis' release on reasonable bail was essential to the restoration of her right to a fair trial, the basis of which was her presumption of innocence. "The fact that a woman of controversial opinions," concluded the Countryman, Emerson and Miller amicus,

> is now in her second year of incarceration for a crime of which she is presumed innocent reflects adversely on the fair working of our administration of justice. The fact that she continues to be held without bail despite a State probation department recommendation for bail and a judicial finding that she is a good bail risk is not only unconscienable, it is unconstitutional.

The movement for bail gained momentum. Franklin left on his

national tour. Sallye Davis, Angela's mother, had already been on the road for days. Between them they had covered a score of cities by mid-November—Chicago, Detroit, Cleveland, Milwaukee, New Haven, Philadelphia, New York, Boston, Denver, Birmingham, Tuscaloosa, Nashville, Memphis. They spoke to however many people came to a rally, or to a person's home. They met with community leaders and solicited organizational resolutions calling for Angela's release on bail.

Word came from Fania in Europe: 6,000 people had demonstrated in Florence for Angela's freedom, 7,000 in Bologna, 4,000 in Frankfurt, 3,000 in Hanover, 3,000 in London, and tens of thousands more in Berlin, Moscow, Leningrad, Sofia, Budapest. But the outpouring in the streets of Paris captured the imagination of us all: 60,000 workers and students had marched to the Place de la Bastille for Angela.

IN RESPONSE to our appeals, Black Congressman John Conyers from Michigan came to California to visit with Angela. He was accompanied to the Marin County jail by Howard Moore. It took a while though, before Congressman Conyers could get inside.

The congressman didn't have his driver's license with him. The lieutenant at the front desk would not accept various papers he did have attesting to his identity as a United States Congressman. The lieutenant said unless he had proper identification he couldn't see Ms. Davis.

Five hours later John Conyers and Howard Moore returned to the jail. Conyers had telephoned an associate in Marin County. The friend had telephoned the sheriff's department with a personal request that Conyers be admitted. He finally got in.

Conyers came to express his solidarity with Angela, and to learn more of the specifics of the case. He left assuring us of his continued support, and his willingness to help in whatever way he could.

Reverend Ralph Abernathy, President of SCLC, also came to visit Angela in the Marin County Jail. His presence caused like consternation in the sheriff's department.

I had been with Angela most of that day in mid-September. It was 4 o'clock in the afternoon and I had just left her and come downstairs. I was standing at the entrance to the jail when a limousine pulled up, and a distinguished-looking gentleman, wearing a long black overcoat and a white carnation in his lapel, stepped from the car.

I recognized Reverend Abernathy at once. He swept passed me, and passed the astonished guards at the front gate without so much as a glance in their direction. He stepped into the elevator. Angela later described the scene upstairs.

Reverend Abernathy emerged from the elevator and quite by coincidence met Howard Moore in the corridor. Howard knew that Abernathy was in the area for several speaking engagements, but he had not expected him at the jail on that day.

Angela had just been taken from her cell to the main visiting area which looked out into the corridor. She was seated in the visiting booth behind a glass window. A representative from Swedish television was on the other side of the glass enclosure, in the hallway. They were talking to each other over the telephone. The Swedish television network had obtained permission from the court to do an interview with Angela. The corridor was bustling with activity as the camera crews set-up their equipment.

Abernathy strode over to the visiting booth. He asked the newsman if he might have a few moments with Angela. Marin County Undersheriff Sid Stinson was also on hand. He had come to supervise security arrangements for the television interview.

The undersheriff surveyed the scene. Angela was having an unauthorized visit with a man who had not identified himself and who had not filled out any visitation forms. It was after visiting hours even if he was accompanied by counsel.

Stinson sputtered and gestured and paced back and forth and Howard calmed him down and assured him it was all right and this was after all Reverend Abernathy, and surely the undersheriff knew who *he* was.

Angela and the Reverend spoke together for a few minutes, exchanged clenched fist salutes. The Minister departed, assuring her of the continued support of the Southern Christian Leadership Conference.

THE LEGAL situation continued to press in upon us. As we moved closer to trial the overwhelming volume of work made it apparent that at least one more trial lawyer was needed. In mid-October we secured the services of Doris Brin Walker. She had an unusual history.

Doris had been a successfully practicing lawyer when she decided to leave her law practice and go to work in basic industry. Fired for her trade union activities, Doris next joined the staff of the Independent Progressive Party (IPP) in the late Forties. She was an extremely able and competent organizer. Eventually she determined to return to her law practice because she felt an obligation to participate in the struggle for the right of women to serve in the legal profession.

When we asked her to join the Davis defense, Doris had been practicing in California for more than twenty years. She had long been associated with the defense of political prisoners.

During the 1950's she had been part of a team of lawyers who successfully defended fourteen members of the Communist Party accused of conspiracy to "advocate the overthrow of the government by force and violence" under the Smith Act. These California defendants were the only ones of dozens across the country to win release on bail pending trial, as the result of an appeal before the United States Supreme Court. They were also the first Smith Act defendants to win reversal of their conviction, also on appeal before the highest Court.

Doris is intensely conscientious, thorough, innovative. Her particular forte is in research, the preparation of argument, the often brilliant development of legal theory. Her early experiences gave her a keen sense of politics, something which is often missed in the best of legal minds. She brought an unusual combination of qualities into the trial team.

The lawyers, of course, were dividing up responsibilities amongst themselves. Doris was asked to begin preparations for our affirmative defense; that is, for our case-in-chief at the trial. She plunged into work, having first to acquaint herself with the entire legal history of the case.

Margaret was in charge of preparing our motion for a change-of-venue. Formal arguments began before Judge Arnason as scheduled. There was never much doubt in our minds that the judge would grant the venue change. Margaret's accounting of the law made it obvious to us that even the prosecution would be hard-put to oppose the motion outright. Two factors contributed to this. First, there was the explosive nature of the alleged crime, in which a leading citizen, a judge, had been killed. In the relatively small community of Marin County he was well-known and well-respected. Second, the pre-trial publicity in Marin County, as elsewhere, had been sensational. Both factors combined to make it more than likely that virtually everyone in Marin had already formed an opinion about Angela Davis — and that most of the opinions were hostile.

The crux of our legal thrust then, was to insist that the defense could not only request a change-of-venue, but that it could name the county to which it wanted the trial moved. The county was to be selected on the basis of constitutional criteria as to what constituted a fair trial — i.e. as to where the defendant could hope to secure a jury of her peers. It was this contention that the prosecution bitterly opposed.

Margaret had enlisted the services of a Berkeley sociologist, Jeffrey Paige. Professor Paige had conducted a series of public opinion surveys at our request in seven northern California counties. Students from the University volunteered their time to assist in the project. A random selection of registered voters — all of whom were potential jurors — were questioned. They were asked their opinions about Angela Davis, race relations, Communism, Communists teaching in the public schools and so forth. From this survey we argued that San Francisco County afforded the most favorable climate for the trial. This and its multi-racial composition, including a Black population of 15%, could give Angela some hope of obtaining a jury of her peers. Margaret argued forcefully and cogently. Judge Arnason promised a ruling by the first week in November.

Howard Moore undertook to argue our motions for suppression. In the course of 14 months of investigation the prosecution had amassed a veritable warehouse of evidence. Through the court's discovery order this evidence had been made available to the defense. Much of it had been obtained in searches of Angela's apartment, her car, homes where she had stayed. The assorted paraphernalia included books, newspapers, private correspondence, notes for lecture preparations, letters to Angela, some of which she had never even seen, clothing, shoes, medication. In particular, however, the prosecution had in its possession three letters Angela had written to George Jackson in June 1970. The argument for suppression was focused on the inadmissibility of this correspondence. The diary, just discovered, and written more than a year after the supposed conspiracy, was not included in this argument for suppression.

The first two letters were dated June 2nd and June 10th respectively. They had been discovered by FBI agents in a search of Angela's apartment in August 1970. The third letter, dated June 22nd, had been sent to George and had been confiscated by Soledad guards in the mail room at the prison.

Howard's argument for suppressing the letters was eloquent. He defended the sanctity of the individual's right to privacy. He demanded to know by what racist chicanery the prosecutor intended to exhibit for public viewing the love and compassion of a Black woman for a Black man and for her people, and thereby establish evidence of criminality.

Judge Arnason interrupted and asked if he could please see the letters. Howard left his customary position behind counsel table and approached the bench. He handed the judge a sheaf of papers. The judge began to read.

Howard returned to counsel table. He waited for the judge to look up so that he might resume his argument. The judge continued to read. Howard cleared his throat. The judge appeared totally absorbed. Howard approached the bench. He cleared his throat again. The judge started and looked up.

With pride Howard said: "Ms. Davis is a fantastic writer, isn't she?" The judge blushed and cleared his own throat, and Mr. Harris looked down at his feet under the counsel table, and Ms. Davis studied the judge's face, her chin cupped in her hands.

ON FRIDAY, October 22nd the California State Supreme Court denied our bail appeal. They refused to allow us to present oral arguments. They sent us a form postcard with a check next to the printed words: "Motion denied."

On Tuesday, November 2nd, Judge Richard Arnason denied the motion for suppression. He denied the change-of-venue to San Francisco. He ordered the trial moved to Santa Clara County.

Ms. Davis was to be transferred to some jail in that county as soon as the necessary security could be provided. A new trial date was left in abeyance.

7

Angela survived indignities. She survived isolation. She survived repeated denials by the courts. She survived Jonathan's death and George's death and Attica and the discovery of the diary and the chains around her waist and wrists.

Black people took great pride in Angela and believed in her and loved her. They wrote to her and told her so. Tens of thousands of letters, poems, drawings, songs poured into the Marin County jail, and later the Palo Alto jail and later the lawyers' office and our home in San Jose. The messages were simple, direct, oftentimes eloquent.

Angela was very strong. Still, I don't think she would have made it through August and September and October and November and on into the following year and through to the end of the trial without the support, encouragement, devotion of the mass of Black folk, and finally of people everywhere.

Coal miners in Appalachia raised $300 for the defense and sent it to Angela with a note saying, "We're with you." Black bus drivers in Pittsburgh went out on a wild-cat strike when several of their number were suspended from work for wearing "Free Angela" badges on the job. The white workers honored their picketline.

A prisoner circulated a petition demanding bail for Angela, and 177 fellow prisoners signed it. He sent the petition to the defense committee in Walla Walla, Washington.

Seventy-five prisoners in the New Jersey State prison raised

$210.00 amongst themselves and had the "Principal Keeper" (the warden) send a check in that amount to the Angela Davis Defense Fund.

A ten year old Black girl in Detroit sent a card to Angela and said simply, "I love you."

GI's on the front-lines in South Vietnam signed over their life insurance to the Angela Davis Legal Defense Fund.

Seventeen political prisoners in Paraguay made Angela a doll. They signed their names on a piece of paper and indicated how many years each had been in prison and their occupations. Most had been incarcerated for more than eight years, all of them without trial. There were five campesinos, seven workers, two students, one electrical engineer, one technician and one accountant.

A message came from Aegina Prison in Greece smuggled out on a piece of toilet paper: "We have the absolute certainty that victory will be ours. It will be a victory of all oppressed peoples and nations, of the whole of progressive humanity in our titanic common struggle against the powers of hatred, injustice, obscurantism and war. . . ."

The twenty-one year old brother, Olen Purnell Jr., in the Tombs prison in New York sent her a poem called, *When I Was A Kid*:

> When I was a kid, know what I did?
> I stole things . . .
> All sorts of things,
> like penny cookies, candy, cake and ice cream
> My father would beat me
> My mother would yell and scream
> They would both get angry, but I would get hungry
> So when I was a kid, know what I did?
> I stole things . . .
>
> (*Daily World*, September 4, 1971)

Angela answered scores of letters. To the sister who knitted her a shawl: "Thank you. . . . Its warmth goes much deeper than they would ever suspect." To the Black dishwasher who wrote an essay on Black women which she had inspired: "I only hope I will be able to live up to the historic role you described about Black women." To the prisoners in San Quentin and the Tombs and the

Women's House of Detention in New York and Alderson Federal Penitentiary for Women and a half dozen other institutions she sent individual messages of love, solidarity, encouragement.

PEOPLE active in Angela's defense were fired from their jobs, harassed by public officials, jailed for circulating petitions, at times beaten by police. There were dozens of incidents all over the country.

The Black meat butcher who headed the defense committee in Baltimore was arrested by two city policemen. Rudolph Williams was handcuffed, with his hands behind his back, thrown into a paddy wagon and beaten with a nightstick all the way to the police station. When they arrived police hauled him from the paddy wagon, knocked him face down in the parking lot of the station house and continued to beat him. Then they took him to Mercy Hospital. His ribs were broken and he had severe lacerations on his legs. The police took him from the hospital back to the station house and booked him on charges of "loitering."

Brother Williams retained counsel and was released on his own recognizance. He called the local branch of the NAACP, urged they conduct an investigation, and notified the district attorney's office that he was pressing charges against the attacking officers. Then he called the next meeting of the Angela Davis defense committee.

Rudolph Tuberville, a member of the Committee to Free Angela Davis in Charlotte, North Carolina, was fired from his job as a juvenile counselor with the district court in that city. Reasons cited included his outside political activities.

The Angela Davis Defense Committee in Charlotte issued the following statement: "Rudy made Angela's fight and the fight against racism his own. Now we must go to his defense. We are prepared to fight repression on a local level. How can we divorce ourselves from it? We plan to consolidate a petition campaign for Rudy with the struggle for Angela."

A Black woman attending Wayne State University in Detroit was arrested for a traffic violation. LaSandra Randolph had a "Free Angela" sticker on her car. She was stopped by two policemen. They said she had been speeding. They asked to see her driver's license. She complied. They began looking through her car. She asked what they were looking for. An officer said: "Since you're such an uppity nigger I'll just keep your driver's license." He did. They did not give her a ticket. They told her to go. She left. They stopped her again a couple of blocks later. One of the policeman said, "You're under arrest. Get your black ass out of there." They pulled her from the car, kicked her to the ground, picked her up and put her in the back of the police car. "We're gonna fix your ass, nigger," the officer said.

Ms. Randolph was released a few hours later. There were no charges. Her husband, Thomas Randolph, was the assistant track coach at Wayne State University. He was also an administrative aide to Detroit City Councilman Ernest Browne, one of three Black councilmen. Wayne State University officials, teachers and students petitioned the Detroit City Council for a public hearing on the incident. Members of the Black policemen's association in Detroit, the Guardians, put "Free Angela Davis" stickers on their private autos.

PEOPLE called our national committee office and asked how they could get into the jail to visit Angela. We asked a brother in the Oakland defense committee to try to coordinate the visiting schedule. All inquiries were sent to him. Regular visiting hours were between noon and 3 p.m. on Thursday and Sunday. She was permitted two twenty minute visits on each occasion. Scores of people went to see her, and hundreds more tried to get in. Sometimes people didn't know anything about our Committee. They just went to the jail.

On one Thursday late in the Spring of '71, Angela and I were together in the lawyer's booth. A matron interrupted and informed Angela that a Ms. _____ was here to visit and would Angela like to see her. Neither Angela nor I knew the name, but Angela thought she should see her. I remained in the booth.

The visitor was an elderly white woman in a wheel chair. She stayed only a few minutes. "I live over in San Rafael," she explained. "I heard on the news about how you can't get bail unless you can find a place to live in the county. Well now," the old woman continued, "I've lived here over thirty years. I have a big house, and I live alone, except for my nurse here. If you need a place to stay you come and stay with me. I just came by to tell you that."

Angela thanked her and tried to explain the reasons why she had been denied bail and did she know about the defense committee? The woman waved aside the explanation of details, and the prospect of committees. Angela floundered for something else to say. The old lady wished her the best of luck and said good-bye. The nurse turned the wheel-chair around and they disappeared down the hallway.

ANGELA enjoyed the support of people in the most unlikely places. A petition supporting her release on bail was circulated by employees in the Marin civic center complex. We only learned of its existence the day of the bail hearing in June. A hundred people had signed the petition — office workers and cooks and janitors and electricians.

At the Marin jail Angela was permitted to make telephone calls to her lawyers. She had to call collect. She telephoned Margaret one evening in May. "My name is Angela Davis," she said, in response to the operator's routine question. "You're Angela Davis?" the operator exclaimed. "How is everything?" Angela talked to her for a few minutes and they joked and laughed and the operator expressed her concern and support.

A few days later Angela again placed a call. Another operator handled it. She said: "I'd like to talk to you, but I can't. The other girl was fired a couple of days ago for talking with you." Angela tried to pursue the conversation, anxious to learn details of the incident, but the operator was unwilling to say more.

After Angela's extradition to California a Black matron in the New York Women's House of Detention wrote to her. It was an extraordinary letter:

My dear Angela,

My thoughts and heart have been with you ever since that sorrowful night. . . . If you have found us beautiful, it was because you made us that way. We related to you and your struggle in so many ways. What little I could do to bring you a bit of comfort was nothing compared to what you gave us. I miss you, and miss worrying and fussing at you about little things. . . . Keep your head up and remember you're always in my thoughts and heart. All power to you Angela. . . .

Angela is, in all manner and temperament, a scholar. She is shy, even retiring. She dislikes meetings, is apprehensive before addressing a large gathering. She prepares her lectures and speeches, even short statements, with great care. At times the preoccupation with precision and detail is compulsive. She is deliberative, rarely, if ever, impulsive.

Above all, she has a unique ability to relate to people. She's patient, intensely sensitive, genuinely interested in what they have to say. More, she conveys a sense of trust, compassion, humanness, that overwhelms (that is to say, disarms) even an adversary.

Angela sustained great control over her emotions. Her mind never ceased to probe, analyze, consider, absorb. This detachment of the intellect was an astonishing achievement. She kept a firm grip on her writing and her books as the one sure realm of relief from the enveloping madness. Her own strength was inextricably bound up with the infinite resources of a people, and therefore her writing always reverted back to the themes of the people — survival, struggle, liberation, self-liberation. Through this bond with Black folk the intellect remained alert and militant, the emotional traumas controlled, then channelled.

Her stamina was that of genius. In the weeks following George's death, with the trial apparently upon us, with our internal problems legion, she poured out thousands of words in poems, essays, short stories, letters:

My tears and grief are rage at the system responsible for his murder. . . .

Of Attica:

For those of us who are committed revolutionaries the days preceding the massacre offered gratifying and invigorating experience. In a figurative sense, it evoked visions of the Paris Commune, the liberated areas of pre-revolutionary Cuba, free territories of Mozambique. The revolt . . . burst forth as if to demonstrate that the brutal killing of George Jackson fell dismally short of its repressive aim. It was a very real affirmation that George's principles and his mission live on . . .

To the thousands gathered in the Central Park Mall in New York City on September 25th to denounce the Attica carnage and demand freedom for political prisoners:

Let this day of protest and solidarity mark a renewed dedication on the part of everyone present. Efforts must be redoubled to transform our ideals of struggle into reality. The fascist juggernaut can and must be smashed before it razes everything in its path. There is one sure path towards this victory. The brothers at San Quentin said it; the brothers at Attica said it; and the same message continues to issue forth from sisters and brothers struggling across the globe. "We've got the answer—unity," in the words of an Attica insurgent.

On the eighth anniversary of the bombing of the Birmingham church in which four Black children died:

Bombings occurred with such regularity in the neighborhood where I grew up that it became known as "Dynamite Hill." Cynthia Wesley, who lived only a few houses away, was well aware of what it meant to grow up in an atmosphere steeped in the terror of racism. She and Carol Robertson were among my sister's closest companions. On that fated morning eight years ago, when their lives and the lives of Addie Mae Collins and Denise McNair were so abruptly and ruthlessly brought to an end, the pain I felt was deeply personal. Yet, I could not avoid being struck by the universal and objective significance of that act of murder.

This act was not an aberration. It was not a fortuitous occurrence sparked by a few extremists gone mad. It was, on the contrary, logical and inevitable. Its matrix was an openly racist world, no aspect of which had to be camouflaged. The racist was explicitly allowed, if not encouraged, to express himself and what he felt by the exigencies of his environment by having recourse to all available means, including the most extreme. The individuals who planted the bomb that extinguished the lives of our four sisters were not therefore pathological, but rather the normal products of their surroundings. Although their identities are known, they are still at large, for the American system of justice does not consider the murder of Black people a punishable crime.

Her commemoration ended this way:

Our responsibility—to Carol, Cynthia, Addie Mae and Denise, to 'lil Bobby [Hutton], Jon [Jackson] and now to George, to our people and to all the oppressed is clear. We must gather up that rage and organize it into an invincible movement which will irresistibly advance towards the goal of liberation. It must smash the capitalist order and its attendant racism and must ultimately begin to build the new society.

ONE MORNING early in October we were sitting in the lawyer's booth and Angela handed me a twenty-eight page typed manuscript. She asked me to read it. It was titled: "Reflections on the Black Woman's Role in the Community of Slaves." It had been inspired by a dialogue with George Jackson.

On May 28, 1970 George had written Angela a very long letter, setting out his views on the role of Black women in the oppressed community and in the liberation struggle. It was an intensely moving letter, honest, passionate, tender, defiant. In it, however, he had endorsed the concept of the female dominance in the Black family, and he had decried what he saw was the crippling effect of women on the Black man's will to resist oppression.

Angela had begun a response to him in her letter of June 2, 1970 — the same letter the prosecution now insisted was evidence of a criminal plot. She had suggested only a few thoughts then. Now, sixteen months later, she continued her reply. In a brief introduction she dedicated these reflections to him:

> If his life had not been so precipitously and savagely extinguished, he would have surely accomplished a task he had already outlined some time ago: a systematic critique of his past misconceptions about Black women and of their roots in the ideology of the established order. He wanted to appeal to other Black men . . . to likewise correct themselves through self-criticism. George viewed this obligation as a revolutionary duty, but also, and equally important, as an expression of his boundless love for all Black women.

The theme of Angela's essay was an assault upon the concept of the Black woman as matriarch. Cogently, passionately, Angela argued that matriarchy was a myth, and wholly without historical foundation given the utter absence of power which defined the slaves' existence. Indeed, she contended, the myth was created by the white ruler to divide the Black community—men from women and women from men. It was designed to create the illusion that the dominance of the female in the family was a primary source of the poverty and wretchedness of the Black condition, thus to turn the anger and frustration of the community, inward, away from the true enemy.

Angela detailed the concrete resistance of the African woman to slavery from Sojourner Truth to Harriet Tubman to the anonymous millions who sacrificed, struggled, survived. Perhaps it was this lack of passivity on the part of Black women that led chauvinistic and male supremacist sociologists to conclude that a matriarchical arrangement must prevail in the Black family.

Angela explored the sexual abuse to which Black women were subjected by the white master. These abuses were not isolated acts of depravity. On the contrary, she insisted, rape must be viewed as an integral part of a consciously enforced system of terror directed against the slave community as a whole. For the rape was intended to be as destructive of the Black woman as it was intended to be emasculating of the Black man.

Angela concluded with an impassioned appeal:

> The myth [of matriarchy] must be consciously repudiated . . . and the Black woman in her true historical contours must be resurrected. We, the Black women of today must accept the full weight of a legacy wrought in blood by our mothers in chains. Our fight, while identical in spirit, reflects different conditions and thus implies different paths of struggle. But as heirs to a tradition of supreme perseverance and heroic resistance, we must hasten to take our place wherever our people are forging on towards freedom.

Born of her love for George, this outpouring in the weeks following his death, became an expression of Angela's love for all Black men and women and children. This love sustained her, generating from within the will to live. To live she had to work. To work she had to write. Writing meant discovery. Discovery meant new ideas, insights, impressions. Freedom the constant theme. Discovery demanded survival. Survival demanded discovery.

Angela interwove the individual and social realms into an extraordinary dialectical arrangement. Through it she simultaneously displayed and reinforced the courage and passion and will of a people acquired over centuries of struggle. She/they emerged from her ordeal infinitely stronger.

8

"The Angela Davis murder trial was moved to Santa Clara County yesterday,"—reported the San Jose *Mercury*, the county's largest circulation daily newspaper—"an event that apparently failed to enchant anyone with the possible exception of the Hotel, Motel and Innkeepers Association." The county's executive officer, Howard Campen, was reported to have gasped, "Oh my God!" when he learned of the trial shift.

Santa Clara County Sheriff James Geary and Dominic Cortese, chairman of the county Board of Supervisors, and other officials called a press conference Tuesday afternoon, November 2nd. The press conference was held at the main jail in San Jose.

Cortese estimated that the trial would cost one million dollars. He said that special security measures would be necessary and estimated that they would cost several hundreds of thousands of dollars. Security costs, he said, would have to be borne by the county. He vowed to "make every effort to recover our costs" from the state government. Asked by newsmen if he thought Ms. Davis would receive a fair trial in Santa Clara County, Cortese said: "Our county is no different from any other county. We're part of a statewide judicial system. Angela Davis or anyone else can receive a fair trial here."

Sheriff Geary said he was sending Undersheriff Tom Rosa and Lieutenant Donald Tamm to Marin County to study security measures. He said that the main jail in San Jose did not have women's facilities. Ms. Davis would have to be, at least temporarily, confined either in the North County Holding Facility in Palo Alto, or at the Elmwood Rehabilitation Center in Milpitas. He said the Elmwood jail was not too good because it was a "minimum security facility." Undersheriff Rosa volunteered that if Ms. Davis was kept at Palo Alto "she could be taken right from her cell to the court [superior court in Palo Alto] through a tunnel without having to go outside." The tunnel is called "the chute" in police parlance, the story said.

John Racanelli, presiding judge of the Superior Court of Santa Clara County, was reported to have responsibility for determining the location of the trial. The jail commander, Captain Wes Johnson, said Judge Arnason had personally toured all Santa Clara County jail facilities, including those in Palo Alto, San Jose and Elmwood. Captain Johnson said that he and Judge Racanelli had escorted Judge Arnason on his tour.

"There were immediate indications," the story said, "that the trial would be assigned to the North County Superior Court in Palo Alto because it has better security facilities." Palo Alto Police Chief James Zurcher said he would "do whatever is necessary" to keep order in the city if the trial is conducted in the North County courthouse. "We'll take care of anything that comes up," he said.

There were two possible locations for the trial: Palo Alto or San Jose.

Palo Alto, 40 miles south of San Francisco, is a university town, Stanford University at its center. It is white, wealthy, in the heart of a military-industrial complex: Memorex Corporation, Hewlett-Packard, a dozen other electronic and aerospace companies in the immediate vicinity—Science Data Processing, Telextronix Corporation, Ford's Philco Company (specializing in missile tracking and guidance systems). Just to the south of Palo Alto are the United States Air Naval Station at Moffett Field, the United States Air Force Satellite Testing Center, and the National Aeronautics and Space Administration's (NASA) Reserve Training Center. Also south of Palo Alto (midway between Palo Alto and San Jose) is the Lockheed Aircraft Corporation. Most of the corporations' executives and engineers live in Palo Alto. By-and-large the technicians and maintenance crews live in San Jose.

Palo Alto is a relatively isolated enclave. It bears little economic or political relationship to the rest of Santa Clara County. Historically, Palo Alto has had social and political ties with San Francisco. This, combined with its academic milieu, has tended to make the community more liberal than might, at first glance, appear likely. The nearest concentrations of Black people are to be found in the communities of East Menlo Park and East Palo

Alto, both of which are in San Mateo County, just to the north.

San Jose, 60 miles south of San Francisco was, up until the mid-fifties, a rural community with less than 100,000 people. It is set in the lush farm country of the Santa Clara Valley. In the last fifteen years it has sprawled out in cyclical spasms, the vineyards and orchards uprooted, the big industries—many of them defense oriented—moving in: IBM, Food Machinery Corporation, Ford Motor Company, General Electric (with two large plants). The canneries, long a main industry, remain in large numbers.

San Jose is rapidly becoming a major urban center, experiencing all of the social crises associated with city life—high property taxes, inadequate social services, chaos in the public schools, an antiquated public transportation system. There are repeated police provocations against the poor, the Black and the Brown. Racism is entrenched, often vulgar and undisguised. The new city dwellers are still provincial enough not to have perfected the more subtle accoutrements of racial conflict typical of a northern metropolis.

There are now nearly half a million people in San Jose. The older white rural residents, still wielding decisive political and economic power, cling fervently to the individualist mores and fundamentalist traditions of a by-gone era. In many ways, as Howard Moore observed, San Jose resembles a southern town.

Approximately 22% of the people in Santa Clara County are Chicano. Many of the Chicano people are not registered to vote. Most could not be considered then, as prospective jurors. Only 1.15% of the people in the county are Black.

Reporters interviewed a few of the Black people in Santa Clara County and asked them if they thought Angela Davis could receive a fair trial. Inez Jackson, on the Board of Directors of ESO, the county's anti-poverty agency said: "She has five strikes against her. She's a Communist, she's Black, she's a woman, she's a radical, and she's an intellectual. When I came to San Jose 28 years ago," Ms. Jackson continued, "I couldn't get a job at my vocation which is teaching school." Ms. Jackson said she found a job with the post office. "By the time my daughter got out of college she couldn't get a teaching job either. We couldn't buy a house and we had the money. These type of things make us bitter."

We talked with people we knew in San Jose and Palo Alto.

Nothing anybody had to say was encouraging. Older residents remembered that the last lynching in the State of California had taken place in San Jose forty years before. Two unemployed men accused of kidnapping and killing the son of a wealthy storeowner had been dragged from the city jail and hung in St. James Park, across the street from what was then the superior court building.

Margaret Burnham insisted upon our right to further contest Judge Arnason's venue decision. The judge agreed to entertain further arguments. Another hearing was set for November 11. Margaret brought additional witnesses before the Court, and marshalled new arguments. She maintained that only in San Francisco could Ms. Davis hope to receive some semblance of a fair trial.

"Depending on results of a Marin County judge's hearing on a change-of-venue appeal by Angela Davis' attorneys," quipped the *Mercury*, "Santa Clara County officials either will launch a frenzied effort to set-up a costly and intricate security program for her trial, or sigh with relief and relax."

Judge Arnason denied the appeal. He ordered that Ms. Davis be placed in the custody of Santa Clara County Sheriff's Department anytime after midnight, November 30th.

Working at a frantic pace our staff and lawyers coordinated political and legal efforts to force a reversal of Judge Arnason's decision. We had less than two weeks before the order was to take effect. Just before Thanksgiving the Santa Clara County Board of Supervisors appropriated an initial $203,677 for "minimal" security provisions for the trial. The money was designated to be used to pay salaries of twenty-two deputy sheriffs, five matrons, one sergeant, one lieutenant and one senior stenographer clerk. The money was also to be used to obtain metal detection equipment. A week later the board approved the appropriation of another $20,000, more than half of which was to be used to purchase two video monitors. Sheriff Geary said the monitors would be used for watching crowds outside the courthouse. Santa Clara County officials still publicly maintained that they did not know in what part of the county they would detain or try Ms. Davis. Neither Judge Arnason nor any other official would inform our attorneys as to exactly when Ms. Davis was to be transferred from Marin County or where she was to be taken. We believed that unless the venue appeal could be won before Angela was physically moved to Santa Clara County we would face a *fait accompli.*

We viewed the decision to shift the trial to Santa Clara County with alarm. Whether in Palo Alto or San Jose the trial was now set to take place in a community isolated from the mainstream of urban life. Regardless of the judge's intentions, the move to Santa Clara County could have no other effect but to isolate Angela, to sever her physically, psychologically and spiritually from the Black communities, where her support was greatest.

Speculating on possible trial locations before the judge's decision, Angela had predicted that she would be tried in Santa Clara. It was an obvious choice. San Francisco was not politically safe. While it would have been eminently reasonable from the point of view of population, adequate facilities, and convenience (all the main trial participants lived in or near San Francisco) it would have enraged the attorney general because of its long-standing reputation as a liberal community. The two most conservative counties in the northern California area, Sacramento and San Joaquin, would have satisfied the prosecution, but would have been totally unacceptable to the defense, and an appeal might have had some hope of success.

Sacramento, the state capitol, would have meant placing the trial in the governor's front parlor, hardly an appropriate site considering his public utterances asserting Ms. Davis' guilt. The San Joaquin Valley is notoriously racist, and moving the trial to the town of Stockton, the county seat, would have been akin to trying Angela in Greenwood, Mississippi. The judge was astute. If he were going to compromise, he would make the only tenable choice.

WEDNESDAY, November 30th. Working around the clock, our attorneys had prepared an appeal against the change of venue to be filed with the state's First District Court of Appeals in San Francisco. The appeal had to be filed by that Wednesday afternoon or the higher court would not review the venue decision. As final copies of the brief were being duplicated our xerox machine broke down. Howard Moore telephoned the court and explained the situation. He was assured that the court would consider the appeal if it was filed before midnight. It was.

Police officials, however, had no intention of awaiting the outcome of any appeals. The venue change could be legally executed anytime after midnight on the 30th. It was.

Late Wednesday evening Kendra Alexander and members of the Oakland and San Francisco defense committees began an all-night vigil in a car parked across the street from the Marin County jail. We still did not know at what time Angela would be moved or where she would be taken.

Angela waited alone, unable to sleep. Earlier in the day we had brought crates and cartons to the jail and helped her pack all of her books, papers and clothes.

December 1st. 3 a.m. A phalanx of sheriff's deputies from both Marin and Santa Clara Counties entered the Marin County jail. They dispatched themselves throughout the building. Several went to Angela's cell and put her in handcuffs, and with a deputy gripping her at each elbow, she was escorted out. The sheriff's men entered and exited the jail through a tunnel which emptied into a secluded parking lot north of the civic center complex. It was unknown to us. Kendra remained across the street from the jail all night.

Angela sat in the rear of an unmarked police car, between Santa Clara County Undersheriff Tom Rosa, and Marin County Deputy Matron Evelyn Gosser. Other police vehicles were behind and in front. The convoy proceeded southward through the darkness, in a driving rain. It took a long, circuitous route. Three and a half hours later Angela arrived in Palo Alto. She was put in a 6x8 foot cell in the basement of the courthouse building.

Just after 7 a.m. Franklin Alexander drove to Marin to tell Kendra that Angela had been moved. At 8:30 Franklin called me at home. He and Kendra had returned to our committee's offices in San Francisco. He told me Angela was in Palo Alto. We called everyone we knew in Santa Clara, and everyone we knew called everyone they knew. By 12 noon, despite the fact that it was a work day, there were two hundred people picketing the Palo Alto courthouse.

I met Franklin at the court. We decided to try to see Angela. We had been informed that all court orders issued in Marin County pertaining to visiting privileges for attorneys, investigators and witnesses would be honored by Santa Clara County. We went inside. The sergeant at the front desk said he didn't have any copies of the court orders. He assured us they would be honored when they arrived. He said he only had the names of the attorneys-of-record. Only they were to be admitted. I produced a xeroxed copy of the court order attesting to my status as an investigator. The sergeant said he had to see the original. We couldn't get in.

A short while later Margaret Burnham and Howard Moore arrived. They asked to see Ms. Davis. The sergeant let them in.

Franklin and I decided to take a walk and survey the new environs. We took a self-guided tour of the courthouse building. Three stories, plush, polished, plastic. Tiny compared to the Marin complex. The basement jail was inaccessible to the public from the inner building. The only entrance was on the outside, down a ramp and through an electronically-controlled steel door. We went into an unoccupied courtroom and counted the number of seats. There were only 68, ten less than the average size of a Marin courtroom. As we walked through the halls we delighted in a shared fantasy. How much fun it would be to conduct a good old-fashioned sit-in, inside one of those sterile chambers. Joyfully we mused over the predictable consternation in official circles.

Our tour ended. Franklin and I went downstairs to the ground floor and into a small room with vending machines, which substituted for a cafeteria. We each had a cup of coffee. Sheriff's deputies rushed in. They told us to get out of the building. An anonymous caller said there was a bomb in the courthouse.

We stood outside engulfed in an effervescent throng of receptionists, file clerks, typists and stenographers. Margaret and Howard and Angèla and all the other prisoners were still in the jail. There was no bomb.

Margaret and Howard emerged from the jail a couple of hours later. Howard looked pale, unnerved. Margaret reported to the now assembled crowd of supporters. They had found Angela perched on the upper bunk of a double-decker bed in a cell the size of a bathroom. She had no clothes and no shoes. She was wrapped in a blanket, her legs drawn up under her chin, her arms wrapped around her legs. Shivering. There was no heat. The toilet had overflowed. The water was ankle-deep on the cell floor. All of her personal belongings were still in Marin. Margaret said she had left Angela a few pieces of paper and a pen.

IN THE days following Angela's internment in Palo Alto our immediate concern was to force the sheriff's department to clean up the jail. We told people the details of her situation. Sheriff Geary's office was inundated with letters, cables and telephone calls. He was responsive to public opinion.

Sheriff Geary and Lieutenant Donald Tamm called a press conference to assure the world that "the Palo Alto accommodations are among the most modern in the state."

Geary said the majority of the letters he had received were from women. The Brooklyn [New York] Women's Club wrote urging him, "as a Christian and in the spirit of Christmas to do all in your power to give her [Ms. Davis] fair treatment." A woman in Fairfield, Connecticut warned that "the entire world is watching the process of justice in America through her case . . ." Another writer compared Ms. Davis' living conditons to those of Lieutenant William Calley, convicted of murdering Vietnamese civilians: "Calley is allowed a nice apartment under house arrest . . . Ms. Davis is not convicted of anything. Do we have two systems of justice in this country, one for whites and one for Blacks?" Sheriff Geary said he was writing some personal letters to reassure the women. Lieutenant Tamm said he had telephoned a couple in Jamesburg, New Jersey to assure them that Ms. Davis was all right.

Meanwhile the sheriff had seen to it that the toilet was fixed, the heat was turned on; a second, padded cell was unlocked and made accessible to Angela as a work area. She now had two cells. Her things from Marin County had been brought to her.

Angela had a way of fixing up her tiny quarters to make them more livable. There was a colorful shawl flung over a cell door to hide the steel grating; a poster on a glass window (glued on with soap) to hide the toilet in the sleep cell from public view; an extra mattress pulled off the lower bunk of the double-decker bed (after a heated argument with the jailers who said it couldn't be done) and dragged into the padded cell, a blanket wrapped around it, newspaper stuffed between the blanket and the mattress to give it more body, making an almost comfortable floor couch; crude book cases fashioned out of cartons, precariously balanced one on top of the other, the books shelved and arranged according to subject; empty cigarette cartons with the tops torn off, the cartons attached to the walls with layers of masking tape, to serve as receptacles for odds and ends (one such carton for letters was marked "outgoing," and another was marked "incoming.")

The padded cell, 6' x 8', was officially known as the safety cell. There was a printed sign above the door that said *Safety Cell*. It was routinely used to confine alcoholics, drug addicts and other inmates classified by their keepers as violent. The walls were soft and pliable. The cell was bare. There was no sink. There was no toilet. There was a hole in the floor to serve as a toilet. Occasionally the drain clogged and fetid water backed up and ran out of the hole, onto the floor, seeping into the mattress/couch. It caused a terrific odor. Angela concocted all sorts of detergents to try to clean it up.

The pressures on the sheriff's department brought other results. Investigators (not more than two at a time) were now permitted to visit with Angela in her cell from eight in the morning until three in the afternoon, every day, without the presence of an attorney. Investigators, prospective witnesses and family were permitted to visit in the evenings for the first time, if they were accompanied by counsel. We could stay until ten o'clock. Angela was permitted to have a thermos-bottle, a jar of instant coffee, a box of tea bags, a package of vita-nuts, a spoon, a small dish of sugar and an odd assortment of cups. She was also permitted a typewriter, radio, television and a recorder (the musical instrument).

She was taken out to exercise with greater frequency. Usually she went to the Elmwood Rehabilitation Center in Milpitas where there was. a real exercise yard. She played volley ball with the other women in the jail. One memorable morning the sheriff's deputies took her to Stevens Creek Park, a vast, secluded forest, at the northwestern corner of San Jose.

WEDNESDAY, December 8th. 1 p.m. Superior Court, Palo Alto. A hearing was scheduled before Judge Arnason. It had been announced the previous Friday. Hundreds of people came to the courthouse — mostly young, mostly Black. It seemed as though every Black family in the county had sent a representative. We jammed into the corridor. The crowd spilled out onto the steps. A few people carried signs — Free Angela! Bail Now!

Fania was back from Europe. Her daughter, Eisa, now six months old, was with her. Charlene was there and Kendra, Bobby Seale and Ericka Huggins came too. We were hoping for an open court hearing after the initial closed session. Everyone pressed in towards the doors leading to the courtroom. We saw Angela for a fleeting moment through the glass window on the door as she walked into chambers, a black shawl draped over her shoulders, her head down, clutching a legal-sized manila folder. People shouted to her. She lifted her head and raised her fist.

Bobby Seale stood on a chair in the hallway and made a little speech. Every time he wanted to say free Angela, he said free Ericka. So many cases. So many trials.

Our lawyers emerged a short while later. Court had been adjourned without an open session. We all moved outside. Doris Walker stood at the head of the steps and spoke and explained what had happened in chambers. The trial would be in San Jose. It would begin on January 31. Sometime before then Angela would be moved again, this time to the main jail in San Jose.

After court Fania went down to the jail with Margaret. She was still holding Eisa. The sergeant said she couldn't come in with the baby. He said he didn't think a baby belonged in a jail. Fania said she didn't think her sister belonged in one either.

The *Mercury* featured a lavish photo display the day after the Palo Alto hearing, trumpeting the arrival of the sensational murder trial: ANGELA MAKES THE SCENE IN SAN JOSE. There were pictures of the leading players, the actual courtroom where the trial would take place, and an aerial view of the San Jose civic center complex showing the jail, and next to it, the courthouse. The caption under the aerial photo said: "The San Jose courthouse where Angela Davis will be tried for murder and conspiracy. . . . She will be jailed at left . . . and brought to justice in the building at the right. . . ."

On Friday, December 10th, the State District Court of Appeals in San Francisco summarily denied our motion appealing the change of venue to Santa Clara County. The trial was now scheduled to begin in 52 days.

9

We had reached the decisive moment in the defense. Two severe blows has been sustained in rapid succession — the refusal of the California State Supreme Court to even consider the bail petition, and the loss of the venue appeal.

We put every available resource we had into organizing efforts in the Santa Clara area, and we picked up the loose ends of a half dozen projects initiated during our October offensive. An amazing sequence of events took place, partly as a result of the Committee's efforts and partly by coincidence — history is often affected by the combined product of consciousness and chance — which ended in our first and critical victory on the eve of trial.

At 4:30 in the morning on Monday, September 20, 1971, a young Black man, John Henry Smith, was stopped by a San Jose city patrolman for allegedly making an illegal u-turn. The patrolman's name was Rocklin Woolley. The incident occurred in front of the Meridian Corners apartment complex where Smith lived. The apartment complex is in a predominantly white, middle class neighborhood. Within a couple of minutes another car pulled alongside the Smith vehicle and two more patrolmen — Robert Watts and Daniel Richter — got out. Both were officially off-duty and out of uniform. They asked Woolley if he needed assistance. He said no. Nevertheless the two off-duty men stayed.

Smith was ordered from his car. He got out. An argument ensued. According to neighbors, aroused by Smith's shouts, the
three officers released a police dog from Woolley's car. The dog
attacked Smith. Then the three officers threw him to the ground,
maced him and clubbed him. Smith broke free. His shirt ripped
from his back, his head bloodied, he ran into the apartment complex screaming, "Help me. Help me. I'm afraid." Then, witnesses
reported, there was a quick burst of gunfire. Smith fell. He was
dead.

Patrolmen Woolley, Watts and Richter maintained that Smith
attacked them with a tire iron. Then they said, he ran towards his
apartment. They feared he was going inside to get a gun. Rocklin
Woolley said he shot Smith. All admitted that at the time he was
shot, Smith was unarmed. He had no gun, and no tire iron.

The San Jose Chief of Police Robert Murphy made a statement
the day after the shooting, defending Woolley's action, and alleging that Smith was "obviously under the influence of something,
and the autopsy would show it." The autopsy, however, revealed
Smith's blood contained no drugs and no alcohol. Patrolman
Woolley made several public statements. He said he felt no re-
morse, and that there was no doubt in his mind that the shooting
was justified.

John Henry Smith was 35 years old. He was a research chemist
for the IBM corporation in San Jose. He was the fifth person of
color to be killed by the San Jose police in 18 months. Another
Black man and three Chicano youngsters had been the earlier
victims.

Immediately after Smith's death a score of small community
meetings were held. Groups called each other for support. An *Ad
Hoc* Committee of Concerned Citizens was formed. The San Jose
Black Officers Association — which had issued a statement brand-
ing Woolley as a "notorious racist" — was among those represented in the coalition.

Four days after Smith's death the San Jose City Council announced that its regular Monday night meeting — scheduled for
September 27th — would be cancelled so council members could
attend the League of California Cities Convention in San Francisco. Enraged San Jose citizens met Sunday afternoon, September 26th, at the Eastside Community Center. The people im-

mediately and unanimously voted to call the Mayor. They told him to be at the city hall for Monday night's meeting. If a majority of the council failed to convene, the citizens said they would go to the convention hall in San Francisco. The council decided to meet on schedule.

Five hundred people overflowed the council chambers. *Ad Hoc* committee spokesmen presented three demands: 1) suspend the three officers pending the outcome of a grand jury investigation (already begun); 2) fire Police Chief Robert Murphy; and 3) establish a citizens board of inquiry with broad community representation to probe the case. The council refused to take any action.

Fran Escalante, co-chairperson of the Community Alert Patrol (CAP), one of the groups affiliated with the *Ad Hoc* committee, told reporters after the session that the next weeks would see some changes in San Jose: "The system has been caught," she said, "and now the people are working together, Blacks, Chicanos, Asians and Anglos to fill the chambers with one big fist."

For the next six weeks between 800 and 1,000 people attended every meeting of the San Jose City Council. Slowly it responded to the pressure. Opposing forces in the city's power structure likewise gathered momentum, attempting to resist the community demands.

On October 12th the city council censured Police Chief Robert Murphy for his public comments defending Patrolman Woolley. Forty-eight hours later Superior Court Judge James Scott ruled that the council had no jurisdiction over Chief Murphy and ordered that the censure be lifted. The council failed to comply. Shortly thereafter, the council agreed to establish a citizens board of inquiry, but sought to generalize its responsibilities to preclude any specific investigation of Smith's death. The newly appointed board met and voted to inform the city council that it intended to investigate the slaying regardless of its official mandate.

On November 3rd — one day after Angela Davis' trial was ordered moved to Santa Clara County — Rocklin Woolley was indicted for manslaughter by the Santa Clara County grand jury. He was arraigned the same day before Judge Scott. He pleaded not guilty and was released on $3,125 bail. Woolley remained on leave from the police department, with pay. The San Jose Peace

Officers Association and Local 170 of the Policemen's Union set up a Peace Officers Assistance Fund, "to insure that justice is guaranteed," according to the association's president, Phillip Norton.

Three days after the grand jury indictment, San Jose City Manager Thomas Fletcher, responding to community demands, urged that Rocklin Woolley be fired and Watts and Richter suspended for 240 working hours. Judge Scott promptly gagged Fletcher, and ordered that no further statements be issued by any members of the San Jose City Council or anyone else connected with the case. The council was effectively silenced. No disciplinary action was taken by the police department against Woolley, Watts or Richter. A few days later, in apparent disregard of Judge Scott's order, Rocklin Woolley gave a lengthy interview to a reporter from the San Jose *Mercury*. The paper ran a front-page story. Woolley told about his life, and presented his version of the killing.

The Angela Davis defense committee in San Jose was already a part of the *Ad Hoc* Committee of Concerned Citizens, when the change of venue for Angela's trial was announced. The two struggles converged.

The key to political success for the Davis defense in San Jose lay with the Chicano community. More specifically, it lay in the unity between Black and Chicano people already achieved in the *Ad Hoc* committee. If Angela's defense was embraced with equal passion we believed we could decisively influence the preparations for the trial, and perhaps affect its outcome.

My husband, Jack Kurzweil, a professor of electrical engineering, and I had lived in San Jose for four years. We had both been members of the Communist Party for almost a decade. Jack had been intimately involved in developing local community support for Angela in the San Jose area. He was also involved in the fight to prevent an official white-wash of the death of John Henry Smith.

Franklin Alexander came to our home early in November. We had called many of the individuals we knew in the San Jose community. The coffee pot perked continuously as we met with successive groups of community activists. The mutual benefits of a joint effort against a common oppressor were apparent. As

Franklin later told the San Jose City Council: "The eyes of the world are on your city, and we will not surrender so easily the life of our sister to the forces that condone the murder of John Henry Smith."

The Community Alert Patrol (CAP) — one of the groups represented in the *Ad Hoc* committee — was an interracial organization led by Chicano people. Its most important work was the monitoring of police activity in San Jose, especially in the eastside barrio. CAP cars, clearly marked and equipped with two-way radios, cameras and tape recorders, patrolled the barrio from approximately 9 p.m. to 3 a.m., Fridays through Sundays. The CAP headquarters, located in the Old Guadalupe Church on San Jose's eastside, had communications equipment licensed by the city with which to monitor police calls. People on duty at the church dispatched CAP patrols to the locations specified on the police radio as incidents occurred. CAP members were under strict, self-imposed rules of non-interference with police activity, but they could photograph and record the events they witnessed. Observation had significantly reduced what had been routine police harassment of Chicano residents. CAP's membership at the time of the trial exceeded 600, and most participated in the patrols on a rotating basis. CAP was one of the most widely respected organizations in the San Jose community.

CAP members were more than willing to help with Angela's defense. And Victoria Mercado, a twenty-year old Chicana, a student at San Francisco State College, who was one of our main organizers in the San Francisco defense committee, agreed to join our national staff, and concentrate her political efforts in the San Jose area.

By early December a new Chicano group had emerged in San Jose—El Comité para la Defensa de Prisioneros Politicos. El Comité focused on Angela's case, and also agreed to publicize the cases of other political prisoners, especially Chicanos. The first efforts of El Comité were directed towards securing assistance from the most important organizations and people in and around the Chicano community.

The support of La Confederación de la Raza Unida, a coalition of more than 70 Chicano groups in San Jose, was essential for Angela's defense. El Comité representatives presented a resolution to La Confederación and secured its unanimous approval.

Equally significant, El Comité successfully solicited the support of two leading priests in the San Jose community, Father Anthony Soto of Our Lady of Guadalupe Church and Father Cuchulain Moriarty of the Sacred Heart Catholic Church.

Leaflets in Spanish and English, explaining Angela's case and containing excerpts from these statements and resolutions, were printed. CAP organized the distribution of thousands—in many cases door-to-door—throughout the barrio. Chicano families began to post placards and bumper stickers around their homes calling for Angela's freedom. I remember one night walking through a housing project in the barrio. Every fourth or fifth apartment had a "Free Angela" sign on the door or in the window.

Activity in the Black communities intensified. The East Palo Alto Municipal Council, an advisory group established by the San Mateo County Board of Supervisors to reflect the feelings of the Black community (East Palo Alto is adjacent to Palo Alto, though it is in another county) sent an open letter to Judge Arnason. The council warned that racism in Santa Clara County would prevent selection of an unprejudiced jury. It called for removal of the trial from Santa Clara, for the release of Ms. Davis on bail, and recommended that the Charles Drew Health Center, a Black community health facility in East Palo Alto, be "permitted to organize a medical team to monitor and administer the health needs of Sister Davis."

Simultaneously, students at Stanford University held their first press conference in mid-December to announce plans for a series of protests in and around the Palo Alto community on Angela's behalf. Reginald Turner, 18 year-old Black chairman of the Stanford defense committee, told reporters that the first protest would be held on New Year's day at the Rose Bowl game in Pasadena, where Stanford's champion football team was to play the University of Michigan. Turner said the action at the game would be "lawful, vivid, meaningful and symbolic." The prospect of significant student protest was underlined by the participation in the press conference of Douglas McHenry, president of the Stanford student body and a central figure in California's Black student movement. McHenry made clear that Angela already enjoyed the support of tens of thousands of Black students in all major Bay Area colleges. Two days after the Stanford press conference, as if to confirm McHenry's observation, more than 2,000 students attended a protest/work meeting at San Jose State College addressed by Fania Jordan and Attorney Margaret Burnham.

Additional organizing efforts in the county continued as we began to approach predominantly white groups for support. It was more difficult to secure invitations to address these organizations, and occasionally our appearances stirred semi-official rebuke. At the invitation of the Social Services Union Local 535 (AFL-CIO) I spoke at a public meeting in the social services auditorium in the county's welfare building in the San Jose civic center complex. The meeting was held during the lunch hour on Friday, December 10th. About 200 welfare department employees attended. My presentation was followed by intense discussion, which went on well-past the normal lunch break. The people were overwhelmingly sympathetic, the response was inspiring, and every scrap of literature was distributed.

A week later the president of the Santa Clara County Deputy Sheriff's Association, Ramon W. Hoyt, addressed a scathing open letter to the county's executive officer, Howard Campen, denouncing my appearance. The controversy simmered for several days. Hoyt said that free speech should be protected but "allowing a public building to be used during a work day as a platform for an extremely militant Communist to blast the same public system is ridiculous . . ." Encouragingly, my right to speak was defended by both Campen and the county counsel, William Seigel.

In the San Jose area we made a tactical decision to refrain from soliciting signatures on the bail petition. It was an extremely difficult decision to make and our staff and Angela argued about it for days. In principle the bail petition committed the signer to nothing more than belief in a fair trial. That was, after all, what the law required. Yet we were certain that the prosecution would challenge any prospective juror who had signed the petition. We believed that the judge would probably sustain the prosecution's objections and rule against us. Ultimately there seemed little point in risking the loss of even one progressive-minded individual from the jury panel. Practically, we had all of California and the rest of the country in which to circulate the petition.

We decided that in San Jose we would concentrate on disseminating information and seeking organizational support for bail and for a fair trial. We also urged opposition to the planned expenditures by the Santa Clara County Board of Supervisors for security arrangements around the trial.

Our immediate tactic was to attend the weekly meetings of the county board of supervisors, and to urge all those with whom we had spoken to call or write the board, urging reconsideration of the security appropriations. Concern about this was widespread. Many people unwilling to evaluate the issues of the trial, could see the inherently prejudicial atmosphere the extraordinary security plans engendered.

On Tuesday, December 7th, several scores of people attended their first board of supervisors meeting. The Angela Davis defense committee in concert with community representatives —many from the *Ad Hoc* Committee of Concerned Citizens —submitted three proposals to the board: 1) that it recommend Angela Davis' immediate release on bail; 2) that it urge that the trial site be shifted to San Francisco in accord with the wishes of the Davis defense; and 3) that it rescind its initial appropriation of $203,000 for security.

Santa Clara County Counsel William Seigel argued vigorously that the board had no authority to rule on any of these proposals. Meanwhile, Undersheriff Tom Rosa took the opportunity to inform the board that unless it appropriated $165,000 at once, to remodel the main jail in San Jose, Ms. Davis would have to commute daily from Palo Alto. Reconstruction, he explained, would have to include the building of plywood walls, reinforced with steel, to meet jail standards and to "insure her privacy." Moreover, Rosa said, they would need "locking mechanisms" and a private entrance and exit for the defendant.

Other law enforcement officials informed the board that the San Jose Superior Court building and adjacent areas would have to be remodeled. Costs were estimated to be about $300,000 over and above the board's initial $200,000 appropriation. Surprised by the motions and counter-motions, the board tabled all proposals and recommendations until their next meeting.

Our protests continued. Drawing upon support from the *Ad Hoc* committee, the Black and Chicano communities and the students, our national committee called for an emergency demonstration at the Palo Alto jail on Saturday, December 18th. Our purpose was to reinforce the urgency of the demands placed before the board of supervisors.

Still reeling from the deluge of telegrams and letters objecting to Angels's jail conditions, the sheriff's department called our office in San Francisco a few days before the scheduled Palo Alto protest. Lieutenant Donald Tamm spoke with Charlene Mitchell to assure her of the full cooperation of the sheriff's department. The lieutenant inquired if we needed sound equipment, parking facilities, or anything else. Astonished by the conciliatory gesture, we asked for nothing, except to be left alone.

Meeting again three days before our scheduled protest, with Davis supporters still very much in attendance, the board of supervisors now appeared as a divided body. After heated debate, peppered with lively comment from the floor, the board voted to cut the Davis trial expenses (a minor reduction, but in the context of the controversy, significant) and it refused appropriation of the $165,000 to remodel the main jail in San Jose. Several board members angrily demanded that law enforcement officials obtain a court order to back up their demands for more money, if they wanted the board to act.

Several hundred people gathered at the Palo Alto courthouse on December 18th. It was a cold, drizzly day. Some folks parked a VW camper in the lot adjoining the courthouse and offered hot coffee as we picketed. Our line was long enough to surround the building. Fania and Kendra went inside to visit with Angela.

We decided to hold a short rally before dispersing. We were bunched together in the parking lot. Kendra came from the jail and mounted the flatbed truck, converted into a speakers platform. She announced that we could be heard inside the jail. There was great excitement. The crowd surged back toward the basement ramp, shouting, singing, cheering. "Angela! Can you hear us? Angela! Angela!"

ACTIVITY tapered off as the Christmas holidays approached. Authorities granted another, temporary, relaxation of the rules. If we prepared it, Angela could have a home-cooked Christmas dinner. Franklin, renowned in our circle as a superb chef, did the honors and friends in the San Jose community contributed their particular specialty. Home-baked cakes and assorted delicacies, in gay wrappings, covered our dining room table.

Angela joined in the holiday spirit. I went to see her the day before Christmas. She presented a little gift, apologizing that it wasn't properly wrapped. She had knitted me a woolen hat, and for my son, Joshua, she made a cap with matching scarf. "Do you think it will fit him?" she asked anxiously. She knitted something for everyone on our staff. We told her that if she kept it up we could sell her work and raise enough money to sustain the committee and the lawyers.

On New Year's Eve some four hundred people gathered outside the Palo Alto jail. The vigil began at five in the afternoon and ended just after three in the morning. It was a clear, very cold, night. We lit a fire in an oil drum brought for the occasion. The sheriff's department didn't enforce the zoning ordinance prohibiting an open fire. Huddled around the drum, bundled in coats and blankets, sipping hot wine we sang. Angela could hear us. She said it was beautiful.

ON JANUARY 5th the board of supervisors convened their first meeting of the New Year. Law enforcement officials came armed with a court order obtained through the office of the county counsel specifying that funds necessary for the renovation of the San Jose Civic Center be appropriated. The board complied. It voted approval of an additional $469,790, over and above the initial $203,000 outlay. Total security costs now approached three quarters of a million dollars.

We had lost our first effort in San Jose. Still, we had succeeded in stirring opposition. The same divisions which had marked the city's power structure during the controversy around the murder of John Henry Smith, now spilled over into the county's seats of power. Resolutions, counter-resolutions, judicial decrees seesawed back and forth as community pressures continued to mount and a renewed campaign for bail unfolded. National attention was focused on San Jose. The trial was scheduled to begin in 26 days.

10

A ngela grew up in the infamous state of Alabama under the terror of "Bull" Connor. We lived on Dynamite Hill, where we never knew from hour to hour if our home was to be bombed like those of neighbors all around us. This reign of terror was at its height when Angela was four years old.

She grew up with the four little girls who were killed in that horrible bombing of the 16th Street Baptist Church. Two of the first words she learned to read were "colored" and "white," labelling where to eat, where to drink water, what restrooms to go to. This was my eldest daughter's introduction to America as a child . . .

I visit Angela as often as possible. I never visit her without coming away with greater strength, inspiration and confidence. This is what enables me to live through these trying days. She is filled with optimism and courage, and gives me insights. I know why Angela has such confidence, such great inner peace. It is because she knows that without a doubt she is perfectly innocent, and she knows that *we* know she is guilty of no criminal act.

She has confidence in you, the people—you—around the world. She has confidence that people are the answer. She wrote to us, "Have no fear, Mother and Daddy, the peoples of the world will set me free!"

We have always been very proud of Angela as well as of our other three children. We are even more proud of the courageous stand she has taken for freedom and justice. I beg you to remember that she has made and is still making a great sacrifice. She is putting her life, as she puts it, on the line. I beg you not to let her sacrifice, or the sacrifice of other political prisoners, be in vain . . .

Sallye Davis
June 25, 1971

I FIRST met Sallye Davis in March 1971 in the corridor of the Marin County jail. We were waiting to see Angela. I said hello and introduced myself. Yes, she knew of me. Angela had told her I was a friend.

I saw her hands first, one gripping the other, clasped together in front of her, knuckles taut; slender, delicate fingers. She was of slight build and average height, her hair brushed back and put up in a bun, handsome features, melodious voice. She swayed slowly from side to side as she spoke. Images of Angela's face in hers.

We talked. She said she had been to the jail a few weeks before and had tried to see Angela, but they wouldn't let her in. She came back the next morning and waited again. She had had to leave for Birmingham later that same day. The tension had been unbearable. She got in finally.

"When I saw her, I started to cry. I couldn't help it. I just started to cry," she said. Now, waiting again, the memory still fresh, apologizing through me to Angela.

In the long months to come we were to get to know each other a lot more. As the center of activity for the trial shifted to San Jose, she stayed with us for much of the time she was in the area. We always called her Mrs. Davis. Even after she had lived with us for a long time she was still Mrs. Davis. It wasn't something anyone demanded of us. She never said anything about it. It wasn't a formality due to emotional distance or because we were white. Everyone said Mrs. Davis—except Howard. Most of the time he called her Mamma. I think she liked that. He had a special way of saying it: Hello Mamma. After the verdict, when it was all over, then we called her Sallye.

Mrs. Davis lives in Birmingham, Alabama. She teaches elementary school. She's been teaching for more than twenty years. She attends church regularly. She is patient, reserved, always conscious of observing proper decorum. She is, above all, a remarkably gentle woman. In all the months we were together, she never once raised her voice in anger. She never once spoke harshly of anyone, not even the prosecutor. Pain. Anguish. Resistance. But never hostility or hatred.

Her demeanor should not be taken for timidity. She is not timid. On the contrary. She is very proud, very strong and very brave. She did whatever it was that had to be done to save

Angela's life. She travelled the length and breadth of this country—endless rounds of meetings, speeches, luncheons, benefits.

Sometimes incidents of abuse and insult marred an appearance. Once she was invited to speak at a Catholic Church. Eighty people picketed the service. A spokesman for the group said it was "reprehensible that the church should allow anyone connected with Communism to speak." Another time a bomb exploded a few yards from her, while she was sitting on an outdoor platform waiting to address a meeting. Luckily, no one was injured.

Mrs. Davis knows of bombs. On that terrible day in September 1963 when Carol Robertson and three other Black children were blown apart in the 16th Street Baptist Church in Birmingham, it was Sallye Davis who drove Mrs. Robertson to the still-smoldering ruins.

Mrs. Davis knows of struggle. She defended the Scottsboro Boys and Angelo Herndon and the Martinsville Seven and Willie McGee before some of us were born. Thirty years ago she was fighting jim crow in Alabama. When sheriff's men barred the way into a church where an integrated meeting was to be held, Sallye Davis gathered the people together and told everyone to sit down outside on the church steps. And the meeting was held.

Mrs. Davis arrived at our home in San Jose for the first time in January 1972. We were having a public meeting in San Francisco on the 8th and she was to speak. It was a very important event. Kendra had been in charge of all preparations and had secured a greater breadth of support than any effort we had yet undertaken in the northern California area. Four days after the meeting Angela was scheduled to appear before Federal Judge William Sweigert in San Francisco and petition once again for her release on bail. The meeting was geared toward that appeal.

We sat around the kitchen table that Saturday afternoon before the rally. Mrs. Davis was working on her speech. She wanted me to read it. "Do you think it's all right?", she asked anxiously.

You see, Sallye Davis didn't come out of the movement of the '60's the way the lot of the rest of us did. She was unfamiliar with the rhetoric, uncomfortable shouting a slogan. And it was so unlike her to raise a fist!

She did it though, for Angela. And she did it in a style that was all her own. Of course, she worried about it too. Was she saying the right things? Would Angela like it?

Two thousand people stood in tribute to Sallye Davis that night as she was introduced. She read her speech slowly, carefully, in that gentle southern cadence. And as she finished, she raised her arm up, clenched her fist, and said firmly: *"Free Angela! Free all political prisoners!"* And the crowd, on its feet, roared back: "FREE ANGELA! FREE ANGELA! FREE ANGELA!"

11

A ngela was taken, with her hands cuffed to a chain around her waist, from her cell in Palo Alto to the federal building in San Francisco very early in the morning, Wednesday, January 12th. It was almost six months to the day since Judge Arnason had first denied her release on bail. Having exhausted all channels of appeal within the state courts, we initiated a new action for a writ of habeas corpus in the federal courts. We were prepared to carry the fight for bail through to the United States Supreme Court.

Federal District Court Judge William Sweigert had agreed to entertain oral arguments. It was the first time since Arnason's denial that a higher court consented to allow a public hearing on the issue. The modest-sized courtroom on the eleventh floor of the federal building was jammed with supporters. The hearing began shortly after 10 o'clock, with an opening presentation for the defense by special counsel, Anthony Amsterdam.

Amsterdam was a professor at Stanford University's Law School, and known throughout the legal profession as an outstanding authority in constitutional law.

Amsterdam's argument focused, as it had before in written briefs, on the applicability and interpretation of Article I, Section

6 of the California State Constitution and Section 1270 of the California Penal Code, both of which provide for a defendant's automatic right to bail "except in capital offenses when the proof of guilt is evident or the presumption thereof great."

"No California court," Amsterdam insisted, "has ever sustained a conviction on evidence as flimsy as that presented in the grand jury indictment against Angela Davis." In detail he contested each element of the charges and the supportive evidence, until he had shredded the last remaining tenet of the prosecution's theory of the crime.

At the same time Amsterdam challenged any interpretation of the law which maintained that the trial judge had no discretion in admitting a defendant to bail in a capital case. Section 1270, he said, did not prohibit Ms. Davis' release on bail. It merely provided that the judge had discretion in the matter, contrary to the normal constitutional provision which considered bail as a matter of right. Ms. Davis' presumption of innocence could and should be affirmed. Bail should be granted. Citing the fact that the trial would probably take between six and nine months according to estimates by both the prosecution and the defense, Amsterdam warned the court that in fact Ms. Davis was being preventively detained in violation of basic constitutional rights. "By the time this case is ended Ms. Davis will have been in custody for two years whether she is guilty or innocent."

Supporting presentations were offered in "friend of the court" appearances by Paul Halvonik, representing the Northern California Chapter of the American Civil Liberties Union, Stuart Weinberg of the California Federation of Teachers, and Eugene Rosenberg of the National Lawyers Guild.

Franklin Alexander spoke on behalf of our committee. He presented the court with several dozen bound volumes each containing a hundred or more petitions urging Angela's immediate release on bail. They contained over 350,000 signatures of women and men in the United States. He explained that if we had included all the petitions circulated throughout the world the court would have before it between one and two million signatures.

Angela was recognized as co-counsel. Calm, firm, scholarly, with the same rythmic quality so characteristic of Mrs. Davis, she pleaded her own cause. Noting the difficulties of adequate trial preparations under the conditions of her confinement she contended that the failure to allow bail materially impaired her ability to prepare her defense. "Many," she said, "myself included, think that the denial of bail has been a political gesture. It erodes the presumption of innocence. Bail is supposed to be the keystone of Amercian democracy, but unfortunately in this country Black people and poor people have been unable to avail themselves of bail . . ." Urging the court to find the courage to act affirmatively she assured the judge that, "if bail is granted many will consider it a victory for the democratic processes of this country." In an appeal to conscience she said, "I am fighting for the right to live."

Judge Sweigert promised a decision within a few days. As court adjourned one of the bailiffs approached Attorney Doris Walker. He told Doris that Ms. Davis didn't need any lawyers. "You should just let her speak for herself," he said.

AS THE trial approached we gave renewed consideration to adding a fourth lawyer to the trial team. Several prospects were considered. We all agreed, however, that if Leo Branton were available, he would be our first choice. He was reputed to be one of the finest criminal lawyers in the country.

Leo had most recently served as co-counsel in the trial of thirteen members of the Black Panther Party in Los Angeles. They had been indicted for attempted murder, after defending themselves during a fierce police assault against their headquarters in December 1969. Leo had also been one of the lawyers, along with Doris Walker, to defend members of the Communist Party indicted under the Smith Act in the early Fifties.

Leo came to the Bay Area shortly before the Christmas holidays, met with Angela and the rest of us at considerable length, familiarized himself with the case and early in January 1972 agreed to join the defense team.

PRE-TRIAL hearings continued. Some motions were argued in open court, others in closed session. Judge Arnason preferred to work in chambers and he did so as often as possible. There were three consequential issues still to be pursued. First, a defense motion relating to discovery (of prosecution evidence); second, a motion calling upon the state to assume the financial burden of Angela's legal defense; and third, and most critical, the manner in which the jury panel was to be selected. Judge Arnason agreed to delay the start of the trial on a day-to-day basis until all issues had been presented. He would, he said, rule on each motion. On January 31st, however, we were to begin using the San Jose courtroom.

Federal Judge Sweigert denied the writ of habeas corpus on Friday, January 14th. In his decision to deny bail, Sweigert admitted that the "almost interminable" delays in the trial came close to the denial of due process in the right to a speedy trial and "perhaps even cruel and unusual pre-conviction punishment." However, he contended that Ms. Davis "may have contributed to or caused the delays" herself by "numerous pre-trial motions."

Doris Walker, on behalf of defense counsel, answered Sweigert's charges of defense-inspired delays: "This . . . has not been the fault of the defense. We have had to go before the court several times to insist that the judge force the prosecution to comply with court orders. It's taken us the better part of a year to get a look at the so-called evidence. [Moreover] the improper and forced joining by the state of Ruchell Magee and Angela Davis ham-strung both defendants for months."

The lawyers began preparations for an appeal to the United States Supreme Court.

The legal duel simmered. Political tempers flared. A major confrontation statewide was brewing. San Jose was in the center of the impending storm.

The county counsel's office in Santa Clara, apparently caught in a cross-fire of political pressures generated within the county, decided suddenly that Ms. Davis had too many privileges, too many investigators, too many lawyers, and too many visitors. With less than a month to go before trial, even granted the day-to-day delay proviso, Byron Athan, representing the county counsel's office, moved to alter the court orders under which we had been operating for more than a year. He sought revisions in jailhouse rules to minimize the concessions granted by the sheriff's department as a result of the December avalanche of protest.

Investigators, Athan maintained, should not be permitted to visit with Ms. Davis, unless accompanied by counsel, and then only two investigators were to be admitted at a time. The effect of such an order was to cripple the work of the defense. We had five investigators and four lawyers. We divided our responsibilities. The investigators did much work to relieve the lawyers of certain tasks so that they could concentrate on legal preparation. By requiring the presence of an attorney everytime an investigator needed to see Angela, the county counsel's office would defeat the whole purpose of an investigatorial staff. Moreover, the proposed order meant that our entire legal/political staff could not meet with Angela at the same time. This dismantled our most effective method of work—collective consideration of critical strategic and tactical issues.

Angela braced herself for the worst.

Our lawyers demanded and got a special chambers session with Judge Arnason. The judge could override the order of the county counsel. He had the final authority. Meeting in chambers on January 10th, they argued for hours. What appeared as an innocuous technical matter was in fact a major political confrontation.

The point, of course, was that Angela did not actually enjoy special privileges. On the contrary. Because the Sheriff's Department insisted upon confining her in isolation, normal privileges, extended to all county prisoners, such as access to television and radio, outdoor exercise, access to lawyers and investigators, had to be specially provided in Angela's case.

The chambers session ended when the judge finally agreed to talk to the sheriff about various unnecessary and arbitrary restrictions. "If you still have some problems [after that] let me hear from you," he told Howard Moore.

The judge did talk to the sheriff. The county counsel's order was quashed. We had no further serious problems at the jail.

Another twist of irony, however, came a few days later. By mid-January, we had expected Angela to be moved to new quarters in San Jose. The remodeling of the main jail was to have been completed before January 31.

I was with Angela one morning in Palo Alto. She asked the sergeant when she was to be transferred. Casually, he informed her that she was not to be moved after all. It seemed that the renovation of the main jail had hit a snag. All the work had been completed, $78,000 had been spent, but a newly installed elevator, which was to transport her from the cell to a tunnel leading into the courthouse basement, could not be made to operate properly. Plans to detain her in San Jose had been cancelled. Angela was to commute after all.

The sergeant had decided that Angela should move from the cells she now occupied to two others just down the hall, which he thought were larger. We could not discern any difference, but the sergeant was firm and suggested that Angela move at once.

Whatever work we had planned for the day was abruptly ended. Cell doors were flung open with abandon. Visiting rules were suspended to allow me to remain through the lunch hour. Radio blaring, cartons piled high in the corridor, we carted her paraphernalia from one set of cells to the other, kidding, laughing, bumping into each other in the tight quarters. I started to feel like we were a couple of college kids settling into a new dormitory; and then the steel doors whined open and shut and lunch arrived and it was on a colorless tray and it was a dry bologna sandwich and there was only a spoon and a metal cup and we were in a jail.

12.

Margaret Burnham and Angela Davis had known each other since childhood. They were the same age, and their parents were close friends. Margaret's father, Louis, had been an organizer for the Southern Negro Youth Congress in the Forties, and had spent time in Birmingham. That's where he first met Sallye and Frank Davis. Trips to Birmingham for the Burnham family, or to New York for the Davis' were not infrequent. When Angela came to New York to attend Elizabeth Irwin High School she lived in Brooklyn not far from the Burnham home. She and Margaret were constant companions.

Margaret had been working for the NAACP Legal Defense Fund in New York only a few months, having recently graduated from law school and passed the bar examination, when Angela was arrested. She became her lawyer the same night.

Angela spent her first night in jail at the New York Women's House of Detention. She was arraigned the following morning before the United States Commissioner, and charged with violation of the Federal Interstate Fugitive Act (a direct descendant of the Fugitive Slave Law). She was returned to jail in lieu of $250,000 bond.

At eight o'clock that same night Margaret, and Attorney John Abt, who served as co-counsel during the extradition proceedings, were summoned back to the Commissioner's Court. Angela was released from federal jurisdiction and placed in the custody of the New York City Police Department to be held without bail pending extradition.

After the hearing Margaret and John were informed that Angela would be 'booked' at the Seventh Precinct police station. They went there only to discover that no one in authority had any idea where Angela was. For the next several hours Margaret and John traipsed all over New York City trying to locate their client. They finally learned that Angela had been taken to the Criminal Courts Building at 100 Center Street for arraignment on the California warrant.

It was well-past midnight when John and Margaret arrived for the hearing. They found the building surrounded by more than two hundred uniformed police and scores of newsmen and cameramen. The streets were clogged with police cars, quiet now, save for the rhythmic whirl of the red lights.

When they got into court John suggested that given the lateness of the hour and the long search for their client, an adjournment until next morning was in order. The prosecutor said: "Do you have any idea what tonight is costing the City of New York?"

I WENT to see Margaret in New York shortly after Angela's arrest. She was still working with the NAACP, and we met at her office in midtown Manhattan near Columbus Circle.

Margaret was sharing an office with another young woman. They occupied a small room, just able to accommodate a couple of desks and chairs. The walls were plastered with posters attesting to the rash of political trials. Margaret's desk was cluttered with stacks of briefs, files, books, newspapers. The telephone rang incessantly. She was alternately writing, answering calls, eating a sandwich and talking to me, her small frame barely visible behind the mass of paper, still perfectly calm, unruffled, with no trace of agitation.

With a finely honed sense of the absurd so characteristic of her humor, Margaret recounted the story of Angela's first days in custody. I could just picture Margaret slipping unobtrusively past the rows of uniformed police, through the frantic throng of newsmen; and then her serene, commanding presence in the courtroom.

Angela and Margaret had a unique relationship, a rare blending of the detached efficiency of lawyer to client, and the intimacy, compassion and love of life-long friendship.

I remember once being in the cell with them. Angela didn't understand why some legal maneuver or other couldn't be executed. She argued with Margaret about it, and finally said, somewhat impatiently: "Well, what have you done in other cases?" And Margaret looked up at her and started to laugh and said: "Baby, I don't know. You're my first client!"

MARGARET assumed major legal responsibilities for the defense. She had been in charge of the change of venue efforts. She was to help prepare our affirmative defense for the trial itself. But it was in the preparations for the selection of the jury that Margaret made her most important contribution. Her work was decisive to the outcome of the trial.

Margaret challenged the way in which the prospective jurors were to be selected. She challenged and won major concessions on the way in which the prospective jurors were to be questioned during what is called the voir dire examination. She conceived of and organized an investigation of over 5,000 prospective jurors in 35 days.

Between December 21 and December 29, 1971 the jury commissioner mailed jury service questionnaires to 9,825 registered voters in Santa Clara County, the names selected at random by computer. By the January 15, 1972 deadline, 5,249 voters had returned questionnaires to the jury commissioner's office. From these 5,249 registered voters, 150 would be picked at random and called as prospective jurors for the Angela Davis trial.

Everything about the selection procedure militated against Black, Brown and working people ever becoming prospective jurors. If perchance such a person finally made it onto the jury panel other factors would probably prevent him from actually serving. In a written brief, in oral arguments and through witnesses presented in court, Margaret challenged the selection procedures.

Only registered voters had received the questionnaires. Every known study confirmed the fact that there was a correlation between voter registration and income level — the poorer the person the less likely he was to register to vote.

Margaret argued that the exclusive use of the voter rolls constituted an unjustifiable restriction on the representativeness of the jury list, and that it should be supplemented with other, available lists of residents. "The Defendant," she wrote, "has a constitutionally protected right to a jury from which no significant element of the community is arbitrarily excluded."

The jury commissioner had no procedures for following-up on those voters who did not return the jury service questionnaire. Again, Margaret argued, it was the white, more affluent voter, who was most likely to return his questionnaire. Only half of those sent out by the commissioner were in fact returned. What of the other registered voters?

The law required that jurors have "sufficient knowledge of English" to comprehend the proceedings. However, one of the questions asked prospective jurors on the questionnaire read: "Can you read, write and understand English?" A "No" response would disqualify him from jury service, although obviously many persons of Mexican descent living in California could speak and understand English without being able to read and write it.

Margaret contended that the question was improper in that it imposed a higher standard of literacy than required by law. It had the effect, she said, of excluding large numbers of Chicano voters from jury service in a county that had a substantial Chicano population.

A juror was to be paid only $5.00 a day for the duration of the trial, plus 15¢ a mile for transportation costs to and from court. It was established that many companies would not pay a worker's wages while he served on a jury. Those few that would often stipulated that they would not pay wages for more than two weeks. Many firms would simply fire a worker who was off the job for more than a few days no matter what the reason.

Margaret argued that the Davis trial was expected to last anywhere from four to six months. An average worker couldn't afford to serve on a jury, and would most likely be excused for reasons of economic hardship. Additional compensation by the court was essential.

Margaret maintained that everything considered, the vast majority of prospective jurors would be white, middle class and housewives, hardly constituting a jury of Angela's peers.

The judge refused to alter the procedures for assembling prospective jurors.

Another vital consideration was the extent to which prospective jurors could be questioned by opposing counsel during the voir dire examination. There are few legal imperatives, and a presiding judge may use his discretion. Many judges, backed by appeals courts, had already begun to severely limit the range of questions allowed on the voir dire. Others had begun to conduct the questioning themselves, without the participation of counsel.

The voir dire is important in any trial. In this one it was critical. Margaret contended that only the most rigorous questioning of prospective jurors would give Angela any hope of selecting twelve who were not hopelessly prejudiced against her. Complex issues of racism, communism, the woman's role in society, academic freedom, the war in Vietnam, were involved in her case.

The judge agreed to allow the widest latitude in the questioning of prospective jurors. And the questioning was to be conducted by the lawyers themselves. It was a major victory for the defense.

Proper questioning of the prospective jurors required that our lawyers have as much information as possible about each one, prior to the actual start of the voir dire. The law required that the jury commissioner supply opposing counsel with the list of prospective jurors — in this case the 150 selected from the pool of 5,000 — at least 72 hours prior to trial.

Margaret asked the court to arrange for opposing counsel to

receive the names of all 5,000 prospective jurors. The judge a-
greed. On January 24, 1972, six days before the trial was technically set to begin, thirty-five days before it actually began, Judge
Arnason signed an order authorizing the jury commissioner to
release the names of all 5,000 prospective jurors. He also instructed the jury commissioner to make available to opposing
counsel the names of the 150 prospective jurors to be called for
the Davis trial as soon as they were known.

Margaret had assembled a core of people to organize an investigation of the prospective jurors.

The prosecutor, of course, had a built-in system of investigation. He had only to call upon local, state and federal police agencies for assistance. He had access to computers and to the records
of every conceivable government bureau. We had no such ap-
paratus. We did have people.

Literally hundreds volunteered their time. We estimated that
by the end nearly 500 people had participated in the massive
project.

At the end of the second week in February we received the
names of the 150 prospective jurors for the Davis trial. Intensive
investigation began on each one, with the preliminary work from
the voter registration records of the 5,000 already completed.

With hundreds of volunteers, many of whom had lived in the
community for twenty years or more, and with organizational
support and friends we were bound to find someone who knew
someone else who knew a prospective juror, or lived on the same
block, or knew their kids, or something, any scrap of information.

We obtained a large street map of Santa Clara County and
placed colored pins in the spot where each of the 150 prospective
jurors lived. Margaret's prediction that most jurors would come
from white, middle class areas was confirmed with chilling accuracy. There was scarcely a pin to be found on San Jose's east side
and central districts where most of the Black, Chicano and working class families lived. The density of pins increased as you
moved into the southern and western portions of the city and up
towards Palo Alto.

All the bits and pieces of information on each of the 150 prospective jurors were collated and then recorded in a master book
prepared for the lawyers' use in court.

Our volunteers worked against a deadline from which there was no respite. The investigation had to be completed by the start of the trial, and by any reckoning it was less than a month away. During the last weeks they worked around the clock in shifts.

The investigation gave us a perspective on the jury panel as a whole. We now knew what kind of a jury we could ideally hope for, and what we would have to settle for.

The fact that we had obtained the list of prospective jurors in sufficient time to conduct the investigation, and the judge's decision to allow maximum latitude in the voir dire examination attested to the growing political potential of the mass movement.

Recognizing and fearing that potential, the ruling circles in Sacramento and San Jose, led by California Governor Ronald Reagan, were to attempt one more counter-offensive in an effort to cripple the defense.

13

W ith the bail appeal stalled between courts, the mass campaign reached a momentary impasse, and California Governor Ronald Reagan seized the opportunity to launch a frontal assault against Angela Davis.

In mid-January Angela, acting as co-counsel, argued a unique pre-trial motion. She asked that the State of California be ordered to pay her legal expenses.

A prolonged struggle by advocates of legal reform had finally resulted in a new state law, only recently signed by Governor Reagan, authorizing the state to pay for court-appointed defense counsel (as distinct from public defenders who were salaried). Angela's intent was to invoke the authority of this new law.

Angela determined to make the argument in order to dramatize the fact that tens of thousands of Black people and poor people are shunted off to jail each year because they cannot afford counsel. Many plead guilty for this reason and hope for judicial leniency. Others plead not guilty and are saddled with public defenders, overworked and underpaid at best, cynical and in league with the prosecutor at worst.

Angela did not expect a favorable ruling from Judge Arnason. She did believe that it was essential to utilize every opportunity to expose the institutionalized class and racial discrimination inherent in the system of criminal justice.

Newspapers reported the day's events in court in front-page stories dripping with sarcasm.

Ronald Reagan, judiciously silent on the Davis case since his initial outburst about terrorists, thugs and hoodlums at the time of Angela's arrest, was now bristling with righteous indignation. He called a press conference in Sacramento on Friday, January 20th.

Reeking with chauvinism he denounced all pre-trial motions by the defense as "delaying tactics." He said Angela Davis was depriving "society" of its right to the speedy administration of justice. He advised that if Angela Davis couldn't pay her legal expenses she ought to "throw herself on the mercy of the court and ask for a public defender."

Reagan's statement was accorded national television coverage. It was on the front-page of most California newspapers.

Two days after the Governor's outburst several hundred Black legislators and other public figures gathered in East Palo Alto for the annual meeting of the California Black Caucus. Present were several United States congressmen and state legislators, as well as city and county officials, newspaper publishers, physicians, attorneys.

Fania Jordan requested and received permission to address the assembly. She won unanimous support for Angela's immediate release on bail. But the caucus resolution went even further:

> WHEREAS, if justice prevailed in this country, Governor Reagan's statement, taken together with President Nixon's earlier statement convicting Angela Davis on nationwide television where he labeled her as a terrorist, would be sufficient legal grounds to dismiss the entire frame-up case against Angela Davis . . . if justice prevailed in this country . . .

THEREFORE BE IT RESOLVED that the California Black Caucus calls upon the Superior Court of the State of California to immediately dismiss the case against Angela Davis on the grounds that it is impossible for her to receive a fair trial anywhere in this country.

The Black Caucus statement went unreported on national television. Not one word of it was printed in any newspaper in California with the exception of the Black press and Communist press. As far as millions of Americans could know the governor's statement had gone unchallenged.

We fought back. We called Reverend A. Cecil Williams, Minister of the Glide Memorial Church in San Francisco. Reverend Williams was a jovial, warm, compassionate, energetic Black man who had long associated himself with the defense of the Soledad Brothers and with Angela. His church was packed virtually every Sunday, its spirited, militant services reputed to be among the best in the country.

Cecil Williams had a regular television show on the local CBS-affiliated network called "Vibrations for a New People." We asked him if he would conduct an interview with Angela in jail, and broadcast it. Enthusiastically he agreed. Judge Arnason provided a court order (another testament to the growing impact of the mass concern expressed for Angela) to allow television crews inside the Palo Alto jail. The one stipulation agreed to by both defense and prosecution was that Angela would not talk about the facts in her case *per se*. She could talk about issues in general. It was also agreed that prior to broadcast both the prosecution and the defense could view the video tape to insure that this provision was respected.

The interview was taped the last week in January. The program was edited and prepared for broadcast. Prosecution and defense attorneys viewed it.

Albert Harris appeared indifferent to the first three-quarters of the program. Angela focused the discussion on the injustices and atrocities of the California prison system. Toward the end, however, he sat erect and his pen flew across the sheets of his legal pad.

Cecil Angela, I asked you to bring some letters which you had received. . . . Could you read several of those letters for me at this time? Some are just very fascinating.

Angela . . . I should say, as a preface, that being in jail . . . the thousands and thousands of letters that come from people all over the world expressing their solidarity with me and all other political prisoners, has been a remarkable source of strength, not only for me, but also for the sisters with whom I come in contact because I always let them know what's happening on the outside, how the struggle for our freedom is advancing. This letter, it's really a beautiful letter written by a very, very young child apparently, and it says, very simply, "Dear Angela Davis: My name is Sarah. I wish that you were free. This is a picture of you when you will be free. Love, Sarah." And on the other side, there's a picture that she's drawn.

Cecil Is this Sarah or of you, when you will be free?

Angela Well, she says that it's a picture of me. You see the smile on my face. I think that's supposed to be symbolic of freedom. I get lots of letters from very young children. . . .

A lot of people somehow have the feeling that the movement is collapsing, but I think that what's happening is that the ideas that a few people have been expressing for a long time are penetrating to the masses of people and you have sisters and brothers who are say five, six years old, who know what has to be done. . . .

[These letters from children] . . . make very concrete something that Jose Martí, the Apostle of the Cuban Revolution said: "Los niños son la esperanza del mundo." Translation: "Children are the hope of the world." And I think this is true and that we do have a revolution moving along and it can be seen in our children and in our youth. . . .

Prosecutor Harris protested vigorously in chambers. The interview must not be televised. It was melodramatic, self-serving. The judge said there was nothing in the interview which contravened his order. In fact, Angela had not spoken one word in her own defense. She had not commented on the evidence. She had not demanded her release on bail. She had not attacked the attorney general, or the governor or the president.

The CBS-affiliated network withstood a wave of gubernatorial pressure and preempted two regularly scheduled shows at prime time to broadcast the one-hour exclusive interview. Hundreds of thousands of people saw it. Demand was so great it was re-broadcast a week later. Then CBS nationally scheduled to broadcast the program coast to coast. They eventually reneged on this offer. Still, we were on the eve of trial and we had reached a vast audience. It was another significant victory and we had off-set the impact of phase one of the Reagan offensive.

In line with this more aggressive approach toward the media we had engaged Stephanie Allan as press director for our committee. Stephanie, a young white woman had several years of experience as a reporter and free-lance writer for the *People's World* in San Francisco and commercial papers elsewhere. She established contacts with press people across the country, and supplied the media in general with daily press releases and information.

(During the trial Stephanie and Rob Baker, from our national office, were to produce a brilliant trial bulletin, called *Frameup*, which was to be a vital source of information to thousands.)

Meanwhile, the political situation in San Jose continued to provoke widespread controversy. The *Ad Hoc* Committee of Concerned Citizens had continued its supportive actions for Angela. Community anger over the murder of John Henry Smith had not been assuaged, and when Patrolman Rocklin Woolley, was acquitted by an all-white jury early in February 1972, there were renewed protests.

At approximately the same time the judge in the Woolley trial, James Scott, chose to intervene in the Davis case. It was phase two of the Reagan offensive.

For that story we must trace an extraordinary series of events commencing on January 24th, 1972 and culminating a month later in Angela's release on bail.

14

Sheriff James Geary, middle-aged, silver-streaked hair, conservative gray suit, looked like a typical business executive. His lieutenant, Donald Tamm, was a youngish man with steel-framed glasses, mod dress, protruding Adam's apple, looking earnest and studious. Neither man wore a uniform with any frequency. Both were reputed liberals. This is not said disparagingly. Their political bent was an important factor in the events to come, though they were susceptible to countervailing pressures, and therefore likely to buckle at critical moments.

Still hopeful of reversing or at least tempering decisions of the county board of supervisors to fortify the San Jose civic center complex for the Davis trial, representatives from the *Ad Hoc* Committee of Concerned Citizens urged that we seek a meeting with Sheriff Geary to see what, if any, relief was possible. On Monday, January 24th, 1972 a meeting did take place in the sheriff's office.

The sheriff received a delegation of some fifteen people from eleven different organizations in the county (Unified Soul, representing 15 Black professional, business, religious, student and community groups, Action for Progress, the Women's International League for Peace and Freedom, the NAACP, Santa Clara University Students for the Defense of Angela Davis, Pan-African Students of San Jose State College, the Community Alert Patrol, El Comité para la Defensa de Prisioneros Politicos, the American Civil Liberties Union and the United Black Dignity Committee of the Veterans Hospital in Palo Alto).

The citizens group expressed its concern for the security measures being assembled for the Davis trial. These measures coupled with the refusal of authorities to allow Ms. Davis' release on bail, made it appear, they emphasized, that Ms. Davis was a dangerous person intent upon escape, and that this was a prejudgment of guilt which would severely prejudice all prospective jurors.

There is no doubt that the position of the citizens group was substantially enhanced by the veritable deluge of support our committee was now receiving in the Santa Clara area. Local unions including the Office and Professional Employees, the Social Service Workers, the California Federation of Teachers, the Laborer's International, the United Auto Workers, the United Electrical Workers, the ILWU, demanded Angela's release on bail. The Joint Strategy and Action Committee [JSAC] of Santa Clara County, the largest and most influential inter-denominational religious organization, prepared a splendid booklet detailing the issues in the case for distribution to all of its member churches. Accompanying the pamphlet was a news release containing the text of a JSAC resolution urging Angela's release on bail.

Sheriff Geary stated that he did not understand why Angela Davis was not released on bail, that his job would be much easier if she were. He said he did not consider Ms. Davis dangerous nor intent upon escape. He stated that a fairer and more public trial could indeed be held, and other facilities were available.

Astonished by the sheriff's conciliatory posture, participants in the meeting asked him if he would agree to hold a press conference with them, and make his opinions known publicly. The sheriff readily accepted the invitation.

The next day, Tuesday, January 25th, a joint press conference was held in the Antioch Baptist Church in San Jose. The Black minister of that church, the Reverend C.W. Washington, was among those most active in Angela's defense. He presided over the conference. The press came, including television and radio stations. Of the regular media only the San Jose *Mercury* deemed the story worthy of release.

Sheriff Geary confirmed in public what he had said in private. He emphasized that he saw no reason why Ms. Davis could not be immediately bailed.

Meanwhile, Judge James Scott, who was now the Presiding Judge of the Superior Court, acted to implement the second half of the Reagan scenario. Scott sent a memorandum to the Sheriff's Department concerning regulations for the Davis trial. It was written as a memorandum rather than a court order so that it would not be subject to judicial review. The Sheriff's Department hastened to comply.

On Thursday, January 27th, Fania Jordan, Charlene Mitchell and Franklin Alexander were summoned to the sheriff's headquarters to receive the details of the Scott Memorandum. They met with Lieutenant Donald Tamm and Undersheriff Tom Rosa, who informed them that:

1) No demonstration which advocated the freedom of Angela Davis could be held within "sight or sound" of the courthouse. This had been interpreted to mean that no such protests could be held within an approximate one-mile radius of the courthouse. Further, Judge Scott held that he could ban any demonstration anywhere in the State of California which he determined to be within "sight or sound" of the courthouse, via media coverage.

(Judge Scott's order was based upon an admittedly loose interpretation of Section 169 of the California Penal Code enacted by the State Legislature on September 18th, 1970. That was the law that had its origins in Judge Campbell's Salinas courtroom, eighteen months earlier, when the Soleded Brothers case had begun.)

2) A "peaceful assembly" could be held within the one-mile perimeter of the courthouse, in a county-owned parking lot, 500 yards from the building, under severely restricted conditons: a) a permit had to be obtained form the Sheriff's Department at least 24 hours prior to the planned assembly; b) there could be no picket signs, posters, banners, etc. of any kind, which advocated anything; c) no speeches could be made which could be heard beyond the limits of the people present in the parking lot (effectively prohibiting the use of sound amplification); d) there could be no singing or other verbal expressions in unison by the people present; e) there could be no symbolic gestures such as clenched fists by the people present.

In addition, the Sheriff's Department spelled out three of its own provisos for the Davis trial:

1) Courtroom #1 of the Superior Court, where the Angela Davis trial was to be held, seated sixty people. Thirty seats were to be reserved for the public, and thirty seats were to be reserved for the press. The press would, in addition, have access to a large

room seating 105 people to view the trial on closed-circuit television. The public would be provided with no such facility.

2) Courtroom #1 would be accessible to the public only through the rear entrance. The front entrance would be locked, and wired with an alarm system. Access to the rear entrance would be through a secured covered walkway. The walkway would be fenced off. Surrounding the fences would be a concentration of armed guards.

3) All persons, including press and potential jurors, entering the Davis trial would be processed through an elaborate security check. Public and press would be subjected to two detailed body searches. They would be issued numbered passes for seats inside the courtroom. Each spectator or reporter would be photographed before being permitted to enter the courtroom. This procedure would be followed daily for each individual, no matter how many times that person had been to court.

Fania, Charlene and Franklin were then taken on a guided tour of the secured area and shown the 12-foot cyclone fences, the surveillance equipment, the searching areas, etc. They were not permitted to ask more than a few questions. When Fania asked about peoples' rights under the U.S. Constitution, Undersheriff Rosa remarked, "That was written a long time ago."

Fania, Franklin and Charlene returned to our national office in San Francisco. Our staff met that night. Franklin took a felt-tipped pen and sketched a map of the courthouse area directly onto the wall of the office. He explained to us exactly what had been told to him. There were outbursts of disbelieving laughter as the labyrinth of restrictions unfolded before us. Our discussion was anything but morbid. Enraged, yes, but also spirited, ebullient, anticipating the fight we knew we could make. Not only *could* we make a fight. We *had* to make one if the campaign itself was to survive.

It was another atrocity in a long series of abuses and outrages. This one directed against the committee and its supporters—Angela's life-line. It was a clear-cut, definable political issue: the transgression of elemental constitutional rights. We could make a challenge without the frustrating constraints of legalistic intrigue. We would violate their laws and rules and protocol. We would shatter their precious decorum, we would break through the stony silence of the media, we would get Angela out. I think all of us at that moment felt a sense of impending victory, though none of us could predict its exact contours.

This euphoria was authentic, though it may seem to others to have been premature and inexplicable. It wasn't. It had to do with the moment as we were living it, the dynamics of the struggle itself. Fania and I were positively joyous as we drove home to San Jose after that meeting. And early the next day, seeing Sallye Davis in the kitchen with her morning cup of coffee, I remember embracing her and telling her we would have Angela out in a matter of weeks. It was just a sense, a feeling, and I can recall it now vividly, as I felt it then.

THE NEW regulations were to take effect Monday morning, January 31st—the first day pre-trial hearings were to be conducted in San Jose. In consultation with members of CAP and Unified Soul and others in the San Jose community we agreed upon a tactical approach.

The first essential was that the courtroom be filled to capacity that Monday morning. We agreed that no one was to submit to a strip search, though we would submit to the frisk, and walk through the metal detector and allow photographs to be taken. (These procedures had been standard throughout the months of pre-trial hearings in Marin County.) To dramatize the need for a larger courtroom those who could not get into the courtroom would be asked to remain on the line at the rear gate, at least through the morning session. If there were enough people on that line, and if the situation seemed reasonably calm, we would ask a few people to leave the line and join us in a peaceful picket-line at the rear entrance of the courthouse, thus testing our constitutional right to protest.

We arrived at the courthouse about 6:30 in the morning. It was very cold, frost still on the grass. The sky was clear. The sun rose over the courthouse building as we huddled in small groups sipping cups of coffee. The tension from the cold combined with the tension of the day. We waited for our numbers to grow. They did. People stood silently in a line at the rear entrance to the court.

The line stretched from the fence further and further down the road, passed the sheriff's headquarters, the main jail and on towards the street. The morning grew brighter and warmer.

The deputies opened the gates at about 8:30. People filed quietly into the court. There were no incidents. The gates were ordered closed. The courtroom was full. There were still scores of people on the line.

Franklin and I sat down on the curb. I slipped my arm through his. Fania sat down next to us. We looked at each other. There were more than enough people to do what we wanted to do. "Shall we?" Franklin asked. He was smiling. "Let's go," I said. Fania went quietly up and down the line talking to small clusters of individuals explaining our intentions to conduct a peaceful picket. Most already knew something of the plans. She assured the people that those who remained on the line were, as far as we could ascertain, in no danger of arrest. Those who wanted to join the picket should consider it carefully, arrests were probable. Moreover, we only wanted a few people—enough to make our point. Mass arrests were too costly and not necessary, at least not yet.

It was time. Franklin and I got up. We told the folks we'd be back in a few minutes. We were going to get the picket-signs which were in Franklin's car. Fania stayed with the line. Everything was very cool, calm, low-keyed.

Franklin and I walked slowly towards the parking lot. I still had my arm through his. We joked a little bit. We brought the signs back to the demonstration and placed them face down in the roadway, near the line of supporters, in front of the gate. People gathered around us, Franklin made a little speech. He was very calm. He wasn't soap-boxing. He was just explaining what had to be done: "We're going to ask a few of you who are willing to risk being arrested, to pick up these signs and join Fania in picketing this building. We're going to ask the rest of you to please remain standing on line."

Fania swept passed Franklin, bent down and picked up a sign. She started walking, a kind of graceful, elegant step, almost a dance. People surged forward, grabbed a sign and fell in behind her. I scrambled for a sign. It said: WE DEMAND A LARGER COURTROOM! There were seventeen of us. As we had previ-

ously agreed Franklin did not join the picket. We did not want
him to be arrested. We walked in silence for a while. Then we
took up various slogans. Victoria Mercado and Fania were walking together, leading the chants. Tension dissipated. I felt good,
really good.

We kept it up for about 15 minutes. We'd get tired and stop
chanting and just walk. Franklin hovered over us like an expectant father, waiting for the sheriff's men to make their move.

Lieutenant Tamm emerged from the courtroom, walked
through the fence and surveyed the scene. He was in full uniform. He looked hopelessy out of place. He was very agitated. He
talked into his walkie-talkie for a few moments. Then he picked
up a bullhorn and started reading to us from Section 169 of the
Penal Code. We knew the text. Fania started singing. We sang
freedom songs. We took up the chants again. Someone shouted
FREE THE IRISH! Free the Irish? Oh my God. Well, why not?
Then Fania and Victoria again, WE HAVE A RIGHT TO DE-
MONSTRATE!

The lieutenant finished reading Section 169 for a second time.
Then he said: "I want you to pay very close attention to what I am
saying. I ask you to listen carefully." Then he read 169 a third
time. FREE ANGELA! FREE ALL POLITICAL PRISONERS!
WE HAVE A RIGHT TO DEMONSTRATE! The lieutenant
talked into his walkie-talkie again. We continued to chant. Then
there was silence.

We heard the gasp from the people standing on line as the
troops arrived. There must have been a hundred sheriff's men.
They marched in lockstep. They carried three-foot clubs in hori-
zontal position at the ready; they wore army green flack jackets,
and heavy black boots; helmets, with the visors up. Tear gas
masks and cannisters hung from their belts. So did the guns.

They halted a few feet from us. The commander gave an order.
Quickly, efficiently they parted ranks. About half, marching in
formation, surrounded us, cutting us off from our supporters still
standing on the line. We continued picketing. We were singing
now. I don't remember what we were singing. I felt dizzy—we
were walking faster and faster, in a tighter and tighter circle and
the building, faces, fences were spinning past me. I thought about
taking my glasses off, but I didn't know how to negotiate getting

my glasses off and into my purse without dropping my sign. I didn't want to drop my sign and I couldn't stop walking now. It was too late.

The remaining soldiers marched lockstep into our ranks. I could see their faces clearly now. They looked very young and very scared. All that gear and military paraphernalia—the momentary panic turned into uncontrollable gaity. It suddenly seemed terribly funny. One of the men grabbed Fania, another Victoria. Then one came towards me.

As I was being led away, I heard Franklin shouting after us— "... and there will be hundreds and thousands more to take your place."

They led us into a holding area in the Sheriff's Department building. Each officer stayed with "his" demonstrator. Fania started chanting again. We all took up the cry. WE HAVE THE RIGHT TO DEMONSTRATE! We started singing and clapping, swaying in rhythm to the music. We made an awful din.

Bob Lindsay, chairman of the Communist Party of Santa Clara County, arrested with us, was the last man brought into the holding area. He's a tall, lanky fellow, with a mop of white hair, in his early fifties. He's seen a lot of protests and a lot of busts. As he entered the room he gazed upon us in studied awe. Here we were in custody, about to be carted off to jail, singing . . . The astonishment, perhaps born of the years of McCarthyite purges and the memories of grim-faced Communists marched off alone—to prison, faded. He grinned and joined in the singing.

It was 10:15. The preliminary booking process was completed in the holding area, the men and women were separated, not to be reunited until a court appearance later that afternoon. The women prisoners were escorted onto a bus. We were to be driven to the Elmwood Rehabilitation Center in Milpitas. There the booking process would be completed, and we would be confined until bail was arranged.

As we boarded the bus a great cheer went up from the folks on our line at the courthouse. We cheered back. I saw Franklin. His arms were up, his clenched fists waving, his face all lit up in the sunlight. He was shouting something, but I couldn't hear what it was.

The side windows of the bus were frosted. We couldn't see out.

However, we discovered that we could open the windows a couple of inches from the top. We did. The matrons did not object. We were driving through the main streets of San Jose toward the freeway. We were still shouting, singing, chanting. Everytime we passed a Black person walking down the street, Fania would yell: FREE ANGELA! Startled the brother or sister would look around for the source of this frantic cry. Occasionally they would see the bus in time, grasp the essence of the situation, and shoot a fist into the air, bringing more unrestrained cheers from the captives. By the time we got to the Rehabilitation Center we were hoarse.

We were led into the jail one-by-one. Those still to be admitted were kept in the bus. The sergeant at the front desk asked again for my name, address, date-of-birth, etc. I told her to look in my wallet. She did, She typed out all the information in triplicate. She told me to put my possessions (wedding ring, watch, purse, etc.) onto the counter. She made a list, and put each item into a manila envelope. Upon release I'd get it all back.

Just before I was led into the inner sanctum of the jail another matron told me to face the wall, stretch my arms up and lean forward against the wall. She searched me. Then she told me to take off my shoes and socks. I did. She looked at the soles of my feet. (The reason for this was a complete mystery to me. Later I asked Ginny Proctor. a friend, arrested with us, the purpose of this inspection. She told me it was to check for needle marks, and also to see if any dope was taped to the arch of my foot.)

Now inside, sitting on a bench. In front of me was the familiar ink roller for fingerprinting, next to that a small room, unoccupied. Behind me, in a glass enclosure, was what was called the drunk tank. It was a large room, padded walls, with an open toilet.

A matron came and told me to go into the small, unoccupied room. She closed the door most of the way behind us and told me to take my clothes off. I peeled them off, awkwardly. Naked. She told me to face the wall. Then she told me to do two deep-knee bends. I did. Nothing fell out. She carefully felt each item of clothing, and threw them back at me as her search was completed. She told me to get dressed.

Our arrival caused quite a stir in the jail. Many of the sister prisoners knew Angela because she came at least once a week for exercise and they played volley ball together. Shouts and cries came from the various cells back and forth around us. We told people what was happening, what we were doing, other news.

We were lodged in the drunk tank. We had barely gotten settled when a matron came in and announced that we were to be driven back to the courthouse — this time, the municipal court, for a hearing at 1 p.m. We would, we were told, probably be released on our own recognizance (this meant that we would not have to post a cash bail).

We trooped back onto the bus. As we approached the courthouse complex, our cheerful temperament restored, we resumed singing. The bus pulled up at the rear to the superior court building. The sheriff's deputy driving the bus muttered aloud about all these damn fences everywhere and how the hell was he supposed to know where to go to get us to the proper municipal court entrance. He discussed the situation with the two matrons accompanying us. One got off, presumably to discover the correct route, and disappeared behind a fence. We never did see her again. Meanwhile, the other matron told us to get off the bus. We did. The area around the courthouse was now deserted, Angela's court having adjourned for the day. Suddenly we realized that we were right back at the scene of "the crime."

What happened next seemed perfectly natural. We started picketing again, Fania and Victoria leading us with renewed enthusiasm in our morning chants: WE HAVE THE RIGHT TO DEMONSTRATE! FREE ANGELA! FREE ALL POLITICAL PRISONERS!

Lieutenant Tamm re-emerged from somewhere in the courthouse. Red with rage, arms flapping frantically above his head, he shrieked to the deputies in charge of this motley crew of convicts: "What the hell are they doing here? I thought they were all arrested. What the *hell* is going on?"

Nervously, the matron ordered us back onto the bus, counting us to make sure she hadn't lost anybody. I told her not to worry. The worst that had happened was that she had picked up a few more of us. Someone ordered us put in handcuffs. Someone else ran off to get enough of them to chain us together.

We were handcuffed in pairs. On the bus again. We drove around the block and finally pulled up in front of the municipal court. As we filed into the building, our chained hands raised in clenched fists, shouting and cheering, we were greeted by hundreds of supporters who had flocked to the courthouse as word of our arrests had spread. I spotted Charlene in the crowd, and I heard her shout FREE THE SAN JOSE 17! Instant slogan.

As we went into court we were quiet. The women prisoners sat in the jury box. The men prisoners sat in the front row of the spectators section. In came the press corps and as many of our friends as the tiny courtroom could accommodate. Everyone was exchanging militant salutes, except my husband Jack. As he came in, our eyes met, he smiled plaintively at me and gave a little wave with his fingers.

Formal proceedings went quickly. The judge would agree to release us on our own recognizance (O.R.), if we promised to refrain from any further demonstrations in or near the courthouse. Otherwise we would have to post cash bail. I think Bob Lindsay spoke for all of us when he told the judge, "That means to exercise my constitutional rights I have to purchase them. I do not accept O.R." The spectators burst into applause. An angry judge cleared the courtroom, except for newsmen. Each of us, in turn, refused the conditions of release on O.R. Bail was set at $350 per individual. The women were returned to the Elmwood facility. The men remained at the main jail in San Jose.

In the drunk tank again, the spirit of camaraderie, the quiet celebration of a day's work. We talked amongst ourselves. We knew that security checks were being run on all of us. The county had just installed a new computer at the jail, which tied into a central computer in San Francisco, which tied into an even more central computer somewhere else. Push a few buttons and your whole life history flashed on a screen in Milpitas. Ginny Proctor and Vivian Raineri, who were sisters, twenty years my senior, kidded that if the jailers discovered who their father had been they might throw away the key and leave the two of them in jail forever. H.E. (Mac) McGuckin had been one of the organizers for the I.W.W. going back to the years before the First World War. They told us that he had accumulated enough arrests in his lifetime to jam any computer for a month.

Victoria Mercado: she appeared at first to be tough and brooding. Under the outer armor there was a principled and compassionate human being.

Victoria was born and raised in California's Salinas Valley. She had lived in Watsonville most of her life. As was true of most Chicano youngsters she spent much of her childhood and adolescence in the fields harvesting apples, tomatoes and squash — for Del Monte. She'd gotten involved in Angela's defense after spending the summer of 1970 on the Venceremos Brigade in Cuba. She had met Fania in Cuba. They'd become good friends.

Night came. I lay down on the floor of the cell. I took my jacket off and folded it over for a pillow. (It was a very special jacket. My mother had given it to me years before — a brown, suede jacket. It was pretty frayed now, but I loved it, and wore it often. I'd been arrested in it before — in '64 during the Free Speech Movement at the Berkeley campus.)

My eyes wandered over the other faces in the cell . . . then they closed. I could see Franklin again, as he had been that morning. I fell into a deep sleep.

I was awakened by the singing. Ginny and Vivian were singing. Then we all were. It was very late, well past midnight. The mood was different, still jubilant, but more subdued, and the singing was passionate and resonant. We sang for a long time. At two o'clock on the morning of February 1st we were bailed out.

WE HAD broken the sound barrier. Newspapers and television across the country reported the arrests. Though the stories were garbled, the picture of Fania being taken off to jail, a club pressed to her neck, told millions across the country and throughout the world that the time to act was now. The following days appear in my memory as a blurred array of meetings in cluttered rooms, mimeograph machines cranking out thousands of leaflets, telephones ringing incessantly (we received calls from everywhere, Chicago, New York, Memphis, Berlin, London, Paris, Frankfurt.)

Late on February 1st we received word that a warrant had been issued by the sheriff's department for Franklin's arrest, apparently charging him with violation of Section 169 for his actions the day before, even though he hadn't picketed. Originally we had intended to have no further arrests at the courthouse, at least not immediately. We had made the point and we were gathering momentum to hold a very large demonstration in a couple of weeks. But the warrant for Franklin's arrest altered our tactics.

Another pre-trial hearing began on Wednesday morning, February 2nd. Supporters once again gathered on line waiting to go into court. Suddenly a car careened down the street. It turned into the driveway at the rear of the courthouse and came to an abrupt stop directly in front of the gate. Victoria was driving; Franklin was in the front passenger seat.

An astonished deputy sheriff peered anxiously through the cyclone fence. Franklin leaped from the car, positioned himself directly in front of the gate and held a sign aloft: *Free Angela*. It was his final gesture of defiance before being led off to jail on the prior warrant.

As he was taken into custody Franklin dropped the sign. Charlene Mitchell retrieved it, held it up and was herself arrested. As she dropped the sign, Christina Nuñez of the Community Alert Patrol retrieved it, was arrested and so it went as three more people did the same.

(Undersheriff Tom Rosa, who had met with Charlene on several different occasions, appeared shaken by her arrest. He ordered deputies to bring her into his office, rather than to the prisoners' detention area. Charlene told us afterwards that as she was sitting in Rosa's office quite unguarded, with the door wide open, two deputies walked by and saw her. One said to the other, pointing his thumb in her direction, "Who's that?" His partner replied, "Oh, some pie-card or other.")

We bailed each of those arrested. There were now a total of 24 people facing trial for activities during the two days of protest at the courthouse.

Two days later we held a press conference. The press came. Franklin spoke. The authorities had ten days in which to lift the ban on demonstrations within sight or sound of the courthouse. We would enforce a self-imposed moratorium on further protests until Monday, February 14th. On that day we would assemble hundreds of people in the parking lot across the street from the courthouse. It would be a peaceful assembly, but we would carry banners and make speeches and sing in unison and make any gestures we thought appropriate to convey our desire for

Angela's freedom. Either the sheriff's department would arrest all of us, or it would grant a permit for the assembly.

At 9 a.m. on Monday, February 7th Sheriff Geary announced his intention to hold a press conference at noon to respond to our demands. Rumor had it that he would grant permission for the protest on the 14th. But before he could say anything at a press conference, the now-infamous Judge Scott issued an oral order (to be followed by a written one, he assured Geary). The sheriff was to make no further comment on any matter relating to the Angela Davis case, or be held in contempt of court.

Meanwhile, Kendra Alexander had organized another press conference for Thursday morning, February 10th, this time in San Francisco. The press again came. Representatives from seventeen different groups in the Bay Area crowded around the microphones. Everyone from the Urban League and the YWCA to the Communist Party endorsed a statement denouncing the "arrests of people exercising their constitutional rights of assembly in demonstrating their support of Angela Davis," and joined the call for people to converge on the San Jose courthouse the following week. "Our experience has always been," Kendra said, "that the only way to protect a right is to exercise it and this is what we will do on Monday."

We went ahead with plans for the demonstration. All of the groups associated with the *Ad Hoc* Committee of Concerned Citizens in San Jose, especially the Community Alert Patrol, devoted much time and energy in preparation for it. Many communities in San Jose were leafletted door-to-door. *Constitution Suspended!* read the headlines on our flyers. The Angela Davis defense committees throughout the Bay Area mobilized their members and we had assistance from sisters and brothers as far away as Los Angeles. We hung huge banners on billboards in San Jose announcing the demonstration.

Fanned by the openly racist appeals from public officials, especially Judge Scott and Governor Reagan, racist elements within the area began to make open appeals for violence. Threats filtered into our national sub-office in San Jose. Fania, Franklin or I were to be killed. Our banners were torn down, or mutilated — "Kill the nigger" scrawled across Angela's picture. Tensions mounted.

The sheriff meanwhile had interpreted Judge Scott's gag order against himself to also mean that Angela Davis was likewise not to be permitted to make any further public statements, and on Tuesday morning, February 8th, Judge Arnason vacated (nullified) a previous order of his own which had allowed Angela to have one media interview per week. We interpreted Judge Arnason's action to be a result of the gubernatorial pressure arising from the interview conducted by Cecil Williams which had, despite all the controversy, been aired on KPIX, the local CBS affiliate, the night of February 7th. For some thirty-six hours chaos reigned.

Our attorneys argued vigorously in open court that Judge Arnason was capitulating to political pressures emanating from both the Santa Clara County counsel's office and the governor's mansion. Moreover, Judge Scott's various decrees were creating an intolerable situation. In Leo Branton's words, we demanded to know who was running the Angela Davis trial, Judge Scott or Judge Arnason.

By Wednesday afternoon, February 9th, both Judge Arnason and Sheriff Geary issued statements clarifying their respective positions. The judge was not ordering a prohibition on media interviews with Ms. Davis. As long as the sheriff said it was all right, she could have as many as she wanted. The sheriff said he would permit interviews "consistent with security requirements and upon written request of the media and the consent of the inmate and the inmate's attorneys."

Three days later the sheriff's department issued a permit allowing us to hold the rally in the parking lot across the street from the courthouse, with sound amplification, banners, etc. The tide was turning.

On the day of the rally — Monday, February 14th — one final and potentially deadly, racist assault occurred. Rodney Barnett, a young Black student from Sonoma State College, who had been working with the defense in the San Jose area for several weeks, was leaving our committee's offices in San Jose a few minutes before noon, enroute to the rally. He was burdened with material for the demonstration. As he walked down the street and towards his car, someone shot at him with a rifle from a passing car. The bullet missed his head by inches, and crashed through the plate glass window of a nearby pharmacy, as Rodney fell to the pavement. He was not injured.

More than a thousand people assembled "within sight or sound" of the courthouse. The rally was broadcast live over KPFA and reached thousands of radio listeners throughout the Bay Area (including Angela). It went off without incident. As one final act of bravado, Franklin Alexander summoned Lieutenant Tamm to the microphone and asked his permission to have the assembled crowd march silently across the street and past the courthouse, to "tour" the security facilities. The lieutenant made a little speech expressing his respect for the discipline and "professional" way in which the protest had been conducted. He granted permission for the "tour." A long line — more than a thousand strong — filed silently across the street and around the superior court.

We never heard another word from Judge Scott. We had established our right to demonstrate. And although the 24 people arrested were eventually convicted by an all-white jury several weeks later (the judge gave suspended 30-day sentences, six months summary probation and no fines), no one has since been prosecuted under Section 169 of the California Penal code, to our knowledge. And there have since been many demonstrations on behalf of political prisoners in California.

THE PROTESTS had done something more. They had shifted the balance of power within the county's political structure in a progressive direction, at least temporarily. The confrontation had brought the racist element out into the open, and then forced its official repudiation. We had also served notice on the court that we would tolerate only so much and no more. If Judge Arnason wanted the trial to be conducted with decorum, then a certain degree of respect for constitutional law and due process was going to have to be observed.

Finally, of course, the protests rekindled the spirit and momentum of the mass movement across the country. The fight for Angela's release on bail was to be resumed within the context of a new political situation: we were, for the first time since her arrest, assuming an offensive posture in the political arena.

15

Friday, February 18, 1972. New York City. 11 A.M. Kendra, Franklin and I were sitting with the California delegation to the Twentieth Convention of the Communist Party. The convention was being held at the Towers Hotel in downtown Brooklyn. We were listening to the debate on the main resolution presented the day before. There were well over 1,000 delegates, observers and guests. The atmosphere was typically "convention"—much activity, groups in the rear of the hall, whispered conversations in sundry corners, papers rustling, constant streams of people walking in apparently random motion.

Charlene Mitchell burst into the room, wove her way through the bustling throng, and over to our table. She extended both arms around all three of us, and whispered: "Howard just called. The California Supreme Court will abolish the death penalty at noon today, California time." She didn't say anything else for a few moments. We all sat there stunned. Slowly, very slowly, my brain unravelled the import of this announcement. Kendra's eyes flooded with tears. She seemed overwhelmed, unable to remain seated. She started pacing, working her hands, repeating softly, in ecstasy and disbelief, "Oh my God! Oh my *God!*"

The implications of the decision for Angela's case were manifold. The most immediate and obvious fact, the cause for overwhelming psychological relief, was that there was no longer any possibility of a death sentence should there be a conviction. We had almost never spoken of that—except once, Angela and I had discussed it briefly. It was one of those horrifying realities, contemplated in the sub-conscious realm of the nightmare, never to be articulated.

The decision would also mean that our prospective jurors could not be asked their opinion of the death penalty during the voir dire examination. Many a progressive-minded individual had been dismissed from a jury panel in a capital case in the past, for expressing opposition to the death penalty. We had a chance for a better jury. It was, as Howard jubilantly declared, "a whole new ball-game."

And then, finally, in the recesses of my mind, the idea germinated and then burst forth to the surface—*we could win Angela's immediate release on bail.*

Angela had been denied bail under Section 1270 of the California Penal Code—which section applied *only* in capital offenses. If such a category of offense was abolished, 1270 would be rendered a nullity. There would be no legal grounds whatsoever for Judge Arnason to continue to deny bail. In fact, the judge, in his denial in June of '71, had specifically affirmed that if Ms. Davis were eligible (under his interpretation of 1270) he would have no hesitation in granting her release on bail.

Charlene urged us to remain inside the convention hall. No general announcement to the comrades should be made until Howard called again to confirm the court's decision. That would be a few minutes after 12 noon, California time, 3 p.m. in New York. We waited. But we couldn't keep the news totally to ourselves. We scurried around to other delegations, and told a few friends close to the case. Little ripples of excitement bubbled across the convention floor. I couldn't stand it. I left the hall, and paced the length of the outer corridor.   Howard's call came a few minutes after three o'clock. Yes. Yes. Charlene was nodding her head frantically to tell us it had happened, even as she continued listening to Howard. Delerium. Charlene hung up and gave us the rest of the news. Howard had called Judge Arnason. A hearing was scheduled in chambers for 1 p.m. in California. Howard would call us again as soon as the hearing was over. Everyone was very optimistic.

We ran back into the convention hall. Charlene worked her way forward to the front of the room and told Henry Winston the news. Winnie stopped the convention. For the first time that day the hall was absolutely silent, no movement, no rustling of papers, people frozen in anticipation of some major development. Winnie was so excited. He put himself and his thoughts together. He made the announcement. Pandemonium.

SAN JOSE, California. 1 p.m. Howard Moore, Doris Walker, Margaret Burnham and Angela Davis were in Judge Arnason's chambers. The judge was present. Harris had not yet arrived. For the first time in anyone's memory he was late. He was forty-five minutes late. The hearing started at 2 p.m. Howard spoke in almost one continuous sentence, scarcely pausing for breath:

> Judge Arnason, Mr. Harris, I requested this conference this morning because I had gotten word through the news media that there would be an opinion today on the . . . from the Supreme Court of California . . . and the news media indicated that the California Supreme Court had declared the death penalty in California to be unconstitutional as being in derogation of Article I, Section 6, prohibiting cruel or unusual punishment, and I indicated that the purpose in requesting this chambers conference was to make a Motion for Bail on behalf of Ms. Davis. I now so move the court to admit Ms. Davis to reasonable bail pending trial. . . .

The prosecutor hesitated, pondered, asked for more time to consider the implications of the court's decision. Harris said:

> Well, I will tell you. I first saw this at noon, and then I had some copies made and came down here and I am sorry it took me as long as it did . . . I have read the decision . . . It certainly does hold the infliction of the death penalty unconstitutional . . . and that certainly does have significance in respect to the question of bail. No question about that. Now precisely what the significance is, is a different propostion. I haven't had chance to digest it and to think about it.

> The impact of the decision on the whole administration of criminal justice is going to take a little time to reflect on. . . .

The hearing was adjourned at 2:00 p.m., California time.

NEW YORK City. 5:40 p.m. The four of us, Charlene, Franklin, Kendra and I paced back and forth in the corridor outside the convention hall waiting for Howard's call. It finally came. Charlene talked to us as Howard talked to her. A bail hearing would be held in chambers beginning 10 a.m. on Wednesday, February 23rd. It looked good. Very good. There was much work we had to do. Charlene waved her arm. "Howard, just a minute . . . Bettina, give me something to write on . . . Yes . . . Howard? . . . Someone, I need a pen . . . O.K. . . . Go ahead . . ." We read over her shoulder, the four of us crunched into the phone booth, and protruding from it: Must arrange bail money. Angela wants us back. Telegrams Arnason. Black Caucus . . .

It was, of course, a fluke of historical circumstance that the California Supreme Court decision came when it did. The story of how it happened is yet another example of an extraordinary pattern of converging issues and movements.

Back in 1966 an all-white jury found a young Black man, Robert Page Anderson, guilty of first degree murder and fixed the penalty at death. Within a few months Anderson resolved to appeal the death penalty. He retained a white attorney, a professor at Stanford University's Law School, associated with the NAACP's Legal Defense Fund. The lawyer's name was Anthony Amsterdam.

In 1968 Amsterdam argued Anderson's appeal before the California State Supreme Court. The court refused to consider the constitutionality of the death penalty. However, it did order a new trial for Anderson on the penalty phase of his case.

At this juncture Amsterdam left the case, and Anderson was assigned a public defender. A second trial was held. The jury again imposed the penalty of death. A motion for a new trial was denied in the lower court. Anderson began the long process of appeal through the higher courts for a second time. In the fall of 1971 the California Supreme Court agreed to hear his second appeal. Suddenly, Anderson's public defender died, leaving him without counsel on the eve of his Supreme Court hearing.

Now . . . The California Supreme Court was most anxious to hear the Anderson case. It had resolved that it wished to render a decision on the constitutionality of the death penalty. Further, the Court was anxious to rule prior to any decision on the death penalty from the United States Supreme Court, thus to insure that all of its options were still open when it made a decision. However, the United States Supreme Court was expected to render a decision in a death penalty case before its 1972 term expired in June. To the justices on the California court time was a critical factor.

With the death of Anderson's public defender, the California justices determined to find Anderson new counsel and proceed with the hearing as quickly as possible. Late in November 1971, Anthony Amsterdam received a totally unexpected telephone call from the offices of the Supreme Court. Would he, the court asked, resume as counsel for Robert Page Anderson, and along with another attorney, Jerome B. Falk, argue the death penalty case before the Court? Amsterdam and Falk agreed. The hearing was set for January 6, 1972.

Amsterdam, meanwhile, was special counsel for Angela Davis on the matter of bail. He was scheduled to argue her appeal before the federal district court in San Francisco on January 12th. The two issues converged.

The implications for the *Davis* case were immediately apparent to Amsterdam. He went to see Angela. He informed her about the Anderson case, but expressed only cautious optimism as to its implications, more in the nature of gentle kidding than serious consideration. There was no way to know, he told her, just how the justices intended to rule—whether they in fact wanted to abolish capital punishment in toto, or whether they wished only to modify its applicability, allowing capital punishment to prevail. Angela, wary of false hope, did not mention the Supreme Court's intention to hear the Anderson case at all, lest she stir false expectations in any of us. We had gone to New York only dimly aware of the fact that Amsterdam had argued the Anderson case a month earlier, and without any idea at all, that a decision from the court was imminent.

In fact, the court's six to one decision, contained in a 47 page opinion written by the Chief Justice C.J. Wright was historic. Observing the dramatic decline in executions throughout the United States (there had been none since 1968, a testament to mounting popular oppostion to the death penalty) the justices concluded, for the first time in legal history, that death constituted *unusual* punishment. This, combined with the mass of psychological data attesting to its cruelty, allowed the court to conclude that the death penalty was in violation of the State Constitution, protecting against the infliction of "cruel or unusual punishment."

The court's decision did not mean Angela's automatic release on bail. Hers was an intensely political trial. Pressures were im-

mense. We had built an impressive political movement in her defense. The last few weeks in San Jose registered now with fresh significance. We had five days in which to mount the most massive, irresistible effort to insure victory. Bail was within our grasp.
. . *at this moment* . . . We had only to seize it.

WE STAGGERED our departures from New York. Franklin left at once. I was to leave on Sunday, February 20th, Kendra on Monday, the 21st. Charlene was to remain in New York for at least another week. Fania, somewhere in the Mid-West on a speaking tour, had to be reached with the news, but she was to remain in the field.

We had two essential tasks. First, hundreds and thousands of telegrams had to reach Judge Arnason with one message: *Bail Now!* Second, we had to arrange for bail money to be on-hand by Wednesday morning. We wanted to have access to a quarter of a million dollars. It was imperative that we get Angela out at once, if bail was set. The attorney general was sure to appeal her release. The Supreme Court could modify its decision to preclude her release. Time was critical. Once the judge granted bail we had to have Angela out on the streets before any appeal could be filed.

I went home to my parents' house in Brooklyn and converted their normally tranquil environs into a cental headquarters until my Sunday departure. My most important, immediate responsibility, was to arrange to have the bail money on-hand. Second, I was to try to reach members of the Black Caucus in Congress, urging that they wire Judge Arnason at once.

I discovered to my chagrin that it might be a terrible week-end to try to accomplish anything. It was a three-day holiday, Washington's Birthday.

In May 1971 a farmer from Fresno, California had gotten in touch with the chairman of the Communist Party in northern California, Mickie Lima, and offered to post his land as bond for Angela's bail. We didn't know who he was at the time, but a thorough investigation established that Roger MacAffee did indeed own property valued at more than $300,000, that his finances were in excellent order, and that he was willing and able to post bond. With bail denied in June, we thanked Mr. MacAffee, and told him that if and when the occasion arose, we'd be in touch.

On this Friday night, I telephoned Roger MacAffee at his home in Caruthers, California, a little town just east of Fresno. He was home. I had never spoken with the man personally, but he was easy to talk to and beside himself with enthusiasm when I explained the situation. Yes, of course he would post his land as bond, but much work had to be done to fulfill legal requirements to do it. He and his staff worked around-the-clock from the time of my call until late Tuesday night putting the books in order, having the land properly assessed, and doing a dozen other related things so that he could appear in San Jose by Wednesday morning with the necessary papers, properly notarized, prepared to post his property as collateral for bail.

As a back-up to the MacAffee arrangement I tried desperately to reach Aretha Franklin and her attorneys. In November 1970, just after Angela's arrest, she had made a public statement, offering to post up to $250,000 in cash, if and when Angela was eligible for bail. Ms. Franklin had put the money in escrow, and one of her attorneys was authorized to withdraw it for the purposes of posting bail. The problem was that, being a holiday week-end, I would not be able to reach an attorney before Tuesday morning. Upon further inquiries we learned that Ms. Franklin and her attorneys were out out of the country, and would be unavailable until Monday, February 28th. It would be too late.

We tried to figure another back-up to the MacAffee collateral. The reason for our concern had to do with the nature of the law regarding property bonds. The procedure was this: property could be posted as bond directly with the court. However, the prosecution could contest the value of the property. A legal wrangle could delay Angela's release long enough to allow the attorney general time to appeal an adverse ruling by Judge Arnason. Property could also be posted with a bail bondsman, who might or might not contest the validity of its assessed value. But a bondsman would, in any event, collect a fee of ten percent of the bail he posted. Thus, for example, if Arnason set bail at $250,000, we would have to pay a bondsman $20,000 in cash before he would accept the MacAffee property as collateral on a $200,000 bond.

Cash was a sure thing. If we could assemble the full amount we could post bail directly with the court, and the full amount would be returned upon the final disposition of the case. The attorney general could not in any way contest a cash bail. Release would be immediate. We never did succeed in arranging for cash bail. We had to hope that MacAffee's property would qualify with a bondsman. We did insure ourselves of upwards of $20,000 in cash to pay a bondsman's fee.

I called all over Washington, D.C. on Friday night, and by a stroke of luck I reached a member of Congressman John Conyers' staff at home. He drafted the text of a telegram and promised to reach every member of the Black Caucus in Congress for approval. He did. A few hours before the bail hearing (in the early morning hours on Wednesday) we received a telegram from Washington:

WE HAVE LONG MAINTAINED THAT THE DENIAL OF HABEAS CORPUS TO ANGELA DAVIS IS AN ABRIDGEMENT OF HER RIGHTS AS GUARANTEED BY THE U.S. CONSTITUTION . . . WITH THE RECENT DECISION OF THE CALIFORNIA SUPREME COURT ABOLISHING CAPITAL PUNISHMENT IT WOULD APPEAR THAT THE ORIGINAL GROUND FOR PROSCRIPTION OF BAIL HAS BEEN ELIMINATED. IF THAT BE THE FACT THEN WE URGE THAT REASONABLE BAIL BE SET AND THAT ANGELA DAVIS MEETING SUCH BAIL BE RELEASED IMMEDIATELY PENDING THE DETERMINATION OF HER TRIAL.

Every member of the Congressional Black Caucus signed the telegram (John Conyers, Shirley Chisholm, William Clay, Ronald Dellums, Charles Diggs, Walter Fautnoy, Augustus Hawkins, Ralph Metcalfe, Parren Mitchell, Charles Rangel, and Louis Stokes). A similar message was sent by New York Congresswoman Bella Abzug.

In San Jose, Jack, my husband, had been working on placing a full-page advertisement in the *Mercury* urging Angela's release on bail. The ad was to be signed only by attorneys practicing in Santa Clara County. Working at a frantic pace he gathered all the signatures together and arranged to have the ad appear in Wednesday morning's paper. It did. Two hundred and ten lawyers in the county had signed the statement. A week before another full-page ad urging Angela's release on bail had appeared in the Los Angeles *Times* signed by leading personalities throughout the world: Coretta Scott King, Ralph Abernathy, James Baldwin, Julian Bond, Dalton Trumbo, Yves Montand, Simone Signoret, Melina Mercouri. . . .

From our national sub-office in San Jose leaflets were hastily drawn, printed and distributed to summon supporters to court on Wednesday. They said simply: BAIL ANGELA OUT!

ARRIVING home in San Jose late Sunday night, I spent most of Monday and Tuesday with Angela in Palo Alto. I don't remember much of what we did or talked about. Mostly, I think, we waited. Every fiber of her being now strained, concentrated toward one thing — to be free at last.

I do recall that we had a terrible scare on Tuesday afternoon. The 18-year old white girl in the cell next to Angela had been accused of murdering two small Black children. Her attorney applied for her release on bail. The girl returned from court Tuesday afternoon to announce to us that her judge had denied bail despite the Supreme Court's decision. We knew that such a precedent would be just the lever the attorney general needed to shove the door closed in Angela's case. The twisted irony of such a fate! Angela's face froze in despair. The matron came in. She said there was a telephone call for Angela, from her attorney, Margaret Burnham. Angela left to take the call. I remained locked in her cell.

Angela returned a few minutes later. She was smiling, her face relaxed. Margaret had clarified the situation. The judge in the other case had denied bail, but "without prejudice," pending the outcome of the Davis hearing. He had made no substantive decision. We waited. Eighteen hours to go . . . seventeen . . . sixteen . . . fifteen . . .

16

Wednesday, February 23, 1972. The day began in typical fashion — Jack dashing off to school to teach a 7:30 class, me darting around the house getting Joshua ready for school; this morning, frantic to get to the lawyers' office and then to court.

In mid-January, with the trial definitely slated for San Jose, our lawyers had rented a suite of offices on North First Street, just across the way from the eastern-most edge of the civic center. Our offices were on the second floor. On the first floor was a bail bondsman's office, run by a man named Steve Sparacino.

Our office was bedlam. Last minute gathering of papers, Doris, Margaret and Howard rushing in and out of rooms. Leo was in London, England for a week, wrapping up affairs in another case. I gave Howard the telegram from the Black Caucus. He tucked it into his shirt pocket, slipped the ad from the *Mercury* into a legal folder bulging with paper. The three lawyers walked over to the court, with me, Kendra and Franklin tagging along behind. No one said anything. The lawyers disappeared behind the 12 foot fence. Our long vigil began. Small clusters of anxious supporters scattered across the courthouse lawn, on the steps of the municipal court, near the fence, everywhere.

I looked for Roger MacAffee. I hadn't met him yet, but he was unmistakable even in the large crowd. He was standing near the fence. Husky, crew-cut, red-faced, about 35 years old, wearing a checkered sport shirt, slacks, and a green sweater, with a little blue cap perched on his head. He looked like a farmer. He talked like a farmer. All morning, and over lunch and for a good part of the afternoon he talked to me about his dairy farm, his ideas about collective farming, his experiences raising cattle in Cuba after the Revolution. . . .

The hearing began in Judge Arnason's chambers at 10:10 with Angela and all counsel present. It was a long session. The legal minds probed the intricacies of the Supreme Court's decision, dissected each of its implications. Finally, Assistant Attorney General Albert Harris conceded the main point. He agreed that, ". . . the California Supreme Court, by its ruling in effect providing that there are no capital offenses punishable with death seems to have eliminated the only no bailable category under California law, so it is my conclusion, and it is the conclusion I think of the people I have consulted in my office and of other district attorneys I have consulted, we are in a situation in California now where all offenses are bailable. . . ."

But he had not yet given up the battle. In agonizing detail he emphasized the dangers in releasing Ms. Davis from custody. She had fled in August of 1970. She would flee again. She was conscious of her guilt. It was foolish, a travesty of justice, to release her now. Then he fell back on his one remaining legal argument. Technically, the Supreme Court's decision would not become final and binding for thirty days. This thirty day period, he said, "is not simply an arbitrary starting time . . . but is for a particular purpose, and that purpose is to allow the parties to the lawsuit to petition for a rehearing. . . ." Harris expressed his confidence that the attorney general would appeal the Supreme Court's decision, that a rehearing was possible, that a reversal, at the very least a modification of the court's decision was possible, even likely. Vigorously he pursued this line of argument, embellished it, dramatized it. Judge Arnason could not, should not grant bail until the thirty-day period had expired, and only at that time, if there was no modification of the court's opinion, should bail even be considered.

Doris Walker shot back. "Everyone in this room, particularly the lawyers and you, judge . . . knows perfectly well that that decision is not going to be reversed. The rehearing is not going to be granted. As reasonable people, we are well aware that a 6-1 decision of this importance, decided by the Chief Justice himself . . . is not going to be changed and therefore we have a basic substantive change in the law. Ms. Davis has been in jail now for in excess of 16 months. The interests of justice require that the realities of the situation be acknowledged, that bail be set subject to reasonable conditions, effective immediately. . . ."

Howard Moore spoke: "Virtually the whole world is looking at this case to see if simple justice can be accomplished, if this woman can be released on bail. We have received . . . telegrams from the entire Black Caucus, representing the considered thought of some 25, 40 or 50 million people in this country asking for simple justice, that bail be granted to Ms. Davis and granted now . . . This is the eve of trial. We are ready for trial. We would like to be prepared. We feel we can win this case, but we feel we should have — we need — we are asking the court grant Ms. Davis bail now. . . ."

Albert Harris chafed, returned to his 30-day theme. Arnason bristled: "Let's just get off this subject entirely . . . I am satisfied that Ms. Davis is entitled to bail. The only question is whether it will be effective today, tomorrow or whatever date I designate and I propose to make an outline as to what I think the bail conditions should be. . . ." The judge then outlined, in considerable detail, the conditions of release he would impose. Bail was to be in the amount of $102,500; Ms. Davis was to live in Santa Clara County, released in the custody of some responsible individual residing in the county; Ms. Davis was to report to a probation officer in Santa Clara County once a week; Ms. Davis was not to attend or speak at any public meeting whatsoever (though she could attend church); Ms. Davis was not to travel beyond the six counties comprising the Northern California area, without the express permission of the court or the probation officer; Ms. Davis was not to travel by air; Ms. Davis was not to possess firearms. . . .

Our lawyers began to contest the various aspects of the judge's proposed conditions, especially the infringement on Angela's constitutional rights to freedom of speech and assembly. The judge noted that the noon hour was approaching. He proposed a short break for lunch.

The judge asked the representatives of the sheriff's department if Ms. Davis could be confined in the jury room during the lunch hour. They agreed. It was just a gesture, but a decent one. Angela was normally confined in a small, barred, holding cell, with no windows and little ventilation in the basement of the courthouse. It had been recently painted and the pungent odor made her severely ill. Once she had passed out.

Court recessed for lunch.

Howard, Margaret and Doris emerged. Outside, we knew nothing of what had taken place in the hearing. They would say almost nothing. From facial expressions and abbreviated nods we surmised that things were at least all right. The lawyers scrambled for the office. We did not know it, of course, but they were hastily drafting a bail order to present to Judge Arnason that afternoon, for his consideration — omitting several of the stipulations they considered unreasonable and unfair.

We went out to lunch. Roger MacAffee and I went to Pete's Steak House, about a block from the civic center. I was hungry, but it was hard to eat. Roger was still telling me about his dairy farm. I think he was as nervous as I was. This was his way of dealing with the tension. I nodded and grunted here and there. I don't remember anything he said.

Court reconvened at 1 p.m. We resumed our vigil. Silence. Pacing. Kendra and I kept bumping into each other. We had the whole civic center in which to pace and we kept bumping into each other.

They haggled in chambers for one hour and fifty-five minutes. The judge would not relent on his stringent conditions. Harris raised every conceivable technical objection he could conjure. Then he resumed his morning argument, objecting to bail in principle.

But the judge had made up his mind. He finally alluded to the "wide-range of interest [that this case] has. . . ." He continued. ". . . if you think that interest has waned, you [ought] to just take a look at the mail that I have received in the last two days and the telephone calls none of which I have personally taken, but which my staff has taken, from virtually, not every state, but from a tremendous number of states, and telegrams from foreign countries and it is — it is a case of amazing interest. . . ."

It was 2:45 p.m. The judge said: "I have decided that nothing useful would be gained by delaying the [bail] order and when the appropriate order is prepared and written and submitted to me for approval I am going to sign it, and I am not going to wait for 30 days or any other period of time. I think it would only prolong the agony and I don't think that would do us any particular good."

The judge wanted to go onto other matters. The issue of bail was settled. There was something about new equipment in the jury assembly room and he wanted the opinions and approval of counsel and. . . .

Doris Walker interrupted. "Can we do it today, judge?" Howard Moore said: "Get it done this afternoon?" And the judge said: "Well, if the order is prepared. Before she can be released, of course, she has to comply with the conditions of the probation officer. . . ." Doris said: "We'll start scurrying around. . . ."

The judge still wanted to pursue other matters. Harris was flushed and brooding. The judge finally relented. At 2:55 p.m. court was recessed.

Howard, Margaret and Doris walked out, and through the expectant throng of supporters, their faces emotionless. "Well, what happened?" We were desperate. "For God's sake, what happened?" Howard was bounding off toward the lawyers' office. Kendra was closest to him. He turned to her, his voice choked with emotion, he said hoarsely: "We got what we came for . . .", and then he broke away at a run. I don't think he could have said anything more even if he'd wanted to. Kendra screamed: "*She's free! She's free! Angela's free!*"

REPORTERS scurried off in all directions. Albert Harris held an impromptu press conference in front of the courthouse. No, he would not appeal the judge's decision at this time. He wanted to concentrate on trial preparations. Angrily he maintained that the bail order was in violation of the law.

Franklin and I returned to the office with the lawyers. At 3:06 Howard, Margaret and Doris locked themselves in Howard's office and began drafting the final bail order:

> Good Cause Appearing Therefore, the Motion on behalf of Defendant Angela Y. Davis to be admitted to reasonable bail is hereby granted, and the Defendant is hereby admitted to bail on the following terms and conditions, namely 1. Bail shall be in the sum of $102,500. . . .

In the street dancing crowds surged through the civic center and out onto North First Street, blocking traffic, cheering, laughing, crying. Others circled back into the civic center complex and stood at the tunnel leading down to the prisoners' exit at the main jail. Angela would come out here to be returned to Palo Alto. People were singing, *Ain't gonna let nobody turn me 'round.* . . .

THE REFRAIN echoed off the walls of the tunnel.

Angela emerged in handcuffs, flanked by two deputies. They put her in an unmarked car. She turned around and looked out the rear window. She was smiling and waving (awkwardly) and laughing. . . .

Back in the lawyers' office, we cabled Leo Branton in London. Bail granted. We telephoned Sallye Davis in Birmingham. "Hello Mamma," Howard said. We telephoned the airport in Des Moines, Iowa, and after what seemed an interminable delay, reached Fania. (We had spoken with her the night before and she had given us her schedule hour by hour). She was just about to board the plane when she heard her name called over the public address system. She didn't believe us at first. . . .

Kendra, Margaret and Stephanie Allan, NUCFAD's press director, left the law office and drove to Palo Alto. They would wait with Angela. Shortly after 4 p.m. the bail order was completed and typed in proper legal form. Doris and Howard ran back to court. Franklin and I sat down in the office with Roger MacAffee and a bail bondsman from San Francisco to work out the final details for Angela's release. But it was not to be so easy. The bondsman called his office in San Francisco to obtain final permission to issue a $100,000 bond with the MacAffee property as collateral. His superiors balked.

It was after 4 p.m. Who could we approach to authorize a $100,000 bond at such a late hour?

Angela knew, of course, that there could be a problem in arranging her immediate release. She had prepared herself, I think, for such an eventuality, and probably expected to spend one or two more nights in jail. But we wanted her out. Tonight.

4:35 p.m. Howard and Doris returned from court. The bail order was signed. Howard started to argue with the San Francisco bondsman. We had had firm assurances from his office. But it was to no avail. We made a few calls. No luck. It was getting late. Howard perked up. "Let's ask Sparacino?"

"Who?", I asked.

"Sparacino, downstairs. . . ."

We had nothing to lose. We went downstairs. Steve Sparacino ran one of the biggest bail bonding businesses in the county. He was wealthy, owned real estate too. He was at least willing to listen. His office was very posh. Sparacino eased himself into a big, leather, swivel chair behind a mahogoney desk. Howard put the proposition to him. Sparacino nodded gravely and noncommittally. Roger talked non-stop for ten minutes, shoving document after document onto Sparacino's desk, assuring him of his intergity and his financial soundness. Roger was talking shop. He knew his business.

Sparacino nodded again. He observed that he had $100,000 bonds right there in his desk drawer. He could sign one just like that. He snapped his fingers to dramatize the point. It was 4:50 p.m. In ten minutes most businesses would be closed for the day. Sparacino looked at the clock on the wall behind him. "All right, Mr. MacAffee, let me have the phone number of your real estate man in Fresno." Roger rattled off the number. Sparacino dialed. The office was still open. Roger's finances were authenticated. Satisfied. Sparacino hung up. He hesitated. He rubbed his chin, swiveled around in the chair. His partner came in. He was a younger man. He urged him to do it. Sparacino said: "O.K." It was one minute to five.

Howard, Franklin and Roger stayed with Sparacino to negotiate the details. I raced out of the office, leaped into the car and drove to Palo Alto. It was rush hour. The traffic was bumper-to-bumper on the freeway. I got to the jail at 5:30.

Dusk. The sky turned gray. A light drizzle fell. But it was not cold. I parked and ran towards the ramp leading down into the jail. A huge crowd was already gathering. People surged around me, calling my name, demanding news. "We'll have her out in a couple of hours," I shouted.

Captain Johnson and Lieutenant Tamm of the sheriff's department were waiting for me at the jail entrance. Captain Johnson was a very typical-looking cop — crew cut, brisk, efficient manner, an exaggerated air. I had already had several angry exchanges with him in court. I was in no mood for another one. "What took you so long?" he wanted to know. I wondered how the hell he already knew Sparacino had agreed to post the bond. I mumbled something about the traffic and hurried on inside.

The matron took me in tow. Jail routine. I still had to be searched. She was incredibly thorough. She led me down the corridor. I could hear Angela laughing and talking. I went inside. Kendra, Margaret and Stephanie were standing about, crowded into the cell, The remains of a spaghetti dinner were on a metal tray on a chair. Everyone was munching on part of an orange. Angela was curled up on the bed. She wanted to know if I was hungry. There was some salad left. No. Then she sensed that I had come with more than celebrations. She got up. I could hardly talk. I said, "We'll have you out in a couple of hours. . . ." She fell back onto the bed. Then she jumped up. "I'll have to pack. Just look at all of this junk!"

We pitched in together. Cartons were assembled. The matrons brought more as we needed them, and unlocked the door to the cell. Without regard for Angela's carefully assembled order of things, we hurled books, papers, folders, clothes, into one box after another, and hauled the cartons out into the corridor, piling one on top of the other.

At a quarter to seven, Howard, Doris, Franklin and Roger MacAffee arrived at the jail. All the papers were in order. The final arrangements were made.

Franklin, Kendra and I met briefly. The sergeant volunteered to let us use his office. With us was Tony Estramero, co-chairman of the Community Alert Patrol. We had to arrange for Angela's departure and insure her safety. Tony had everything well-in-hand. He laid out the plans. The sheriff's department wanted Angela to leave via a back entrance away from the crowd. We insisted however that she'd walk out the front door. Victoria Mercado would drive her car down the ramp to that entrance. Another car driven by Franklin would be in the lead, and a third car would bring up the rear. Angela was to go directly to my house in San Jose. Later, after the celebrations, she could be taken to Emma Sterne's old home in Willow Glen, where she was to live.

There was a pay telephone in the sergeant's office. Franklin called our house and spoke with Jack. Franklin did not identify himself. He said: "Open your back gate." I knew Jack would understand.

The jail was buzzing with activity, deputies rushing back and forth, going nowhere. Angela came out into the corridor. No handcuffs. She embraced Roger MacAffee. She walked slowly towards the exit. She was wearing light colored corduroy slacks, a long-sleeved black sweater. A lavender shawl was draped across her shoulders.

The first steel door whined open. She paused, quivered, then walked steadily through it, and the next two similarly operated exits. Margaret, Doris and Howard were right behind her. Kendra and Franklin were already outside in the lead car. Stephanie and I remained inside the jail. We peered through the steel grating. Blinding flashes of light as cameras recorded the moment of freedom. We heard the roar of the crowd. We saw Angela's fist go up. She got into Victoria's car. I looked at the clock on the wall. It was 7:14 p.m.

17

J oshua had celebrated his third birthday six days after Angela was arrested. For more than a year, "the case" (as he came to call it), had thrust its way into his world, disrupting the psychological and physical contours of his childhood. It had provoked an awesome range of emotions in the people around him and closest to him—emotions he could perceive, but could not comprehend. And somewhere, in a place inaccessible to him, called a jail, there was a woman whose name was Angela Davis. His mother seemed to love her very much and spent a lot of time with her, but Joshua could not remember ever having met her. Sometimes he wanted to know why Angela never came to visit him.

SCENES from my own childhood: I remember how my mother and father worked very hard and were often preoccupied with problems I did not understand. Sometimes my father went away for a while. He always came back. Love. Fear. Confusion. Love. Rejection. Warmth. Loneliness. Love.

We went to Washington, D.C. once, all three of us. I was six years old. We walked around a building called the White House. Men in gray suits peered down from nearby buildings and watched us. I asked my mother who they were. She said they were counting the number of people on the line. She said it was very important that there were so many people. It was a protest. There were two people and something called the government was trying to kill them. Their names were Julius and Ethel Rosenberg. A lot of people were carrying signs. I wanted to have one too. It was too heavy, but I wanted to carry it: So my mother helped me and I lugged it around.

I remember the night the two people died. We were standing in Union Square. So many people. Silent. I was afraid to utter a sound. There was an announcement. The two people were dead. The crowd swayed and moaned. My mother and father were crying. I had never seen them cry before.

Sundays were very important to me. My father tried to be home, and we would go somewhere special. I remember one Sunday. I must have been about five. We were in a park. My father met a friend unexpectedly, and invited the man to have lunch with us. My father looked down at me and said: "You don't mind, do you?" And I said, very loudly: "Yes, I do. I don't want him to come with us. Tell him to go away . . ."

SUNDAYS. Joshua often played with his friend Hollis—Margaret Burnham's son. Hollis was six years old. He and Joshua were great pals. Once together it was hard to pry them apart. There were always tears and parents promising that they could see each other the next week.

Hollis knew all about Angela, and he understood a lot of things about the case. So while he and Joshua played (they usually assembled some elaborate structure out of random pieces of wood) Joshua asked questions and Hollis explained about jails and the police. Joshua in turn would explain it all to me the next morning as I drove him to nursery school. He told me that he and Hollis had a plan. They were going to get some rope. They were going to go to the jail and tie up the policemen. And they were going to free Angela.

Halloween. The children at nursery school made costumes and masks. Joshua did too. The masks depicted evil, witches and goblins and fearful-looking creatures. All the masks were black. Black was evil. Breakfast a few days later. Joshua opened a box of corn flakes. Eagerly he rummaged through it looking for the prize stored inside. He found it and tore open the package. It was one of those cards with a picture of a ballplayer.

"He has a 'yukky' face," Joshua said to me. I took the card from him and looked at the picture. The ballplayer was Black. I asked Joshua why he had said that. He told me it was because his face was Black. I said I didn't understand what he meant. "We have many Black friends. Hollis is your best friend. His face is dark and he is very beautiful." There was a long silence. When he spoke again it was about something else.

I went to the school and had a talk with Joshua's teacher. I told her about the incident. I said that I thought Halloween masks ought to be made in all colors and depict varying fantasies. It was harmful and wrong for the children to be allowed to associate blackness with evil.

The school was moderately well integrated. There were Black and especially Chicano children. But in a society permeated with racism, only conscious resistance to it could prevent the children from absorbing its poison.

Joshua loved Hollis. He loved little Angela Eisa. Fania, Kendra, Franklin, Charlene, Margaret, Mrs. Davis always showed him great affection and he responded to it, and yet he associated the trauma affecting his life with them. The Halloween caper at school had served to reinforce and legitimize an impression.

CRISIS. Joshua came home from school one day; he was moody and irritable. I was not yet home. Jack was busy making supper. Many people were in the house. We were to have a staff meeting later. Ignored, frustrated Joshua lashed out at Franklin: "I don't like you. I don't like you because you are Black."

I came home a few minutes later. Joshua was sitting alone in the living-room, crumpled up on the couch. I asked him what was wrong. Bursting into tears he told me what he had said, and that it was very wrong, and he was going to tell Franklin that he was sorry.

Franklin came into the living-room. He looked at me reassuringly. He didn't say anything. He picked Joshua up and ruffled his hair and hugged him. Comforted. Relieved. Joshua started laughing. He pointed to a chair and asked Franklin to write the word "chair" on a piece of paper. This was Joshua's favorite game. Franklin got some paper and a pencil and wrote down the various words as Joshua pointed to this and that. After a while Franklin wrote down the word "Black"; then the word "beautiful"; then "Black is beautiful". After supper he read Joshua a couple of stories and kissed him and put him to bed.

CHRISTMAS. Joshua saw the array of presents on our dining room table, and asked me if they were for him. I told him no, they were for Angela. "Oh ", he said uncertainly. Pause. "All of them?" he asked wistfully. "Yes", I said, "all of them." Another pause. "How come?" he wanted to know. I tried to explain.

I told Angela about it, and the other things that had happened. It was hard to talk about.

A couple of days later she sent me a note in the mail. It helped. At the end she said: "Give Joshua a big hug and a kiss . . . Tell him he can have any of those goodies all wrapped in Xmas paper." It was after that that she knitted him the cap and scarf.

Mighty political conclusions were to be drawn about Angela's release on bail. They were all true. But the most important thing to me at that moment when she walked into the house was that Joshua saw her. When I came home from the jail later that night I found Angela sitting in the dining-room with Joshua on one knee and Hollis on the other. There were close to a hundred people jammed into the house. Everyone was talking at once, champagne flowing, wild celebration. But it didn't matter to Joshua anymore. Angela had finally come to visit him.

THE TRIAL

18

T wo days after her release on bail Angela went to San Francisco to attend the trial of the two surviving Soledad Brothers, John Clutchette and Fleeta Drumgo. The trial was in its seventeenth week. John and Fleeta had not seen Angela since July when they had all met in the men's mess hall at the Marin County jail and George was still alive.

Outside, word spread that Angela was at the trial. By noon a crowd of several hundred people had gathered on the steps of the Hall of Justice. On the day her trial opened—Monday, February 28th—in chambers, prosecutor Albert Harris protested Angela's presence at this "assembly", charging that she had violated the terms of her release. Judge Arnason seemed perturbed; but there were no reprisals.

John and Fleeta's trial had begun on November 8, 1971. Judge Spiro Lee Vavuris addressed their 120 prospective jurors. "These men," he said, "may be Black, but I want you to treat them as if they were as white as newly fallen snow."

"Under our system of justice," the judge continued, "there is no difference between Black, Mexican and white."

Inez Williams, Fleeta's mother, had written an article, that was

157

really a poem, about the white man's justice and her son and his trial:

Fleeta, John and George were arraigned in
Salinas, Monterey County, on Monday,
February 14, 1970. There were only five Black
people in the courtroom.

We stood outside as the van drove up from Soledad . . .

They were chained together.

They fell out of the van.
            I started screaming. Why
            are they treating them like
            that?

But these people are mad. They are vicious.

            What happened to "innocent
            until proven guilty"?

They acted like they wanted to hang them right then.
Newsmen were running over each other taking pictures.

            I turned around and people
            were running and laughing as
            if they were going to a circus.
            It was May Day.

            Oh my God. . .

Of the 120 prospective jurors for the Soledad Brothers trial only seven were Black. Fifteen percent of the people in San Francisco are Black. The jurors were drawn from the list of registered voters. Ex-prisoners are not allowed to vote.

In the corridor outside the courtroom there were always at least twelve heavily-armed guards picked from the city's tactical squad. Inside the courtroom there were ten bailiffs. A bullet-proof plexiglass shield separated the spectators from jurors, counsel, defendants and judge.

John and Fleeta were flown to court every morning from San Quentin prison in an army helicopter which landed on the roof of the Hall of Justice. The men were shackled. Once inside the courtroom the judge allowed the chains to be removed. He said the men could wear regular clothes instead of the prison uniform.

All those wishing to attend the trial were searched before being allowed inside the courtroom. The men were frisked. The women had to go into a little booth with a matron and undress. (When Angela's turn came that morning the matron only frisked the so-called accused murderess — lightly and quickly.) Each person was then photographed and assigned a specific seat in the courtroom. You had to sit in the assigned seat.

The judge told the prospective jurors that they should not be concerned about the guards in and around the courtroom, or the unusual security precautions. "This courtroom," he said, "is a bastion of democracy."

The prospective jurors were questioned. Several admitted feeling intimidated. One man said his fear was based on the media coverage and the tight security, which indicated to him "that there is something I should be afraid of."

A jury was finally picked. All the jurors were white. There were also four alternate jurors. Two of the alternates were Black.

INEZ had written:

> How can my son get a fair trial? Will the jury want to know why he was first imprisoned? Are they going to start with January 13, 1970?
>> Are they going to start with May 31, 1946, when he was born?
> Will they know the truth when they hear it? Will they see through the lies? Will they care?
>> And, are they ready and qualified to judge my life?

Formal presentations were to begin on December 21, 1971, four months to the day since George Jackson's death. At the insistence of defense counsel the judge declared George Jackson innocent. He could not be tried posthumously. The presumption of innocence still prevailed, technically.

Defense attorneys came to court the morning of December 21st carrying an eight foot by four foot model of Soledad Prison's "Y" wing. John and Fleeta were alleged to have murdered the white guard in that wing of the prison. After the guard was killed, Soledad prison officials had arranged for that section of the prison to be completely renovated, thus to obscure forever the details of the alleged attack. The defense exhibit reconstructed "Y" wing as it had been that day.

Security guards at the Hall of Justice at first refused to allow defense attorneys to bring the model into court. When informed that it was a defense exhibit, the guards insisted upon taking it apart to look for "tools of violence" hidden within. The first day's session was delayed for thirty minutes while the guards disassembled the model.

The chief prosecutor, William Curtis, made his opening statement. He did not talk very long. Most of his presentation dwelled on the role of George Jackson in the alleged murder. The defense objected strenuously. George could not be tried posthumously. The judge grew impatient with the defense.

The prosecutor said he would establish that a murder had occurred; that it had happened on January 16, 1970; that it had taken place in the "Y" wing of Soledad prison. He said he would present witnesses who would testify that they saw George and John and Fleeta kill the guard and then hurl his body from the third floor tier to the television room below.

The defense made its opening statement. Attorneys Floyd Silliman and Richard Silver began by trying to tell the jury something about the racist and repressive nature of the California prison system. The prosecutor objected. The judge sustained the objection.

Then the defense tried to explain the "snitch" (informer) system within a prison — the guards' use of reward and punishment to force inmates to betray each other. The prosecutor objected. The judge sustained the objection.

Then the defense tried to explain the particular role of the captain of the prison guards at Soledad, Charles Moody, who had conducted the initial investigations resulting in the grand jury's indictment. Moody, the defense contended, had engineered the assassination of three Black prisoners at Soledad on January 13th, 1970, three days before the death of the white guard. Black and white inmates were put out in the exercise yard together for the first time in many months when the expected fisticuffs erupted. The prosecutor was on his feet objecting. Silliman plowed on. The judge sustained the objection. What had happened on January 13th 1970 was not relevant.

The prosecutor said he intended to call twenty inmate witnesses against John Clutchette and Fleeta Drumgo. Two thirds of the inmate witnesses had been paroled since February 1970. Eighteen of the twenty inmate witnesses were white. Captain Charles Moody was no longer at Soledad Prison. He was now officially titled as the prosecutor's Chief Investigator.

The prosecution proceeded with its case. Several Soledad guards testified, as did the prison's chief medical officer, an autopsy surgeon, a criminalist, and a finger-print expert. None of these witnesses succeeded in linking either John or Fleeta with the death of the guard. Spiro P. Vasos, the latent finger-print examiner for the California Department of Justice, testified that none of the finger-prints on a flashlight found at the apparent scene of the crime, or on the walls in "Y" wing near the place of the alleged assault, matched those of either of the two defendants.

All twenty of the inmate witnesses were presented to the jury. Relentless cross-examination by the two defense lawyers revealed the contradictions and inconsistencies of each witness, and between the different witnesses. The defense—fighting the prosecutor all the way—succeeded in eliciting admissions of the deals and threats used to secure testimony. Captain Moody figured prominently in each case.

William Worzella was one of the inmate witnesses. He had been released from prison. Silliman cross-examined him first. He established that Worzella had told Richard Draper, a defense investigator, that, "there is no way I can have my parole revoked and go back to prison." Silliman continued, "Isn't it true that you became a prosecution witness between January 17 and January 21 [1970] to save your own life?"

Worzella replied: "I asked for protection. That's all I can say."

Attorney Silver took over the cross-examination and asked Worzella about his relationship with Captain Moody. Worzella said: "I was afraid of the things he could do . . .I have a fear of Captain Moody." Silver asked: "Why do you have this fear?" Worzella answered: "He is tough and emotional . . .You just have to be there where the boss is."

One of the two Black inmate witnesses was Manuel Green. On cross-examination Silliman asked him if there was any antagonism between himself and the defendants. Green answered that there wasn't any, "other than I'm a snitch."

Thomas A. Yorke was a key prosecution witness. He was the

other Black inmate. Yorke had been convicted of manslaughter in 1968, had attempted escape from prison in August of 1970, and had nevertheless been paroled in December 1971, just as the Soledad Brothers trial began.

Under cross-examination Yorke related his ordeal in the weeks following the guard's death. He said: "I thought there were no means to which Captain Moody wouldn't go—one way or the other."

Yorke said he was secretly transferred to different prisons all over California. On each occasion he was accompanied by Captain Moody. On each occasion he was alternately threatened with death if he refused to testify or offered his freedom if he would cooperate. Once, Yorke said, Captain Moody told him: "Tom, if you don't make up your mind soon as to whether you're going to testify, I'm gonna have to put you back on the mainline."

Yorke explained that the mainline was the general prison population. He said that if he had been put there it would have meant "sure death" because of the inmate code against informants.

Laughter, incredulous gasps, sometimes issued from the spectators section as witness after witness squirmed his way through some version of the killing. Most of the spectators were supporters of the Soledad Brothers. The judge said the laughter was "cynical."

Once the judge stopped the proceedings. He ordered absolute silence in his court. "I'll hold you all in contempt," he said, "and give you five days and fine you $500. You don't know me. I can be as rough as broken glass."

"I have sat in the courtroom," Inez had written:

and watched the guards dragging Fleeta around
with a chain around his neck, hands cuffed, arms chained
to his side, chains on his feet.

> Me, his mother, sitting there watching the man giving my
> child some more of his
> justice . . .

THE CASE went to the jury on Thursday, March 23, 1972. Deliberations continued for three days. On the fourth day the jurors asked to be returned to court to receive further instructions. The foreman told Judge Vavuris that the jury was deadlocked eight to four. He didn't say in which direction. The judge ordered the jurors to resume deliberations. He instructed the minority to subordinate its views to the majority.

Just before noon on the fifth day, Monday, March 27th—the day formal arguments were to commence in the trial of Angela Davis—the jurors returned with their verdict. They found the defendants, John Clutchette and Fleeta Drumgo, not guilty on all counts.

NOT GUILTY

Inez Williams
ran from the courtroom and
collapsed in the arms
of a comrade
weeping

John and Fleeta were surrounded by
Prison guards and
Taken from court and
Shackled and
Shipped back to
San Quentin.

FLEETA DRUMGO and John Clutchette were returned to prison to continue serving their indeterminate six months to fifteen year sentences.

When the guard was killed at Soledad in January, 1970 John already had a parole date set. He was supposed to have been released on April 28, 1970. Fleeta was scheduled to have appeared before the Adult Authority in April 1970, and had had an excellent chance of getting a release date.

After the acquittal the Soledad Brothers Defense Committee launched a campaign for John's immediate release.

John Clutchette went home on May 23rd, 1972.

Fleeta Drumgo is still in San Quentin's Adjustment Center, awaiting trial as one of the San Quentin Six, accused of murdering three guards and two inmates at San Quentin the day George Jackson was assassinated. John Clutchette wasn't charged with those murders because he was visiting with his mother at three o'clock in the afternoon on Saturday, August 21st, 1971. Even the warden couldn't change that fact.

TWO DAYS after the acquittal of the Soledad Brothers Angela Davis made the opening statement for the defense in her own trial:

> Members of the jury, we were correct in our understanding of the case of the Soledad Brothers. Monday morning as you sat there listening to the prosecution's opening statement . . . the ultimate fruits of our labors were attained. The 12 men and women who for a period of many months had listened to all the evidence which the prosecution could muster against the Brothers, entered a courtroom in San Francisco and pronounced the Soledad Brothers *Not Guilty*. If George Jackson had not been struck down by San Quentin guards in August of last year he too would have been freed from that unjust prosecution . . .

And later in Angela's trial, Leo Branton introduced into evidence a certified copy of the entry of acquittal in the case of the Soledad Brothers. Prosecutor Albert Harris objected. It was, he said, irrelevant and immaterial. Leo Branton responded:

> The prosecution has offered, in this case, a certified copy of the indictment against the Soledad Brothers. In his opening remarks he said that the reason the Soledad Brothers had to be freed by the events of August 7th [and the reason that Ms. Davis was supposed to have joined in that alleged conspiracy] was that time had run out on them. I think this certified copy of an entry of acquittal shows far from time running out. Time is just beginning . . .

19

T he trial was to begin exactly 500 days after Angela's arrest. We had come a long way.

"One might have hoped," James Baldwin had written a few weeks after the capture of one of America's Most Wanted fugitives, "that by this hour the very sight of chains on black flesh, or the very sight of chains, would be so intolerable a sight for the American people, and so unbearable a memory, that they would themselves spontaneously rise up and strike off the manacles . . ."

They had. Not right away of course, and not all of them, and not alone. It had taken over a year, and the support of more than half the world's people, and countless demonstrations, arrests, beating, petitions, writs, appeals. But it had been done.

Bail! It deeply affected the character of the prosecution itself.

The day the trial opened Albert Harris announced his intention to delete one section from the indictment against Angela Davis. Before the jury was called in, he said, the government would move to strike overt act number one from the indictment.

Overt act number one charged that Angela Davis had participated in a rally at the state building in Los Angeles on June 19, 1970 with Jonathan Jackson, "pursuant to the conspiracy and to carry out its objectives." At this rally Ms. Davis, the indictment charged, "advocated the release from lawful custody of George Jackson, Fleeta Drumgo and John Clutchette, also known as the Soledad Brothers."

The prosecution's case, of course, rested on the assumption that the purpose of the August 7th events at the Marin County courthouse had been to free the Soledad Brothers. In fact, the decisive element in the prosecution's case against Angela was motive. Unless Harris could construe a credible motive for Angela's participation in this alleged plot, his circumstantial case against her simply collapsed.

From the beginning then, Harris had to portray Angela in crudely racist terms. He had intended to argue that Angela, driven by a political fanaticism (as evidenced by her speeches) and an irresistible passion (as evidenced by her June 1970 letters to George Jackson) had committed herself to this reckless criminal enterprise.

By the time the case finally came to trial, however, the political situation in the country had changed. In the wake of the Attica Uprising especially, there was a growing popular awareness of the racism and brutality of the prison system. Angela's early denunciations might now seem not only reasonable and just, but prophetic. Moreover, a movement of unprecedented international proportions had just secured her release on bail.

Considerable embarrassment could result from a direct challenge to Angela's first amendment rights to freedom of speech. Some members of a jury might be inclined to accept defense contentions that this was a political trial after all. World opinion certainly would. A more subtle political approach, based upon an appeal to racial and sexual prejudices and stereotypes was more likely to win a conviction without the liability of widespread public criticism.

With Angela's July 1971 diary in his possession Harris decided he would do better to abandon all references to Angela's political views and rest his entire case on the theory of irresistible passion. So he moved to strike overt act number one from the indictment.

"There will be no evidence offered by the prosecution," Harris stated in his opening presentation to the jury, "of the exercise by the defendant of her right to free speech and assembly under the first amendment . . . The case of the prosecution does not rest in any degree upon the nature of the political views of the defendant. The claim that the defendant is a political prisoner is false and without foundation . . ."

Harris continued: "Her own words will reveal that beneath the cool academic veneer is a woman fully capable of being moved to violence by passion . . . Her basic motive was not to free political prisoners, but to free the one prisoner she loved . . . The motive was not abstract. It was not founded . . . on any need, real or imagined, for prison reform. It was founded simply on the passion that she felt for George Jackson . . ."

The criminal plot Angela Davis conceived, Harris said, "was simple, but ingenious and very nearly successful."

As part of the scheme, Harris inferred, Angela Davis had seduced young Jonathan Jackson, to assure his allegiance. "We will present evidence," Harris said, "that the defendant and Jonathan Jackson shared living quarters" in the three weeks immediately preceding the events and that Angela Davis and Jonathan Jackson spent the night of August 6th, the night before the revolt, together in a San Francisco motel.

Harris then recalled the meeting at the Marin County jail between George Jackson and Angela Davis on July 8, 1971. "The evidence will show," Harris said, "that the defendant and George Jackson used this meeting, their only physical meeting that I know of, as an opportunity for a close passionate physical involvement."

The evidence, he said, would consist of the testimony of at least one San Quentin guard who had observed the meeting.

"Her motive," Harris emphasized time and again, "was passion, simple, human passion, a passion for George Jackson, the Soledad Brother, a passion that knew no bounds, no limits, no respect for human life, not even the life of George's younger brother . . ."

Angela was to be portrayed in even cruder racist terms. She had not loved George Jackson. She had craved him, as an animal craves its mate. Angela—shrouded in the centuries-old white mystique of Black sexuality; obsessed with desire; sinister, calculating, ruthless.

Having been forced by public outrage to abandon one element of his case—the overtly political element—Harris had been simultaneously compelled to inflate and embellish the other side of his case until it had become, quite literally, a parody of itself —Angela transmogrified into a demented, savage creature.

Harris was in an incalculably weaker position. Angela as a political fanatic would have been difficult enough to convey. Angela as a maniacal she-wolf was a hopeless caricature. Harris had been forced into a position of forfeiting the one thing he needed more than anything else to win his case: a credible motive.

20

The trial began at 10:11 o'clock on Monday morning, February 28, 1972.

Windowless courtroom. Artificial florescent lighting. Slick, shiny wood-paneled walls. Twelve vacant, green cushioned swivel chairs for the jury. Two flags drooping dully behind the judge's bench. The press corps—primed and polished—flinging witticisms at one another across the room.

All the seats in the spectators section were filled. Thirty seats were reserved for the press and thirty-four seats for the public.

(Our demonstrations had won us four additional seats. Chairs from a recently-demolished church had been obtained and squeezed into the room.)

The judge said: "This is the time and place set for the trial of the case of the People of the State of California against Angela Y. Davis, Case No. 52613 . . .

"Are counsel ready to proceed?"

Howard Moore stood and said: "Ready for the Defendant."

Albert Harris stood and said: "Ready for the People, your Honor."

The inexorable logical madness.

THE COURT clerk drew the names of the first twelve prospective jurors from the pool of 150. He read each name aloud. The voir dire had begun.

It was a fascinating business: lively, intense, dull, funny, grueling, terrifying. The prospective jurors were scared—and honest, unpredictable, hostile, coy, affable, alert. They were frequently uninformed or misinformed; still, perceptive, intelligent, at times compassionate. Only a few were combative and opinionated.

The majority of prospective jurors questioned during the voir dire were middle aged and white collar workers, usually employed in the electronics or defense industries (or some member of their family was so employed). Several were clerks, accountants or managers in large department store chains. Perhaps a third of the prospective jurors were under forty, and many of these were students. There were only a handful of blue-collar workers, and almost all were excused for reasons of economic hardship. One or two prospective jurors came from old, established agricultural families in the Santa Clara Valley. A few were private entrepreneurs—small shop owners, building contractors, real estate brokers.

One prospective juror was Black; four were Chicano.

The vast majority were apolitical, anxious to avoid conflict. They tended to say whatever they thought examining counsel wanted to hear. It took a while then, before they felt sufficiently at ease to reveal any approximation of what they really believed.

One of the prospective jurors had read a portion of Angela's book *If They Come in the Morning*. Another had seen "Free Angela" badges because they were worn by other workers at his job. Another said she had never heard of Angela Davis at all before walking into court.

One juror had a cousin in the New York City Police Department and two other cousins who were guards at Dennamora State penitentiary. Another had a "favorite uncle" who had been on the San Francisco Police Force for twenty-five years. Several had served in various branches of the Armed Forces as career officers for ten, fifteen and twenty years. One juror had a father working for the Tehachapie Correctional Institution. Another's father had just retired from the Santa Clara County Sheriff's Department after twenty-five years of service, with the rank of captain. One prospective juror said her nephew was a deputy sheriff in the state of Washington. It turned out he was the *only* deputy on the tiny island of Lopez, off the coast of Washington, with a population of less than a thousand and no jail.

Two prospective jurors expressed a strong fear of serving on the Angela Davis jury. One was a postal employee who said that people on his mail delivery route had already warned him that if he served and didn't vote one way or the other he could (he quoted them): "Forget about ever coming to my place again . . . I'll go down and pick up my own mail." Another prospective juror, a Chicana, said her husband worked at General Motors and that the case had caused a terrific debate in the plant. She said she would be afraid for her husband if she served and had to make a decision one way or the other. Both were excused.

Several prospective jurors said they could not be fair to Angela Davis and asked to be excused. They were. One man, for example, said he and his family had fled Czechoslovakia after the 1948 Socialist Revolution. Now, he said, he was a successful businessman, owning his own restaurant. Another juror, near hysteria, said she felt so deeply about what had happened to Judge Haley that she couldn't possibly sit on the jury.

Most of the prospective jurors stood in awe of the law and the judge. They knew they were supposed to be "fair and impartial" and so that's what they said they would be, no matter what else they might say in answer to a substantive question. It was left to us to guess how badly they might be affected by their prejudices and misconceptions.

One juror said he thought Communists should go back where they came from. He did not elaborate. Another said he saw the "Communist Party as a threat to the United States." Several said they thought Ms. Davis was "probably guilty." A couple said they could go along with a person's right to be a Communist "up to the point where they advocate the overthrow of the government by force and violence."

One woman said she thought Communism was a "very effective and good system for underdeveloped nations, and I don't have any opinions about the American Communist Party. I am not anticommunist." Another said she knew only "vaguely" about the U.S. Communist Party because "it is not taught in the schools. It is not allowed to be taught."

One elderly lady, asked if she thought the fact that Ms. Davis "dropped out of sight" after the August 7th events indicated a "consciousness of guilt," replied: "I do seem to recall that she was not available. I think I might have been inclined to have been unavailable myself. It was a reasonable thing to do."

A young man, asked if he was married, said he wasn't although he had been engaged three times. "You just haven't quite made it yet?" Leo Branton asked sympathetically. The young man, a student said, "No," and then added hastily, "But I'm not a male chauvinist or anything like that."

Several jurors expressed opposition to the war in Vietnam. One woman's husband had served in the Army Airborne in Vietnam. Asked her views on the war she said: "I don't believe in it myself, and neither does my husband."

Many of the jurors said they rarely, if ever, had contact with Black people, that they had no Black friends and they had never had a Black person to their homes. They said this was as a result of "circumstance," not prejudice. One juror said that she did not think that Black people were treated as equals, but that they hadn't been aggressive enough in demanding their rights. Their current protests, she said, "are about 100 years too late." Several expressed agreement with the main conclusions of the Kerner Commission Report that white racism pervades society.

The two most hostile and intransigent prospective jurors were both financially well-off, white and in their late forties. Howard P. Atkinson was a building contractor. He had owned his own company for nineteen years. He also owned real estate. He said he agreed with fair housing laws and rented to Black families. Asked if he approved of the Black families he said, "If they pay the rent, yes."

Asked his opinion about Communists, Atkinson said: "There are different kinds of Communists. If you are speaking of Russia, I would say that Russia would like to control the world . . ." Communists obtain their objectives, he said, "by infiltrating other governments and trying to gain control from within." Atkinson said if Ms. Davis failed to testify in her own defense during the trial he would certainly conclude that she was "hiding something."

William E. Hotaling, the other hostile juror, was a manager for IBM Corporation, and had lived in the county for about seven years in the suburban community of Saratoga, about ten miles south of San Jose. He told Leo Branton that he was against Communists because Communists were against the government of the United States and he was for the government of the United States. Toward the end of his voir dire the following exchange took place:

Q. [by Leo Branton] In a case where you were charged with murder, kidnapping and conspiracy to commit certain acts, would you be satisfied to have your case decided by twelve Black people?

[Harris objects. He is overruled]

A.   I would say if we had twelve Black people here and they were fair-minded, I would say yes, I would sit in a courtroom with them.

Q.   Would you be satisfied to have your fate decided by twelve Communists?

[Harris objects: "This is going, your Honor, a little too far." The judge sustains the objection. Leo Branton reframes the question. It is virtually the same and a second objection is overruled.]

A.   [Hotaling replies with a sarcastic question of his own] And are you going to find twelve fair-minded Communists in the United States who will try me in court for these three charges?

[The judge interrupts and says to Hotaling: "Do you understand the question? If you don't understand the question, indicate you do not." Leo Branton snaps back angrily, first at the judge and then at Hotaling]

Q.   I understand. The reason I asked that question is you don't think I could find twelve fair minded Communists do you?

[Hotaling is more subdued and pauses for a moment]

A.   I don't know . . .

Q.   Would you be satisfied to be judged by twelve Black Communists?

[Harris objects: "Well, your Honor, I think this is really the most ludicrous point . . ." The judge overrules the objection. Leo Branton revises the question anyway]

Q.   Let me broaden the question . . . Would you be satisfied to be judged by twelve Black *women* Communists?

[It takes Hotaling fully five minutes to reply]

A.   I would take my chances, yes.

ON THE afternoon of March 9th—only eight court days after the start of the voir dire— twelve prospective jurors had survived three stages of questioning and were tentatively seated. We had challenged Hotaling and Atkinson and one other prospective juror for cause. All three challenges had been denied by Judge Arnason.

The first option to accept the jury or exercise a peremptory challenge would pass to the prosecution. And then the option would pass to us.

Crowded into a back room in the lawyers' office we sweated, smoked, argued, fretted, comforted each other—and contemplated our next move.

Two Black psychologists were working with us. They had been in court each day to observe the voir dire. They offered some important insights about some jurors: sensing moments of tension or distress; noting the choice of words, intonation, patterns of speech, type of dress, mannerisms.

We assessed each of the twelve on a scale from one to ten, with ten being very good. we graded four at three or under (and joked that Atkinson and Hotaling owed us points); and seven of the jurors at about five or six. We had confidence in only one—the one Black woman on the panel, Janie Hemphill.

Even with Ms. Hemphill it was a weak jury. The three or four hostile jurors could too easily swing a wavering, uncommitted majority toward conviction. Ms. Hemphill and two or three other jurors might hold out for acquittal. At best that would mean a hung jury, and it would hang in favor of conviction. We had to peremptorily challenge at least two, and possibly three jurors. With any luck that would shift the balance of power on the panel in a more positive direction.

In any criminal trial the defense and prosecution have a fixed number of what are called peremptory challenges during the jury selection. This means that either side can remove a prospective juror from the panel without giving a reason. In addition, both sides have an unlimited number of causal challenges. But, to exercise a causal challenge counsel must show that the bias of a particular prospective juror will prevent him from being "fair and impartial." The granting of a causal challenge is at the judge's discretion.

The strategic object then, in the jury selection process, is to win as many causal challenges as possible against hostile prospective jurors, and to conserve the peremptory challenges so that they can be used in a crunch as the selection process draws to a close.

In this trial we could exercise only twenty peremptory challenges. And, we had to select a total of sixteen people—twelve regular jurors, and four alternates. The jury selection became a suspenseful, terrifying game of chance.

We knew there were some good people still remaining in the first pool of 150 prospective jurors. But how quickly would their names come up? And how long could we hold on to Janie Hemphill?

21

J anie L. Hemphill is a tall, dark, handsome woman. She sat front and center in the jury box. She was the central figure on the panel—physically and spiritually.

Ms. Hemphill and her husband had lived in Santa Clara County for sixteen years. They had three children, ten, twelve and thirteen. Mr. Hemphill was employed as a sheet rock hanger in the construction industry. He had been a construction worker on and off for twelve years. Before coming to San Jose Ms. Hemphill said she had lived in Corcoran, California and before that in Chandler, Arizona. She was born in Texas and grew up in Oklahoma.

Ms. Hemphill said she started working before she was twelve, picking cotton and cutting onions. She said that since high school she had done so many different jobs that it was "kind of hard just to state them all . . ." Babysitter, domestic worker, nurse's aide, short order cook, dishwasher, factory worker.

For three years, she said, she and her husband had managed the Pink Elephant Liquor Store in San Jose, and then they had tried to go into business for themselves. For a short while they had operated a night club, but then it folded, and her husband went back into the construction industry.

"You've had a difficult time, is that correct?" Howard Moore asked, concluding his voir dire.

"Yes, I have," Ms. Hemphill replied.

Albert Harris questioned Ms. Hemphill for two and a half hours.

He began: "You wouldn't feel personally resentful to me if I asked you questions that, in another context, another place, might be somewhat personal?" Ms. Hamphill said she wouldn't hold it against the prosecutor. Harris proceeded.

He established that the night club she and her husband had operated was called the Club Mandingo. And it had been located in San Jose.

Then he said:

Q. There was a raid on the night club on September the 12th of 1971?

A. Yes, there was.

Q. And your husband was arrested, isn't that right?

A. Yes, he was . . . But then he went to court for that . . .

Q. [Harris interrupts] Yes, ma'am . . . and he pleaded guilty to a charge of operating a gambling game in that night club?

A. Yes, he did.

Q. And then he was sentenced to, I think, probation and paid a fine for that violation?

A. Yes.

Q. Yes, ma'am. And in connection with that incident, isn't it true that an accusation was filed under the Alcoholic Beverage Control Act to revoke the license held by you and your husband to operate that night club

A. Yes.

Q. Yes, ma'am.

Harris dwelled on the liquor license revocation for more than two hours. It was not a criminal proceedings, he conceded. And Ms. Hemphill explained that she and her husband had already decided to close their night club, even before the revocation proceedings were begun. She said that they had barely been able to survive financially before the raid. The raid itself had finished them.

But charges had been brought against her under the Alcoholic Beverage Control Act, Harris insisted. Didn't she feel that that experience would make her somewhat biased against the State of California? And wouldn't that affect her judgment in this case? Ms. Hemphill said she couldn't see any connection between the two cases. They were completely separate issues. Harris pursued the point. Ms. Hemphill explained it again. Harris persisted. Ms. Hemphill explained it again.

The judge interrupted. He urged a short recess.

THE RECESS ended. Harris resumed his cross examination. Leo objected: "I resent in the deepest possible way what Mr. Harris is doing here . . . It's unforgivable . . . He has attempted to embarrass Ms. Hemphill . . . This is the very kind of white racism we've been talking about."

"Now I resent that . . .", Harris bristled.

"Now, now . . ." The judge motioned for order, his hands patting the air. "Let's be polite."

The judge overruled the objection.

Harris proceeded:

Q. But charges were brought against you and your husband. Don't you think that fact will tip the scales to some extent—be it ever so slightly?

A. No.

Q. It won't?

A. No.

Q. That would have no effect upon you ma'am?

Ms. Hemphill looked straight at the assistant attorney general and through him. she said: "No . . . For so many years I have had to blot out so many things . . . I could blot this part out. There's a lot of things I have had to blot out of my life."

Harris blanched, looked down at his feet, and sat down.

He could not challenge Janie Hemphill for cause.

She/we had won.

LATE on the afternoon of March 9th the first option to accept the jury or exercise a peremptory challenge went to the prosecution. Harris exercised his first peremptory against juror number one. She had told Howard Moore that she did not live in a middle class neighborhood. She considered herself, she said, to be a member of the working class.

A student at San Jose State College, majoring in economics, took her place. He was quickly passed for cause.

The option to accept the jury or exercise a peremptory challenge passed to the defense.

Leo Branton said: "We pass the jury your Honor."

The courtroom erupted in one sustained gasp.

Hotaling and Atkinson were still on the jury.

If Harris also passed the jury . . .

It was a bluff. In passing the jury Leo hoped to give us an advantage over the prosecution by providing the defense with one extra peremptory challenge.

Harris flushed.

The judge said: "The challenge passes to the prosecution."

Harris stared down at the papers on the table in front of him. He shuffled a few. He looked up. He said: "We challenge juror number two."

Juror number two was a young woman whose husband was a graduate student at Stanford University. They lived in Escondido Village—a housing complex for married students—on the campus. Harris had asked her a lot of questions about whether or not she had seen any student protests on the Stanford campus, and had she seen any members of the Santa Clara County Sheriff's Department in action on the campus? She said she hadn't. Harris wasn't taking any chances.

A middle-aged man of Italian origin, who worked as an accountant for the Memorex corporation was seated in her place. He was quickly passed for cause.

The challenge passed back to the defense. It was five minutes to four. Leo asked for a recess until Monday morning, March 13th. It was granted.

Outside, reporters fell all over Leo. What would he have done, they asked, had Harris called his bluff, and passed the jury too? Leo said: "I would have dropped dead!"

Harris had made a fatal error. Leo was certain he would.

We knew, the judge knew, the press should have known, that Albert Harris would never go to trial with a Black woman on the jury. And certainly not with Ms. Hemphill.

Janie Hemphill had given us a vital edge. Her continued presence on the jury panel had enabled Leo to force Harris to use up his second peremptory challenge before we had used our first. Now if and when it came down to the wire, we would have the tactical advantage. We would have that one extra challenge.

FIRST thing Monday morning we excused juror number seven, William E. Hotaling.

Mary M. Timothy, a medical researcher in the Department of Urology at Stanford University's Medical Center took his place. She had only recently moved to Palo Alto from Stockton, California—a rural, predominantly conservative community. During our investigation of the jury we had learned that her twenty-eight year old son had been a conscientious objector to the war in Vietnam. Later he had been arrested during a student protest at Berkeley for allegedly assaulting a police officer. We had talked with a few people who had known the family. The parents had stood by their son on both occasions.

Harris spent a long time questioning Ms. Timothy about her son. She remained calm; her answers were direct and to the point. There were no grounds for a causal challenge.

Ms. Timothy was seated.

The challenge passed back to the prosecution. Harris excused juror number one, the student at San Jose State College who was majoring in economics.

An employee for the United States Postal Service took his place. But this prospective juror was quickly excused. He was one of the two jurors to have expressed fears about serving on the Davis jury.

Ralph E. Delange, a maintenance electrician for the Memorex Corporation became juror number one. We were ecstatic. Ralph Delange was one of the best prospective jurors on the list. People in the San Jose community who had known Delange and his family assured us that he was a very decent human being, with many progressive, even radical views, despite a rural upbringing in Montana, and a four-year stint with the U.S. Navy around the time of the Korean War.

He was passed for cause.

The challenge passed back to the defense. We excused juror number six, Howard P. Atkinson.

Luis Franco, born and raised in Mexico, now a citizen of the United States, employed as a technician at IBM, took Atkinson's place. He told the court that he had served in the United States Army for four years, and had been stationed in Chicago. The Army, he said, had no category for Mexican people. They have only three ethnic categories: white, Oriental and Negro. They listed him as white, he explained, though he considered himself a Mexican-Amercian.

Franco said his main interest, aside from his family (he was married and the father of two teen-age sons) was painting. In the evenings he took art classes at San Jose City College.

"I am curious all the time," he told Doris Walker during his voir dire examination. "Instead of reading about crime or robbery I read about something that is new."

Luis Franco was passed for cause.

The challenge passed back to the prosecution.

Harris excused Janie Hemphill.

A prolonged hiss issued from the spectators section.

Rosalie Frederick, self-employed as a picture-framer, and the head of her household, with three young children, replaced Ms. Hemphill. Ms. Frederick was another of the prospective jurors we had hoped to draw. Several people in the community had known her ten years earlier. She had been on the fringes of the civil rights movement in the early sixties. She was passed for cause.

The challenge went to the defense.

It was almost four o'clock. We asked for a recess until the next morning. Harris did not object. Court was adjourned.

BACK in the lawyers' office . . .

We had had incredible luck. We had pulled Timothy, Delange, Franco and Frederick in one day. The whole character of the jury had changed.

We reassessed the panel: we rated four at eight or better; five at between five and seven; and three under five. It was a much stronger jury. There were nine salaried workers, two of them in basic industry. Of the three not working, one was a retired librarian, one was self-employed (Ms. Frederick) and one was a young mother whose husband worked for a large electronics firm as a production supervisor. There were eight women, four men. It was an unusually young jury: two in their twenties, six between thirty and forty, three in their fifties, only one over sixty. Several had openly expressed opposttion to the war in Vietnam. None had expressed vehement anti-communist views. A few had indicated some degree of social relationships with Black people.

If this jury hung it would hang in favor of acquittal. An outright acquittal was conceivable.

Still, we agonized over the decision to pass the jury. Four of the prospective jurors on the panel worried us. One had been born and raised in Georgia, and attended segregated schools. Her brother-in-law was a patrolman in the San Jose Police Department. On the other hand, she was young, and she was the one who had read portions of Angela's book *If They Come in the Morning*—"out of curiosity," she had said.

Another prospective juror, employed by Sears Roebuck in the accounting department, had told us emphatically that she liked her job. She was responsible for collecting payment on overdue accounts. That really irked us.

Another juror had been a career officer in the United States Navy, a graduate of Annapolis. He had admitted that he might not be totally fair and impartial because he had been trained to consider communists as "the enemy." We had challenged him for cause. The challenge had been denied. He was not abrasive or hostile, and Angela especially, thought that he had been listening intently to the voir dire questions and the responses. She thought he would be all right.

Our greatest concern was with the juror whose father had recently retired from the Santa Clara County Sheriff's Department after twenty-five years of service. Howard had conducted her voir dire. There was something about it, not what she had said, but the way in which she had said it, that disturbed us greatly. The more we analyzed her responses, the more we became convinced that she had seriously misrepresented her actual views. Still, it was hard to be sure, and still harder to know what, if anything, to do about it.

We talked on into the night—around and around and around. Finally we decided. There was unanimity. We would accept the jury. There was no way to peremptorily challenge any juror without risking the whole panel. And we had to hold on to at least Delange and Timothy.

Tuesday, March 14th. 9 a.m. The Judge's Chambers. We told Judge Arnason we were prepared to accept the jury. Harris chafed. He wasn't ready. Janie Hamphill had been his last challenge. He said he didn't want that to be his final challenge. It would look bad. The judge told him he'd never live it down anyhow. He wanted Harris to accept the jury.

Reluctantly Albert Harris agreed.

COURT convened. The twelve prospective jurors were in the box. The judge said: "The challenge passes to the defense."

Angela stood up:

We have long contended Judge Arnason, that it would be virtually impossible for me to receive a fair trial in Santa Clara County. As you know, we have made a number of change of venue motions challenging the ruling that the case be tried in this county.

As I look at the present jury I see that the women and men do reflect the composition of this county. There are no Black people sitting on the jury. Although I cannot say that this is a jury of my peers, I can say that, after much discussion, we have reached the conclusion that the women and men sitting on the jury will put forth their best efforts to give me a fair trial.

I do not think that further delay in the jury selection process will affect in any way the composition of the jury, and because we have confidence in the women and men presently sitting in the jury box, I am happy to say that we accept this jury.

Reporters bolted for the door.

22

With no pause in the proceedings the selection of four alternate jurors was begun. It was to be a long and tedious process. Twenty-three prospective jurors were either excused or challenged, in three and a half days.

We knew the names left in the pool. We were waiting for the best names to be drawn. As it turned out their selection was decisive to the outcome of the trial. How and why is the story of yet another historical quirk, in a case that had already seen many.

FOUR alternates were accepted and sworn.

Number one was Michelle Savage, a twenty-year old secretary-receptionist for the Syntex Corporation in Sunnyvale. Ms. Savage had just registered to vote under the new State law lowering the voting age to eighteen. She said she would turn twenty-one in a couple of months, in May. Asked her feelings about serving on the jury, she said: "The only thing is I don't think I could judge Ms. Davis unemotionally. I don't feel that I could condemn her — it is an awful big decision to make and I don't know that I could do it."

Upon further questioning and explanations from the judge, Ms. Savage said that she understood that her responsibility as a juror was to judge the facts. She said she thought she could do this, and if the facts warranted a conviction, she would convict Ms. Davis.

Alternate number two was Robert Seidel, a sixty-nine year old retired service engineer, who had worked for the Food Machinery Corporation (FMC) in Santa Clara County for thirty years. Mr. Seidel had immigrated to the United States from Denmark in 1924. Asked if he had been forced to flee Denmark due to political repression, Seidel replied, "It is unknown there."

As a service engineer with FMC, Seidel explained, he had done a lot of traveling. installing equipment and helping to set up new plants jn various parts of the world. He said he had worked for a time in South Africa. Asked his opinion of apartheid, Seidel said he thought it was wrong. "They are all men, women, human beings," he said.

Asked if he had any social contact with Black people, Seidel said that he did: "I belong to a social club called Inter-Cultural Counsel, formed by a lot of immigrants and we have a monthly social evening and there are some Black people there — they immigrated from Georgia!"

There was much laughter in the courtroom. Seidel said he and his fellow club members all "have a bit of fun about it at our gatherings."

Alternate number three was Barbara L. Deutsch. Ms. Deutsch occasionally worked as a secretary for her brother who owned a Midas Muffler shop in Santa Cruz. She also owned some property.

Alternate number four was Samuel J. Conroy who was employed as a mechanical engineer designer for Ampex Corporation in Sunnyvale. His wife was also employed at Ampex as a senior clerk.

IT WAS in the final hours of the jury selection that an unexpected and thoroughly bizarre incident unfolded.

An eighteen year old girl telephoned the court. She was nearly incoherent according to the court clerk who spoke to her. She said she had to see Judge Arnason. The clerk succeeded in eliciting from her the nature of the problem. She had just read a newspaper and learned that her mother had been seated as one of the jurors in the Davis trial. She was certain from the newspaper accounts that her mother had lied on the voir dire. She had to talk to the judge.

A meeting in chambers was arranged. Angela and all counsel were present. The girl, pale, tremulous, said that her mother was in actuality, fanatically hostile to Black people. She gave specific and detailed information. Her mother was on the jury for one reason and one reason only, she said — to send Angela Davis to prison for life. The girl said: "God help Angela Davis if my mother is on that jury."

The juror was called into chambers. She vehemently denied her daughter's accusations. But the incident had tainted her beyond redemption. The judge requested the juror to herself ask to be excused. She refused. Defense counsel pleaded. She refused. The judge renewed his appeal. Reluctant and bitter, the accused juror finally agreed to leave voluntarily, but only after it became clear to her that the judge would hold a public hearing on the matter if she didn't.

Michelle Savage, the first alternate, became juror number eight and Robert Seidel became alternate number one, Barbara Deutsch became alternate number two and Sam Conroy became juror alternate number three. A new fourth alternate was selected.

John W. Tittle, a nineteen year old student from West Valley Junior College became the youngest juror in U.S. history. State and federal law had recently been changed to allow 18 year olds to vote, and a new state law permitted 18 year olds who had registered to vote, to serve on juries.

(Midway through the trial itself there was another, unexpected, change in the jury. On April 24th one of the jurors notified the judge that she was too ill to continue on the panel. Certification was obtained from her physician and she was excused. And so it was that Robert Seidel became juror number four.)

The jury selection completed, a ten day recess followed. Formal arguments and the presentation of witnesses was set to commence on the 27th of March 1972.

THEN it happened. Shortly after 11 o'clock on Friday morning, March 17th, word reached our office that the California State Supreme Court had modified its decision abolishing the death penalty. The result could be Angela's re-imprisonment.

Affirming that the punishment of death could no longer be exacted by virtue of the decision, the court nevertheless held that "The underlying gravity of these [formerly capital] offenses endures and the determination of their gravity for the purpose of bail continues unaffected by this decision."

In other words, the court was modifying its decision so that Section 1270 of the Penal Code, under which Angela had been originally denied bail, would remain intact, unaffected by their abolition of the death penalty.

The modification appeared as an amendment to a footnote.

Somber. Disbelieving the madness of the reality. Angela could be sent back to prison by an amendment to a footnote.

We gathered late that Friday afternoon in Leo Branton's apartment in San Jose.

Someone went out and brought back some cold cuts and cheese and bread and a jug of wine.

We talked strategy. Call everybody and anybody with any measure of political influence in the State of California who will listen. Ask them to call the attorney general's office. Urge the attorney general not to make a motion for the revocation of bail. We were certain that if the attorney general did not take the initiative, Judge Arnason would not himself revoke Angela's bail.

Angela was stretched out on the floor of the living room on her back, her long, slender form rigid and still. There were no tears.

Monday morning, March 20th, in the judge's chambers. Assistant Attorney General Albert Harris announced that he would not move to revoke bail.

The issue was closed. The strength of the mass movement had held.

23

Albert Harris divided the presentation of his case into three parts. Phase one was to reconstruct what had occurred on August 7, 1970 at the Marin County courthouse. Phase two was to establish the motivation for Angela's involvement in the alleged plot — her passion for George Jackson. Phase three was to establish the dimensions and details of the alleged conspiracy, and Angela's role in it.

Harris announced his intention to call 104 witnesses. He said he would introduce approximately 200 exhibits into evidence. These exhibits would include detailed diagrams of the inner and outer areas of the Marin Civic Center, a score of photographs of the events themselves as taken by a reporter-photographer for the San Rafael *Independent-Journal,* all of the guns and ammunition involved in the day's events, the clothes and related possessions of the deceased, Angela's letters and the diary, and a veritable volume of paper: sales receipts, cancelled checks, prison records, telephone company records, parking lot records. . . .

PHASE one. The crime.

Harris called thirty-nine witnesses to describe what took place at the Marin County courthouse on August the 7th, 1970. They were: three of the jurors in Judge Haley's courtroom; James Kean, the photographer from the *Independent-Journal,* and another from the same newspaper who took a number of additional photographs; four members of local police departments in Marin County, including one chief of police; three California highway patrolmen; seven San Quentin prison guards; eleven deputy sheriffs from the Marin County Sheriff's Department; two representatives of the Marin County Coroner's Office; one pathologist; and Gary Thomas, the assistant district attorney, wounded in the gunfire on August 7th. There were five additional witnesses: two clerks from different sporting goods stores in the Los Angeles area; two men who happened to be in the Marin Civic Center on August 7th, on unrelated personal business, and witnessed the events; and the criminalist from the California Department of Justice who reconstructed the scene of the crime.

Through these witnesses Harris had to present four critical elements of proof to establish his case against Angela Davis. Harris had to prove: 1) that there was a plan, i.e. a conspiracy to carry out the objectives of the August 7th action; 2) that the object of the conspiracy was to free the Soledad Brothers, George Jackson, Fleeta Drumgo and John Clutchette; 3) that pursuant to this conspiracy Jonathan Jackson and three San Quentin prisoners, James McClain, William Christmas and Ruchell Magee kidnapped Judge Harold Haley and Gary Thomas and three women jurors; and 4) that Judge Haley was killed in the course of the commission of a felony, i.e. in the course of the kidnapping.

This is the story of what happened on August 7th, 1970, as told by the prosecution's own witnesses.

The Marin County Civic Center, which houses the offices of most of the county's agencies such as the unemployment office, the probation department, the office of public health, as well as the hall of justice, the sheriff's department and the county jail, is a twenty-five minute drive north from San Francisco, across the Golden Gate Bridge. The civic center is also approximately six miles north of San Quentin State Prison. Prisoners accused of crimes committed within that prison are automatically brought to trial in the Marin County Civic Center.

James McClain was a Black prisoner in San Quentin serving an indeterminate sentence for assault on a police officer. New charges were brought against McClain by the San Quentin authorities in March of 1970. He was accused of having stabbed at a guard at San Quentin on March 2, 1970.

In June 1970 McClain was prosecuted for this alleged attack. McClain acted as his own lawyer. He won a mistrial after an all-white jury failed to reach a verdict.

A second trial was begun on the 3rd of August of 1970 before Judge Harold Haley in courtroom number two in the Marin County Hall of Justice. Assistant District Attorney Gary Thomas prosecuted McClain, and James McClain again represented himself.

On August 7, 1970 the McClain trial was in progress. Two Black San Quentin prisoners — Ruchell Magee and William Christmas — had been called as witnesses by McClain. William Christmas, handcuffed and shackled, was seated in the corridor immediately outside the courtroom in the company of a San Quentin guard, waiting to testify. Ruchell Magee was testifying, having been called as the first witness for the defense that morning.

At approximately 10:45 a.m. a tall, very young, light complected, Black man, wearing a light-colored trench coat and carrying a blue satchel, entered Judge Haley's courtroom and took a seat in the second row of the spectator's section. This young man was Jonathan Jackson.

There were few people in the courtroom: one or two San Quentin guards, a bailiff, the court clerk and reporters, the twelve jurors, the prosecuting attorney and the judge.

Shortly after he sat down, Jonathan stood up and said: "All right, gentlemen. This is it. Everybody freeze." He was holding a pistol.

Everybody froze. The judge remained seated behind the bench.

Jonathan Jackson handed the pistol to James McClain. Simultaneously he reached down and picked up a .30 caliber carbine with a collapsible stock.

Jonathan handed a sawed-off shot gun to McClain. According to several witnesses McClain then asked Jonathan: "Did you bring the tape?" Jonathan reached into the blue satchel and pulled out a roll of white adhesive tape which he handed to McClain.

McClain approached the judge's bench. He proceeded to tape the shot-gun to the judge's neck, with the barrel pointed upwards towards the chin.

At about this time Ruchell Magee stepped from behind the witness stand and ordered a San Quentin guard to "take off these shackles." They were removed.

Sometime in the course of these events, and here the testimony was contradictory and unclear, William Christmas apparently entered the courtroom. His shackles and handcuffs were removed.

McClain ordered the judge to call the sheriff. There was a telephone inside the courtroom. Judge Haley did so and is reported to have told the sheriff: "The inmates are holding us as hostages. They have guns. Don't do anything rash." McClain reportedly seized the telephone from Judge Haley and shouted at the sheriff to "call your pigs off."

Meanwhile, several jurors were ordered to leave the jury box and stand in front of it. Gary Thomas was told to stand at the head of the line. One of the men — it is unclear who — took out a roll of thin copper wire and began to wire Gary Thomas and three of the jurors together, first binding the hands, and then passing the wire around the neck and back to the next person and so on. McClain objected, several witnesses testified. He said that the wire might hurt the people if it went around their necks. He said they should be wired around the waist instead. This was done.

While the jurors were being wired together, a couple with a baby entered the courtroom. How and why they came in was unclear in the testimony. In any event, someone was reported to have said, "Let's take the baby." McClain, witnesses testified, said, "We aren't taking any kids."

One of the jurors wired into the original group of hostages was shaking uncontrollably. She was an old woman. McClain released her, and led her back to a seat. Another juror was taken in her place. McClain asked this woman if she wanted her purse. She did not reply. McClain picked it up and handed it to her.

One witness, Norene Morris, a juror who was present in the courtroom, but was not taken as a hostage, testified that McClain repeatedly assured the women that they would not be hurt, and that he only wanted to use them as a "shield" in order to effect their escape.

Further, Ms. Morris testified, McClain said, "We are not animals and we are not going to act like them," referring to the prison guards.

Ms. Morris said that at one point McClain came over to talk to the jurors. He said he didn't want the ladies to be scared "because he remembered that his mother had been scared the day she came to court, and she didn't come back, and that he hadn't done what he was accused of . . .", Ms. Morris recounted. She said that McClain seemed to be "very gentle."

All of the witnesses agreed that there was much shouting and confusion in the courtroom. There was, they said, heated discussion amongst the prisoners and Jonathan about whom to take as hostages, and how many. The witnesses estimated that about twenty-five minutes elapsed between the time Jonathan took over the courtroom and the time the group left the courtroom.

In the group were: Gary Thomas, three women jurors, Judge Haley, and James McClain, William Christmas, Ruchell Magee and Jonathan Jackson.

By the time they left the courtroom dozens of sheriff's deputies and police officials had gathered in the corridor. All witnesses agreed that there was further shouting and confusion in the hallway before the group entered one of the elevators to go down-stairs and exit the building. Witnesses testified that the group spent perhaps ten or fifteen minutes in the corridor.

Jonathan moved about disarming various police officers. McClain disappeared with Judge Haley for a few minutes. He went back to a holding cell adjacent to the courtroom. There were two other San Quentin prisoners in the cell — brought to the courthouse in connection with another trial. McClain asked them if they wanted to go. One of the prisoners shouted back to the effect that he didn't have enough time left to serve to risk escape.

McClain reappeared in the corridor.

In the meantime, James Kean, a reporter for the San Rafael *Independent-Journal* had come up the elevator and was in the corridor. One of the prisoners, Kean said he thought it was William Christmas, told him to take as many pictures as he wanted. "We are the revolutionaries!" Christmas shouted, according to the newsman.

Kean said he took between twenty-four and thirty pictures. He testified that he was awarded three separate honors for his photography that day—a gold medal from the National Headliners, and one award each from the National Press Photographers Association and the California State Press Photographers Association.

Finally, the group decided to leave the building . They walked first in a southerly direction down the corridor, and then turned around and walked back in a northerly direction. They proceeded to the elevators at the northern end of the building directly under the sheriff's department and exited the building at the north arch.

Outside, scores of law enforcement personnel had gathered. Jonathan continued to disarm officers as the group walked towards the parking lot.

All witnesses agreed that the group walked more than 200 yards across the entire length of the parking lot, from the north arch to the southern most end of the parking lot. They went to a yellow Ford van with a Hertz sign on the side panel. They opened the rear door. All climbed into the van.

Once inside the van Gary Thomas and the three other jurors were untied. McClain was in the driver's seat. Jonathan was in the front on the passenger side. The van had no seats except for the driver's seat.

Testimony concerning the arrangement of the other people in the van was contradictory and confusing, but it would seem—as one likely arrangement—that three women were sitting in the back on the floor toward the left side (the driver's side) of the van. Judge Haley was on the right side, near the front. Behind Judge Haley was Ruchell Magee, and opposite Ruchell, on the left side, in the rear, was William Christmas.

McClain started the van. He drove it only a few feet and it stalled. He told Jonathan he couldn't drive it. McClain and Jonathan switched places. Jonathan drove the van. He proceeded slowly towards the south arch. It was a very "jerky, bumpy" ride.

Several San Quentin guards testified that they had set up a roadblock on Civic Center Drive just past the south arch. The van came to an abrupt halt a few yards from the roadblock. According to the guards, Jonathan extended his right arm out of the window on the driver's side. He was holding a .357 magnum pistol. Others at the scene, including all the deputy sheriffs and highway patrolmen, did not recall Jonathan holding a pistol or pointing it at anyone.

James William Brown, a personnel consultant for the California State Personnel Board in Sacramento happened to be in the Marin Civic Center on the morning of August 7th, conducting interviews in connection with his job. He was in an office on the third floor of the Civic Center, overlooking the South arch, when the first shots were fired. Brown said a bullet shattered a window in the office where he was working.

Brown ran for cover. However, a tape recorder which he was using for his interview, was still on and recorded the shooting. The tape was played in court. The relevant sequence lasted 19 seconds.

There was a single shot, a pause for perhaps a second or two, and then there was a rapid succession of fire..

Four San Quentin prison guards testified they opened fire on the van just as it came to a stop. None of the other officers on the scene from the sheriff's department, the highway patrol, or local police agencies, used their weapons.

San Quentin Guard Melvin C. Curry testified he fired his .38

caliber pistol twice, aiming toward the front of the van from a distance of approximately 100 yards. He had no idea what, if anything, he hit.

John A. Hicks, who had been in the Army and Air Force respectively for twenty-one years before becoming a guard at San Quentin, said he couldn't remember much of anything that happened, except that when he heard the first few shots he opened fire, "in the general direction of van", with a .30 caliber carbine. He said he didn't know what, if anything, he hit.

Prison guard Eugene L. Osborne said he opened fire on the van with a .38 caliber pistol from a distance of perhaps as much as 100 yards, and let go with three shots. He said he was shooting "at the left front window, which was the driver's side." He said he had no idea what, if anything, he hit.

John Wesley Matthews stated that he fired "at least" four shots into the van with a 30-30 Winchester rifle. Matthews testified with absolute certainty. He said he was an expert marksman. He said he was crouched in a firing position behind and to the left of the van.

Matthews said his first shot hit Jonathan Jackson and his body "flew back" from the driver's seat. His second shot, he said, hit James McClain, and his body "flew back". His third shot was in the direction of Ruchell Magee. He said Magee disappeared from view, then "popped up" again. Matthews said he fired again, and Magee didn't "pop up anymore."

Matthews said just after he fired his fourth shot a "gentleman in a gray suit" stood up inside the van and yelled: "Stop shooting. For God's sake stop shooting." Matthews said he stopped and yelled, "cease-fire", several times.

SERGEANT Joseph Murphy, a twenty-six year veteran of the prison guards at San Quentin, testified that it was prison policy to shoot escaping prisoners regardless of the circumstances or the number of hostages. Leo Branton established the details of this policy on cross examination:

> Q. And, to be certain I understand the significance of that policy, sir, does that policy mean that, if people are attempting to escape and that they have hostages and that the guards are at all able to prevent that

escape, that they are to prevent the escape even if it means that every hostage is killed? That is what it means, doesn't it?

A. That is correct.

Q. That means, whether they are holding one judge or five judges, or one woman or twenty women, or one child or twenty children, that the policy of the San Quentin guards and correctional officers is that, at all costs, they must prevent the escape. Is that right?

A. That is correct.

Q. In other words, it is more important to prevent escape than to save human life. Is that correct?

A. Yes, sir.

HAROLD Pennington of the San Rafael Police Department testified that in the 19-second barrage of gunfire the van literally rocked from side to side from the impact of the bullets.

Gary Thomas testified that just after the shooting started he grabbed a gun—a .357 magnum—which he claimed was in Jonathan's hand. Thomas said he fired once in the direction of Jonathan Jackson, once in the direction of James McClain, once in the direction of William Christmas, and he recalled definitely shooting Ruchell Magee in the stomach. He said Magee was still moving after the first shot, so he attempted to fire again. He squeezed the trigger but the gun was emptied of bullets and it clicked. It was after that, Thomas said, that he stood up and shouted: "Stop firing. Please stop firing." At that moment, he said, he felt a sharp pain in his back, his legs sagged under him and he collapsed. He said that he had been shot from outside the van.

Keith C. Craig, the coroner's investigator for Marin County, was one of the first men on the scene after the shooting. He said he climbed into the van as soon as the rear doors were opened. Several San Quentin guards had already removed various weapons and were in the process of taking Gary Thomas out through the front passenger side of the vehicle.

Craig said he ascertained at once that Judge Haley, James McClain and William Christmas were dead. Craig said Jonathan Jackson was still alive, and sprawled in the back of the van. "He was rolling his head back and forth and was moaning . . . I spoke to him, but I got no response. And then I examined him and ascertained that he had died."

One witness testified that Ruchell Magee was severely wounded and slumped over, slightly to the right and behind Judge Haley. Magee was removed from the van and placed on a stretcher to be taken to a hospital. He was unconscious. A gun was still in his belt. It had not been fired.

Keith Craig testified that the four bodies were removed from the scene and taken to Keaton's Mortuary in San Rafael where the autopsies were to be performed.

John H. Manwaring, a pathologist in Marin County, performed the autopsies. He said he had been licensed to practice since 1944, and had done in excess of 10,000 autopsies. He commmenced his work in this case at 4:30 in the afternoon on August 7th and finished at approximately 8:30 that night.

Manwaring testified that Judge Haley had sustained two wounds. He was shot once in the chest with a .357 magnum—a probably fatal wound; and once in the head with a shot-gun, which caused instantaneous death. He admitted that it was possible, given the nature of the wounds and the accumulation of blood in the left chest cavity, that the chest wound came first.

William Christmas was shot once in the back. The bullet tore through both lungs and the heart and exited just below the right nipple.

James McClain was shot once. The bullet entered on the left side, shattered upon impact, tore through both lungs and the aorta. The core of the bullet exited near the right shoulder, and fragments from the casing lodged in the neck.

Jonathan Jackson was shot once on the left side. The bullet entered at the fifth rib and passed through the chest, perforating both lungs and the aorta, and exited just below the right shoulder.

Manwaring testified that in his original autopsy report filed on August 7th, 1970, he had reversed all of the entrance and exit wounds on McClain, Christmas and Jonathan Jackson. In other words, he explained, the trajectory of the bullets was the same in each case, but in his original report, what he now said were entrance wounds, he had previously specified as exit wounds.

Manwaring continued his explanation of this strange error. He said that on August 2nd, 1971—one year after the events—an investigator from the attorney general's office, accompanied by a criminalist from the department of justice in Sacramento, had called him in for a conference. He said they showed him the clothing of each victim. The nature of the holes in the clothing—which Manwaring swore he had never before seen —confirmed what the investigators from the attorney general's office suggested to him; namely, that he had mistaken all of the exit wounds for entrance wounds during the autopsy a year before.

Manwaring might have noted as well, though he didn't, that the new findings were made after Ruchell Magee filed motions to have Judge Haley's body exhumed, and challenged the accuracy of the autopsy reports on all the victims.

On the basis of this conference with representatives of the attorney general's office, Manwaring stated, he amended his report and changed his findings. He said he did not exhume the bodies for further examination before altering his report. He said he had no explanation for the fact that after twenty-five years of experience, and 10,000 autopsies he could make such an error three times in succession, other than the fact that the wounds in each case were "unusual".

The significance of this for the defense, of course, was that it suggested that at some point the attorney general and his investigators had falsified the position of each of the victims at the moment they were shot and/or they had falsified the origin of the fatal shots. Caught in a lie that would be revealed under the scrutiny of cross examination, Manwaring was forced to alter his report and his testimony.

FOUR of the prosecution's thirty-nine witnesses were crucial to Harris' case against Angela Davis. They were: Maria Graham, one of the jurors taken as a hostage and wounded in the gunfire; James Kean, the reporter from the San Rafael *Independent Journal;* Captain Harvey Teague of the Marin County Sheriff's Department; and Gary Thomas, the assistant district attorney.

Harris' first witness was Maria Graham. She was tense, emotional. She testified that during the course of events there were repeated references to freeing the Soledad Brothers.

Ms. Graham said that McClain, in talking to the sheriff on the telephone in the courtroom said that "he wanted the Soledad Brothers freed or they would kill the judge." In the corridor she said, "they kept shouting they wanted their Soledad Brothers' freedom or they would kill the judge and that they had until twelve o'clock to free them."

On cross examination Ms. Graham admitted that in two previous interviews conducted by law enforcement officials— one on August 16, 1970, and the other on April 15, 1971—in which she gave her version of the events as she recalled them then, she had never once mentioned the Soledad Brothers.

Ms. Graham said that, of course, she had read newspaper reports and seen the television accounts of those events, and she admitted that the media often referred to the Soledad Brothers. She told Howard Moore that it was Mr. Harris who first asked her specific questions about the Soledad Brothers. She said:

> *A.*   He [Mr. Harris] asked me if anybody had mentioned freeing the Soledad Brothers. He also asked me if anybody had said: "Free our Soledad Brothers," and I said no.
>
> *Q.*   The fact of the matter is [Howard Moore continued] until you had this discussion with Mr. Harris you had never been able to recall Mr. McClain ever having said into the telephone: "Free the Soledad Brothers or we'll kill the judge," isn't that right?
>
> *A.*   That may very well be true.

NEWS photographer James Kean testified that just before the prisoners went into the elevator, James McClain said to him, "Tell them we want the Soledad Brothers released by 12 o'clock."

Kean said he asked "Convict McClain" if he meant 12 noon or 12 midnight. Kean said McClain replied, "12 noon." Kean said he wrote the two words "Soledad Brother" on a piece of paper in a notebook he normally carried with him when on assignment. Kean emphasized that he considered McClain's message to be a vital piece of information.

On cross examination, however, Kean admitted that he hadn't relayed McClain's vital message to anyone in authority. In fact, he said, he didn't mention it to anyone at all until he got back to the newspaper's offices late that afternoon and told a fellow reporter. Kean also admitted that he "lost" the piece of paper on which he had written the words "Soledad Brother," because it "wasn't important."

Leo Branton continued the cross examination:

Q. And, incidentally, this remark that was made about freeing the Soledad Brothers — it was the last thing that was said just as the group got on the elevator and went down the elevator; is that a fact?

A. Yes. That's right.

Q. You never heard Jonathan Jackson say anything about free the Soledad Brothers; did you?

A. No, I did not.

Q. You didn't hear anybody say it other than McClain and it was the last thing he said as he headed down the elevator; is that right?

A. Yes

Q. As though it were a parting gesture; is that correct?

A. That's right.

Kean also testified he had been a good personal friend of Judge Harold Haley, and that he also personally knew both Gary Thomas, and one of the jurors taken as a hostage, Joyce Rodoni.

Of the other half dozen or so police officers who testified about the events in the corridor none could agree on what it was James McClain was supposed to have said to James Kean. Gary Thomas stated that at no time in the course of the morning did he ever hear anyone mention anything about the Soledad Brothers.

Captain Harvey Teague of the sheriff's department testified he did hear the conversation between McClain and Kean, after McClain had stepped into the elevator. Teague said he heard McClain say, "You have until 12 noon to free the Soledad Brothers and all political prisoners."

"What time was this," Howard Moore asked, "when you were ordered to free the Soledad Brothers and all political prisoners by 12 noon?"

Captain Teague said it was about 11:30 in the morning.

Captain Teague admitted he had been in charge of Angela Davis when she was in custody in the Marin County jail from December 23, 1970 to December 1, 1971 and that he had accompanied her to court for all the pre-trial hearings and that he had heard all of the motions argued. Howard asked:

Q. You gained some appreciation and knowledge of the legal issues involved in this case; did you not?

A. Yes.

Q. And you specifically gained some understanding and appreciation of the alleged importance of the reference to the Soledad Brothers with respect to this case; did you not?

A. I know the Soledad Brothers were mentioned, yes.

Teague admitted that in his first official report recounting his version of the events of August 7th, which he dictated on the 7th, and which was subsequently transcribed, and then signed by him on August the 10th, he had made no mention of the Soledad Brothers, whatsoever.

Another Marin County deputy sheriff also said he heard something shouted just before the elevator departed on the morning of August 7th. He said it was something to the effect, "Free all our Black brothers in Folsom!"

Leo Branton asked the deputy to repeat those words at the exact voice level at which he heard them on August 7th. The deputy said his voice wasn't too good this morning, but he would try. He squirmed, stiffened and shouted, "Free all our Black brothers in Folsom!"

"Right on!" Leo hissed softly under his breath.

THE FOURTH critical prosecution witness was the assistant district attorney, Gary Thomas. Wounded by San Quentin guards on August 7th, he was brought into court in a wheel chair, having been permanently paralyzed from the waist down. He gave short, precise answers to Albert Harris' questions.

Tempers flared on the cross examination.

While denying that he was a close personal friend of Judge Haley, Gary Thomas did admit that he was married to Judge Haley's niece. He also confirmed that he had, on previous occasions, referred to his uncle-in-law as a "saint."

On different occasions Gary Thomas gave law enforcement officials different accounts of what had happened inside the van.

He consistently stated, however, that he did seize a gun and did fire it at various persons inside the van until it was emptied of bullets.

The key part of his testimony was his insistence that he had seen Ruchell Magee shoot Judge Haley in the face with the shotgun. Thomas recalled that he "watched the right side of the judge's face pull slowly away from his skull. . . ."

With full knowledge that major alterations had been made in the autopsy reports, Leo Branton turned on Gary Thomas:

> *Q.* Isn't it a fact, sir, that the first fusillade of shots that came into the van killed both Jonathan Jackson and McClain, and that you thereupon grabbed the gun that McClain was holding, not the gun that Jonathan was holding, and that you turned around and began firing into the back of the van at Christmas and Magee, and that you hit Christmas and you hit Magee, and you possible even hit Judge Haley?
>
> *A.* No.
>
> *Q.* And I ask you, isn't it a fact, that you hit Ruchell Magee, and it was only after you hit Magee that that shotgun went off?
>
> *A.* No.
>
> *Q.* Did you hear the shotgun go off?
>
> *A.* No.
>
> *Q.* You never heard it, did you?
>
> *A.* No.
>
> *Q.* And the reason you didn't hear it, sir, is because at the same moment that that shotgun went off you were hit in the spine by a shot coming from outside the van?
>
> *A.* No.

TWO CLERKS from sporting goods stores in the Los Angeles area were called to testify to establish the registration on two of the guns Jonathan Jackson brought into the courtroom. Both guns were purchased by Angela Davis long before even the prosecution alleged that a conspiracy had begun. One was a .30 caliber carbine purchased on April 7, 1969, and the other was a .380 Browning automatic pistol, purchased on January 12, 1968.

Harris concluded phase one, introducing in evidence dozens of items related to the August 7th events: all of the guns and ammunition confiscated from the van, several paperback books, two of which bore the signature of Angela Y. Davis on the inside front cover, various photographs of the events, and some of the clothing of the deceased. All were given to the jury to inspect.

Harris placed Jonathan Jackson's wallet in evidence. Each item in the wallet was carefully marked for identification: a California driver's license; a student body card for Blair High School in Pasadena, California; a United Artists Movie Discount Card; a photograph of an unidentified five-year-old child; and a crumpled slip of paper with a mysterious telephone number written on it. The number was 588-9073. Harris considered the telephone number to be a very importance piece of evidence. Its significance would be explained later, he said.

There was no money in Jonathan's wallet. Coroner's assistant Keith Craig had testified he found 57¢ in Jonathan's trouser pocket and 50¢ in his coat pocket, and a one dollar bill tucked into the crotch of his jockey shorts.

Harris wanted the judge's blood-stained robes introduced in evidence. We objected. The judge sustained the objection. It would have no probative value, he said, and it could be highly prejudicial to Ms. Davis.

24

*P**hase two. Passion.*
    Harris began with a full reading of the indictment returned against George Jackson, Fleeta Drumgo and John Clutchette, by the Monterey County Grand Jury on February 16, 1970, for the murder of John B. Mills, a guard at Soledad Prison.

"I would like to call upon the prosecution, your Honor," Leo Branton said at the conclusion of the reading of the indictment, "to stipulate that Fleeta Drumgo and John Clutchette, the surviving members who were indicted under that case, are the same defendants who were acquitted by a jury on March the 27th of 1972 of all charges."

"Well, Mr. Branton," Harris was piqued, "having said it, there really isn't much to respond to; is there?" He refused to make the stipulation. He said the point was immaterial and irrelevant. "It has nothing to do with this case."

First witness, phase two, Charles G. Foster. Foster had been a deputy sheriff in Monterey County for ten years. He testified that in May and June of 1970 he was in charge of prisoner transportation and security for that county and was specifically assigned as the escort officer for George Jackson, Fleeta Drumgo and John Clutchette. He was in court with the three Soledad Brothers in Salinas each time they were required to appear.

Foster testified he saw Angela Davis in the courtroom on at least two occasions. He recognized her because he had seen her picture in the newspapers and on television. He said she was in the company of Jonathan Jackson.

On cross examination Foster said the courtroom was generally very crowded, and on one occasion, June 15, 1970, the courtroom was so crowded that all of the spectators could not get inside.

SECOND witness, phase two, James W. McCord. McCord testified that in August of 1970 he was employed as a special agent for the Federal Bureau of Investigation. He stated that on August 17th of 1970. a federal fugitive warrant was issued for the arrest of Angela Y. Davis. She was charged, he said, with crossing state lines to avoid prosecution.

McCord went to Ms. Davis' Los Angeles apartment on the 17th, with four or five other agents, to arrest Ms. Davis.

They broke into the apartment, and searched it (for Ms. Davis) and then departed.

McCord testified that on the next day, the 18th of August, he and four or five other FBI agents returned to Ms. Davis' apartment, this time with a search warrant. The warrant provided for the search and seizure of names, addresses, correspondence and related materials that might assist the bureau in establishing Ms. Davis' whereabouts. In the course of this search he found two letters in a cardboard box in the hall closet. One letter, McCord said, now marked for identification as People's Exhibit 120, was dated June 2, 1970, and commenced "Dear George" and was signed "Angela." The second letter, he continued, now marked for identification as People's Exhibit 121, was dated June 10, 1970, and likewise commenced "Dear George" and was signed "Angela."

He confiscated both letters.

On cross examination McCord told attorney Doris Walker that he had indeed assumed that the "George" referred to in the letters was George Jackson. He agreed with Ms. Walker that it was hardly likely Ms. Davis would have sought refuge at the prison. If the letters had nothing to do with establishing Ms. Davis' whereabout, Doris went on, by what authority had he seized them?

Seeking to squirm from the trap Doris had laid — for if the letters had nothing to do with establishing Ms. Davis' whereabouts McCord had transgressed the lawful limits of his search warrant by seizing them — McCord suddenly claimed that the warrant did not prevent him from taking items which he thought would bear on the substantive (state) charges against Ms. Davis.

McCord also stated that on August 17th when he first entered Ms. Davis' apartment he did not have an arrest warrant with him. He admitted he had never personally seen an arrest warrant, but had been informed of its issuance. He was unable to explain how he intended to arrest Ms. Davis on a federal warrant alleging interstate flight from California, in her apartment in Los Angeles, California.

McCord admitted that the two letters he found in the hall closet on August 18th were not originals, but photocopies. He said he had no idea where the originals were. The photocopies were not wrinkled, folded or soiled. Doris Walker said, "Mr. McCord did you take People's Exhibit 120 and 121 with you to Ms. Davis' apartment when you went there to search it?"

McCord bristled. He resented the implications of counsel's question and he certainly had not.

THIRD witness, phase two, Raymond W. Kelsey. Kelsey had been a guard at Soledad Prison for eighteen years. He testified that in June 1970 he was working in the mail room at the prison. His job was to search all incoming mail for unauthorized correspondence and contraband, especially money orders.

Kelsey stated a letter dated June 22, 1970 and now marked for identification as People's Exhibit 125, handwritten and signed "Angela" and beginning "Dear George," had been confiscated by him and turned over to his captain. Kelsey confiscated the letter because nobody named "Angela" was on George Jackson's list of approved correspondents. The letter signed "Angela" was enclosed in an envelope bearing the name and address of attorney John Thorne. Kelsey said he knew Thorne was George Jackson's lawyer. The Thorne letter contained other items in addition to the letter signed "Angela." He said he didn't know what, if anything, from this letter was ever delivered to George Jackson.

On cross examination Kelsey reaffirmed he knew that the letter and material had been sent to George Jackson by his attorney, John Thorne. Kelsey stated he knew he was not supposed to read any communication between a lawyer and his client. He said he did not make any mark on the letter, signed "Angela," at the time he confiscated it.

Kelsey denied he had read the letter. Leo Branton asked Kelsey how he knew that People's Exhibit 125 was the same letter he had confiscated at Soledad Prison, if he hadn't read it and had made no identifying mark on it. Kelsey said he just knew it was the same letter. Leo persisted:

Q. Did you read any part of it?

A. I read a small portion, and I saw who signed the letter. Then I immediately took it to our captain.

Q. How much did you read, sir?

A. Possibly the first paragraph . . .

Q. Why did you do that?

A. Maybe curiosity . . .

Q. You read enough of it to determine in your own mind that you didn't believe that it was something that an attorney should be sending his client; is that right?

A. Yes.

Q. And so you then took it and had somebody in high authority decide whether or not it should go further, is that right?

A. Yes.

Q. And that was to your captain?

A. Yes.

Q. Incidentally, what's his name?

A. Captain Moody.

Audible gasps issued from the spectators section. This was the same Captain Moody who had been so deeply implicated in the prosecution of the Soledad Brothers.

At the insistence of the defense and with much objection from the prosecution, the judge agreed to order Captain Moody called as a witness, but outside the presence of the jury. He appeared that same afternoon.

Captain Moody testified that in June, 1970, Officer Kelsey did indeed bring him a letter from Angela Davis to George Jackson, now marked as People's Exhibit 125. Moody stated that in the same envelope with this letter there was another letter, from John Thorne to George Jackson, and a pamphlet by Mao Tse Tung called "Combatting Liberalism." Moody testified he removed the letter signed "Angela," put the pamphlet and Thorne's letter back into the envelope and sent it on to George Jackson.

Leo Branton conducted the cross examination:

Q. You would not consider such a pamphlet contraband, would you?

A. No, sir. At that time we had instructions to permit inmates to have pamphlets of that type.

Q. In other words, the policy allowed inmates to have a pamphlet by Mao Tse Tung, but wouldn't let the inmates have a letter that started Dear George and was signed Angela?

A. Would not permit inmates to have correspondence from somebody that had not been approved. All inmates were required to have approved correspondence and visitors.

Captain Moody was asked, on further cross examination, if he had been personally familiar with an inmate at Soledad Prison named George Jackson. Moody said: "Not personally. I knew him and knew him as an inmate of the institution."

"Well, all right," Leo Branton responded, "I don't want to quibble over the word 'personally' . . ." Moody then admitted he knew who George Jackson was "as distinguished from his just being a member of the general inmate population."

Q. As a matter of fact in June of 1970 you had quite an extensive file of your own on George Jackson, did you not?

A. Yes, sir.

Q. And in June of 1970, were you also familiar with a person by the name of Angela Davis?

A. By name only.

Q. By name only?

A. By name only.

Q. Didn't you also have a file on Angela Davis in June of 1970?

A. Not per se, no, sir.

Q. In your capacity at Soledad Prison, prior to June of 1970, had you not received reports from other employees of the state concerning the activities of Ms. Angela Davis outside of prison?

A. Not that I can specifically recall, no, sir.

Fifth witness, phase two, Spiro P. Vasos. This was the same Spiro Vasos who had testified at the Soledad Brothers trial. He was the latent finger-print examiner for the California Department of Justice. His office was in Sacramento.

Vasos testified he received a telephone call from authorities at San Quentin Prison very late in the afternoon on Saturday, August 21, 1971, one year after the events at the Marin Civic Center. He was asked to come to San Quentin.

Vasos said he went to the prison, and directly to the cell of George Jackson. He said Mr. Jackson had been killed earlier that afternoon. He said the cell was very "messy", with articles such as books and papers scattered over the floor. There was a great deal of blood on the floor of the cell.

Vasos testified he took four boxes that were in the cell and filled each one with the papers and other loose items he found on the floor. He marked each box: "Jackson Property." There was a fifth carton in the hallway just outside the cell door, which he marked as "Jackson Property — Hallway." He took all five cartons to his office in Sacramento for finger-print and related analysis.

On August 24, 1971, George Murray, an investigator for the California Attorney General's office, came to his office to look through the five cartons. Vasos said that Murray discovered an 18-page, single spaced, typed document in one of the cartons.

Harris picked up the 18-page document — it was the diary — now marked for identification as People's Exhibit 126. Vasos said it was the same document discovered by Mr. Murray.

Vasos said he was asked to examine the document for latent finger-print impressions. Each page of the document was now stained with the pink chemical Vasos used in his work. He found one identifiable print on the bottom of page two belonging to Angela Y. Davis. He found fifty-two identifiable prints belonging to George Jackson.

SIXTH witness, phase two, George D. Murray. George Murray testified he was an investigator for the California Attorney General's office. He said he went to Sacramento on Monday August 23rd, 1971, and again on Tuesday, August 24th, 1971, and searched through the five cartons taken from San Quentin Prison on August 21st, and marked "Jackson Property."

On August 24th, Murray continued, he discovered a manila envelope in one of the cartons. He opened the envelope. With him at the time was Assistant Attorney General Albert Harris. Inside the envelope they found an 18-page, single-spaced, type-written document. Yes, it was the same 18-page document now marked for identification as People's Exhibit 126. Then. Murray said, he and Mr. Harris read the document. Murray had it xeroxed, and gave the original to Spiro Vasos for fingerprint analysis.

Harris asked Murray on the direct examination:

Q. What was your purpose in looking through the boxes that you have described to us?

A. I was searching for any evidence that might link Ms. Davis to Mr. George Jackson.

Q. And had someone directed you or requested you to do that?

A. Yes, sir.

Q. Who was that?

A. You, sir.

THE JURY was excused. The defense made a series of arguments for the suppression of all the letters and the diary. People's Exhibits 120 and 121 (the apartment letters), the defense contended, were illegally seized by FBI agent McCord in violation of the specifications of the search warrant which clearly delimited the purpose of the search of Ms. Davis' apartment to "unlawful flight."

The seizure of People's Exhibit 125 (the Thorne letter) confiscated by Officer Kelsey and Captain Moody at Soledad Prison was illegal, the defense contended, in contravention of the lawyer-client privilege which prohibits the reading of all such communications and enclosures.

The use of People's 126 (the diary) would constitute a serious violation of Ms. Davis' constitutional right to privacy, the defense argued. And much of the diary, if not all of it, was totally irrelevant to the issues in the trial having been written one year after the alleged plot. It would conjure a vast array of issues of no probative value in the case and could be highly prejudicial to Ms. Davis.

Harris stated the diary was not irrelevant. On the contrary, it was the heart of his case. Harris said he intended to call a Lieutenant Sellmer, a San Quentin prison guard, as a witness. Lieutenant Sellmer's testimony would establish the relevance of the diary. Lieutenant Sellmer had observed the meeting between George Jackson and Angela Davis and their respective counsel on July 8, 1971 in the Men's Mess Hall at the Marin County jail. Sellmer would detail, Harris said, the nature of that encounter — the passionate physical involvement of George Jackson and Angela Davis.

Defense counsel raged. There was no secret about the mutual affection and warmth between George Jackson and Angela Davis. And the defense would gladly stipulate to that fact. But we would strenuously object to any testimony from Lieutenant Sellmer. It could have only one purpose: to sensationalize the July encounter, twisting reality to support the prosecutor's perverted notion of the relationship between Ms. Davis and Mr. Jackson. Furthermore, and to the legal point: Ms. Davis' meeting with George Jackson and all their respective counsel, was protected by the lawyer-client privilege of absolute privacy. No testimony as to the nature of that meeting was permissible.

On April 25, 1972, Judge Arnason ruled on the defense motions to suppress the letters, Lieutenant Sellmer's testimony and the diary.

Judge Arnason denied the defense motions to suppress the June 1970 letters — People's 120, 121 and 125.

With regard to the confiscation of Attorney Thorne's letter by Officer Kelsey and Captain Moody, Arnason held that: "The cases are legion in number holding that inmates have no right of privacy to invade and that jailhouse mail is seizable and admissible in evidence."

Arnason did, however, grant the defense motion to suppress the proposed testimony of Lieutenant Sellmer. He said simply: "A defendant's constitutional right to counsel would be seriously and unlawfully proscribed if testimony of this type was permissible."

And, Arnason granted the defense motion to suppress the 18-page diary. However, he said, if the prosecution could edit the diary "so as to preclude all legally inadmissible material," he would reconsider the decision to suppress it.

Stunned by the judge's decision to suppress the diary, Harris pleaded for reconsideration.

Arnason told him to edit it. For the moment the issue was closed.

RETURNING to open court late on the morning of April 25th, in the presence of the jury, Albert Harris read the June letters into the record.

He read in a monotone:

June 2, 1970

Dear George:

I had abandoned all hope of ever seeing the two letters I have just finished reading. I sit down to write to you, not knowing whether or how this will reach you. . . .

Concerning Black Women: I am convinced that the solution is not to persuade the Black woman to relax her reins on the Black male but to translate the "be a good boy" syndrome into a "take the sword in hand" attitude. . . . To take our first step towards freedom we, too, must pick up the sword. Only a fighting woman can guide her son in the warrior direction. Only when our lives, our total lives, become inseparable from struggle can we, Black women, do what we have to do for our sons and our daughters. . . .

George, we must dig into all the muck and get at the roots of our problems. . . . When we are overly protective we attempt to dissuade our loved ones from accepting the burden of fighting this war which has been declared upon us. We cannot be dismissed as counter-revolutionaries. You'd be surprised how many brothers say this. Nor can it be said that we ought to blot out our natural instincts for survival. Why, why is our condition so wrought with contradictions? We, who have been forced into performing the most degrading kind of labor — a sex machine for the white slave master. . . .

The reign of barbarous capitalist society could not have been secure without the continued subjugation of Black people (and they would use any means necessary). "Divide and Conquer." It never fails. Rape the Black woman and make the survival of the race dependent on that vicious rape. No recourse to the Black male except death. After raping the Black woman, give her a piece of the pie. Make the survival of the Black family dependent on a chasm within. Pound into the mind of the Black male that his superiority, his manhood, has been diminished, has been irreparably damaged by the female of the race. Give him no room, no work with which to objectify his potentialities. Convince the female that he is a lazy son-of-a-bitch. The chasm within.

To choose between various paths of survival means the objective availability of alternatives. I hope you don't take this as an apologetic stance. I'm only trying to understand the forces that have led us, Black women, to where we are now. Why did your mother offer you reprimands instead of the flaming sword? Which is equivalent to posing the same question about every other Black woman and not only with respect to the sons, but the daughters too (this is really crucial). In Cuba last summer, I saw some beautiful Vietnamese warriors, all female. And we know that the Algerian War for National Liberation would have been doomed to defeat from the very beginning without the active participation of Algerian women. In Cuba, I saw women patrolling the streets with rifles on their backs defending the revolution. But also young compañeras educating their husbands and lovers, demythologizing machismo. After all, if women can fight, manage factories, then men ought to be able to help with the house, children.

But, returning to the question: we have learned from our revolutionary ancestors that no individual act or response can seize the scepter of the enemy. The slave lashes out against his immediate master, subdues him, escapes, but he has done nothing more than take the first step in the long spiral upwards toward liberation and often the individual escape is an evasion of the real problem. It is only when all of the slaves are aroused from their slumber, articulate their goals, choose their leaders, make an unwavering commitment to destroy every single obstacle which might prevent them from transcribing their vision of a new world, a new man, onto the soil of the earth, into the flesh and blood of men.

Even dreams are often prohibited or allowed to surface only in the most disguised and sublimated form. The desire to be white, the monstrous perverted aspirations of a so-called Black bourgeoisie, created to pacify the masses, and then there is the naturalistic system-oriented desires of a Black woman who is relating to survival of her children...

The point is: given the vacuum created by the absence of collective struggle, the objective survival alternatives are sparce: ambitions of bourgeois gluttony or — like you said — unconscious crime. One path goes thru the front door, the other sneaks in thru the back and is far more dangerous and seemingly far less likely to reach its destination.

A mother cannot help but cry out for the survival of her own flesh and blood. We have been forbidden to reach out for the truth about survival, that it is a collective enterprise and must be offensive rather than defensive. . . .

Anxieties, frustrations engendered by the spectre of a child dead of starvation focus our minds and bodies on the most immediate necessities of life. The "job" harangue, the "make yourself something" harangue. Exhortations, grounded in fear, a fear brought into being and sustained by a system which could not subsist without the poor, the reserve army of unemployed, the scapegoat. Survival instincts perverted and misdirected by a structure which coerces me to kick my jobless man out of the house so the social worker doesn't stop those welfare checks which I need to feed my hungry child. A labyrinthine network of murderous institutions in order to allow my man no flexibility, no room, lets me receive the checks, lets me in the back door to scrub floors (so the reserve labor force remains alive) and has the audacity to consider that a favor in return for which I must submit to the white rapist and/or subjugate my Black man. The principle of (un)Just Exchange is omnipotent.

Frustrations, aggressions cannot be repressed indefinitely. Eventual explosion must be expected. And we, Black women, have much more than our share of them. But with the revolutionary path buried beneath an avalanche of containment mechanisms, we Black women aim our bullets in the wrong direction, and moreover don't even understand the weapon. For the Black female, the solution is not to become less aggressive, not to lay down the gun, but to learn how to set the sights correctly, aim accurately, squeeze rather than jerk and not be overcome by the damage. We have to learn to rejoice when pigs' blood is spilled. But all this presupposes that the Black male will have purged himself of the myth that his mother, his woman, must be subdued before he can wage war on the enemy. Liberation is a dialectical movement — the Black man cannot free himself as a Black man unless the Black woman can liberate herself from all the muck — and it works the other way around. And this is only the beginning. . . . Women's liberation in the revolution is inseparable from the liberation of the male. . . .

I have rambled. I hope I have not been talking in tautologies. . . .

Jon and I have made a truce. As long as I try to combat my tendencies to remind him of his youth, he will try to combat his male chauvinism.

Revolutionary greetings from Che-Lumumba and the Soledad Brothers Defense Committee. . . .

I love you,

Angela

June 10, 1970

Dear George:

The fifth letter came tonight. . . .

Only you can imagine the intense frustration which has accompanied all my daily actions, gestures, thoughts. I have wanted to reach you for so long. But not all has been frustration: vicarious joy in absorbing 2nd person anecdotes out of your past, in catching glimpses of a letter or two written to your family, all the subtle contests to outpraise a beautiful Black warrior. Discussions with Georgia, hidden conversations with Robert (he reminds me very much of my own father). Working together with Penny, Frances. Hard raps with Jon. Nightly musings about George. Daily speeches about struggle, the Soledad Brothers. Pulling together, keeping together the L.A. Soledad Brothers Defense Committee. Along with my normal ambulations of Che-Lumumba activities and problems. Lectures to brain-washed students who subsequently try to convince me of their various conversions (during oral exams). All this has been the extent of my life-activity. Merge this with high tides of unanticipated joy, and you can begin to reconstruct my life of the last month. . . .

It must be close to 2 A.M. I've just returned from Franklin and Kendra's (50th Street) — the meeting place for the Soledad Defense Committee. My room-mate Tamu, and I have been evaluating the meeting. She has gone back to see after her crying six-month old infant. The meeting: loud, encouraging, overcrowded, with brothers and sisters eager to learn, work, revolt, build. First, an intense effort to deal with the grim reality of what we must do. A brother/friend of mine and Che-Lumumba comrades, UCLA student, leading member of the Black Students' Alliance — found Sunday on a deserted road with two bullets in his head. We have been unable to make any break-throughs. Pigs? Minutemen? Not one clue. What is certain, however: this was undoubtedly a political assassination. I think back to your first letters. Your reflections on preparedness. Absolutely correct. Precautions must be taken — for it is certain that this will not be the last attempt.

Accepting the murder of a comrade in struggle is not easy. Our first instinct is rage — to return the attack even if it be blind. We must learn to plan the attack, gear it towards the total annihilation of the monster and not just stick pins in the soles of his feet. The dead brother was a revolutionary. I am sure his last thoughts must have been similar to what Che said about death. His remarks are more than appropriate in an era of encroaching fascism: "Wherever death may surprise us, it will be welcome, provided that this, our battle cry, reaches some receptive ear, that another hand reaches out and takes up weapons and that other men (and women) come forward to intone our funeral dirge with the staccato of machine guns and new cries of battle and victory." But, Che also taught us that the first duty of the guerilla is to remain alive — to carry on the struggle. Saturday, we will be present at one more funeral.

George, we have an overwhelming amount of research before us — material, concrete facts concerning the California Penal System. Some brothers and sisters have already gone to work on it. We would really appreciate it if you could give us some ideas — as many as you can bear. Pandora's box must be sprung. This is what they fear. Pour out your ideas on how to move in a present day above-ground defense organization.

Correct theoretical analysis does not presently constitute the movement's forté. Generally speaking, there is no great lack of spontaneity because there is no great lack of provocation from the enemy's side. . . . But (there is) a profound deficiency . . . a fundamental problem: strategy and tactics. The lazy become either revisionists or anarchists. Well-worn paths of the past which are embarked upon as a consequence of succumbing to that bourgeois disease of historical amnesia.

To digress a moment on that question of historical amnesia: it is ideological nourishment for bourgeois power — conscious absent-mindedness with regard to the bourgeois revolution or else the transformation of that revolution into an innocuous historical curiosity irreparably inflicted with rigor mortis. Why? Because to take on the burden and responsibility of a revolutionary past would be to realize, as Tom Paine said in 1791: "As revolutions have begun, it is natural to expect that other revolutions will follow." Although the bourgeoisie rose to power by waging revolutionary struggle, it abhors the idea that a continuation of that struggle, this time on the part of the exploited masses, led by their former Black slaves, must mean their destruction as a class. The bourgeoisie has an historical vision. History is a thing of the past, dead, closed; its proper abode the museum. It cannot see the explosive present. The future as history. Although we must deal the blow, it is they who are committing suicide. Good riddance.

Revolutionaries have no excuse when they fall prey to that sickness, amnesia, with regard to history. Our struggle did not spontaneously erupt with this generation, nor with the preceding one. A lot of brothers and sisters don't see this. It is true that the struggle is being intensified; but too, imperialism is closer to its grave as a result of its own internal dynamic. . . .

Revolutionary ancestry can be traced as far as history spirals down into the past. As Black people, we must look back to that first posture of resistance exhibited in face of an unnatural white master/monster who set out to destroy humanity. There is a direct line from Nat Turner, Denmark Vesey, all the brothers and sisters who stood up and revolted all the way to Malcolm X, Huey Newton, George Jackson, Ericka Huggins. Past struggles — the most far-reaching victories as well as the most dismal failures — must be living lessons in revolution. Above all, we do not want to repeat past errors, if knowledge/memory will help us avoid them.

Black capitalism is just another manifestation of the Booker T. Washington error. Du Bois ran all that down.

We know what went wrong with Nat Turner's revolt. And we should have learned long ago the dangers of informers, agents, provocateurs.

Concerning non-violence: the spectre of Sharpesville, South Africa — thousands machine-gunned, kneeling in the streets, protesting apartheid, non-violently. Non-violence as a philosophy is a philosophy of suicide.

Etc., etc., etc., only the simplest, most obvious lessons have been named.

It is very late — my eyes are closing. Perhaps I'll pursue those ideas tomorrow. For the moment I'll unleash my thoughts and allow them to go in their instinctive direction toward wild wanderings, fantasies. George — my feelings for you run very deep. My memory fails me when I search in the past for an encounter with a human being as strong, as beautiful, as you. Something in you has managed to smash through the fortress I long ago erected around my soul. I wonder what it is. I'm very glad. I love you.

Hasta la victoria, siempre

Angela

                                                                June 22, 1970
Dear George:

What activities am I supposed to take off from? Since that day I described to you, my life, all my life-efforts have gone in one direction: Free George Jackson and the Soledad Brothers. Man, I have gotten into a lot of trouble, but I don't give a damn. I love you. I love my people. That is all that matters. Liberation by any means necessary. Those means are determined by the nature and intensity of the enemy's response. The American oppressor has revealed to us what we must do if we are serious about our commitment.

If I am serious about my love for you, about my love for Black people, I should be ready to go all the way. I am. Hence a myriad of problems which I must talk to you about at some point.

We came up to San Jose yesterday . . . for a statewide Soledad gathering/meeting. We are now sitting in the meeting. . . . Jon and I will work on the essay. It should be possible to get it together in some form as soon as we receive the material. I think it is one of the most important things to be done.

I try to avoid artificial modesty. But I must admit that I hardly recognize myself in your words. This doesn't mean that I won't do everything in my power to be that person, that Black woman you see in me. I think the most beautiful Black revolutionaries, men and women, are prisoners of war. I received a message from someone who's getting out soon, yesterday. I love him too, like you do.

It has taken me a while to convince myself that George is not a dream, a wish dream which evaporates when it comes down to hard realities. But you are those realities and everything else. I wish I could touch you, we could touch each other here now.

We must go. A six-hour drive to Los Angeles lies ahead. I will write soon. I am completely free, fired, grades in. There are beautiful plans ahead.

This morning Jon and I were having breakfast, after getting my grade sheets off to Los Angeles air freight. I had left my cigarettes in the car. Jon said, "Stop smoking." I stopped. First time in eleven years I have spent eleven hours without a cigarette. Meanwhile a pipe hangs out of my mouth. It serves the purpose.

                                                    Hasta la victoria!
                                                    I love you —
                                                    Angela

Harris put the letters down. Perspiration poured from his forehead and down the back of his neck. He said: "I think we're ready to call a witness, your Honor. I'm not certain if the witnesses are here or not."

Perhaps a short break would be in order, the judge suggested. Harris looked relieved. "I think we could use it," he said.

25

Phase three. The conspiracy. Harris called forty three witnesses. They were: Spiro P. Vasos, the latent finger-print examiner; Sherwood Morrill, the documents expert from the California State Bureau of Identification; George Murray, the investigator for the state attorney general's office; five San Quentin guards; three police officers; one FBI agent; one auto mechanic; six identification witnesses (civilian individuals who claimed to have seen Jonathan Jackson and/or Angela Davis in the days immediately preceding the August 7th events); nineteen clerks (bank tellers, sales personnel, innkeepers). In addition there was a woman named Mabel Magers, who had known Jonathan Jackson for a few short weeks before he was killed; Otelia Young, who had lived next door to Angela Davis in Los Angeles; and John Thorne, George Jackson's attorney. Thorne's testimony was severely delimited over Harris' heated objections. Thorne invoked the attorney-client privilege between himself and George Jackson, and himself and Angela Davis. His testimony was irrelevent, at best, and to most people it seemed incomprehensible.

As a general defense tactic we resolved to stipulate to that evidence Harris was to present in phase three which was true. That is, rather than have a prosecution witness go on for hours detailing each and every piece of evidence, a defense lawyer would get up and offer to stipulate to the truthfulness of the witness' testimony. Harris was then forced to accept the stipulation and excuse his witness; or prolong the agony with no apparent purpose. He lost with the jury either way.

Harris' case was entirely circumstantial. Thus, his main strategy was to try to establish a preponderance of evidence against Angela, whether or not the cashing of a check or the purchase of two army cots were particularly significant actions in themselves. Through stipulation we hoped to minimize the effectiveness of this prosecution strategy.

Finally, in stipulating to the truth and objecting only to that which was false, we hoped to establish a credibility with the jury. Generally, through the trial, Harris found our tactics disconcerting if not positively destructive of his best (dramatic) efforts.

Spiro Vasos testified that he had conducted an exhaustive chemical analysis of all the weapons, ammunition and assorted paraphernalia found in the van on August 7, 1970, and of the van itself, in an effort to obtain identifiable latent impressions. Harris placed all of the guns and bullets, books and pamphlets on the counsel table directly in front of the jury. Harris picked up each item. Vasos identified it. Harris assigned it a number and a letter for identification.

The judge interrupted to ascertain which identification number belonged to which set of bullets. Leo Branton interrupted to make sure his numbers were recorded in proper sequence. The jurors strained to follow the proceedings.

Harris picked up a plastic bag containing loose bullets. The bag broke. Bullets clattered to the floor. Harris fumbled. Leo Branton said: "Is there something I can stipulate to?", as he bent over to retrieve the evidence. Harris said: "I think to hazard a stipulation at the moment would jeopardize the entire record in the case." Muffled laughter rippled through the courtroom.

Jessica Mitford, author of the *American Way Of Death*, happened to be in court that day to observe the trial. In a perfectly reasonable tone of voice, as though she was simply making a very sensible observation, she exclaimed: "Look at that! His whole case is falling apart!"

The spectators section erupted into unrestrained laughter. The judge, already flushed, buried his face in his hands and turned aside. And Leo, still trying to be helpful, offered another stipulation (which was testily declined).

Finally, Harris got to the point. He asked Vasos if he had found any identifiable prints on any of the guns, the bullets, the clips, or the boxes of shells. He said he had not.

Had he found any usable latent impressions on the van? One, Vasos said, belonging to Jonathan Jackson.

Had he found any identifiable prints on the book titled *The Politics Of Violence?* He said he found one print on page twenty-four and one print on page twenty-six. Both belonged to Angela Y. Davis.

Howard Moore cross-examined. It was very brief.

Q.   All of the materials which have been gathered and collected in this case to be used as evidence have been submitted to you when appropriate for your examination for latent finger-prints. Is that correct?

A.   Yes, sir.

Q.   And the only prints which you found which you have been able to identify as Ms. Angela Y. Davis is the one print on page two of People's Exhibit 126 (the diary) and the two prints on People's Exhibit 43-D (the book titled *The Politics Of Violence*). Is that correct?

A.   That is correct.

Sherwood Morrill testified he had been determining the authenticity of documents for the California Department of Justice for thirty-eight years. An expert in handwriting analysis, Morrill was called by the prosecution to establish that Angela Davis had written various things. We stipulated to the authenticity of at least twelve different prosecution exhibits, including seven personal checks and one firearms transaction record, all of which bore the signature of Angela Davis.

Morrill was asked to examine the San Quentin Visitor's Register, the log kept at the East Gate of the prison. Every visitor is required to sign the book upon entering and leaving the prison, noting the respective times. Sherwood Morrill testified Jonathan Jackson had signed the Visitor's Register on July 27, July 28, August 3, August 4, August 5 and August 6 of 1970. On August 4 and August 5, the name Diane Robinson appeared directly under Jonathan Jackson's name in the Register, in Jonathan's handwriting, Morrill testified. Ms. Davis' writing did not appear in the Register.

THROUGH clerks, sales personnel, police, San Quentin guards, six identification witnesses and sundry records, Albert Harris now proceeded to reconstruct, in meticulous detail, the alleged conspiratorial pattern. The testimony of the so-called identification witnesses was critical to Harris' case. It was through them, corroborating the testimony of guards and police, that Harris hoped to place Angela Davis in the company of Jonathan Jackson in the three days immediately before the August 7th events at the Marin courthouse.

Ms. Davis had frequented the Western Surplus store in Los Angeles, several clerks testified, for many months, going back to 1969. Western Surplus is a large department store with general supplies, hardware, and a sporting goods section where, among other things, guns and ammunition can be bought.

On May 30, 1970 Ms. Davis was seen in the company of Georgia Jackson and her son, Jonathan, at the Western Surplus store. Ms. Jackson, according to the sales record, purchased 50 rounds of .30 caliber M-1 carbine ammunition and 50 rounds of .380 caliber ammunition.

On June 25, 1970 Ms. Davis was seen in the company of another young man (not Jonathan Jackson) at the same Western Surplus store. The young man purchased an M-68 rifle. According to the sales clerk Ms. Davis gave the young man some additional money in order for him to complete the purchase.

On July 6, 1970, according to the Sales Record, Ms. Davis purchased 100 rounds of 9 mm military ammunition and 150 rounds of .30 caliber ammunition, at the same Western Surplus store in Los Angeles.

The next day, July 7, another clerk testified, Ms. Davis purchased two army cots and 50 rounds of .38 caliber ammunition. The army cots cost $14.66. Ms. Davis paid for the cots with a personal check for the exact amount.

On cross examination the clerk admitted she had no independent recollection of the transaction whatsoever. Her testimony was based upon the records kept in the sales book. She examined the sales book. She agreed with defense counsel that someone had tampered with the entries relating to Ms. Davis' purchases. It could be, she said, that Ms. Davis had not purchased any ammunition on that day.

On July 14, 1970 Ms. Davis spent the night at the Bel-Aire Motel in Berkeley, California. Jonathan Jackson and his father, Lester Jackson, were registered at the same motel. Earlier that day all had attended a court hearing in San Francisco for the Soledad Brothers.

On July 17, 1970 Ms. Davis rented an apartment at 162½ East 35th Street in Los Angeles and moved in.

Otelia Young was Angela Davis' neighbor on East 35th Street. She was supposed to establish that Jonathan and Angela had "shared living quarters." The clear implication of her testimony, however, was to the contrary.

Ms. Young was an elderly Black woman. She had lived on East 35th Street for almost four years. She didn't live there any more.

Ms. Young said she worked five days a week, 12½ hours a day, from seven in the morning, until eight-thirty at night.

Yes, Ms. Young said. She remembered Angela Davis very well. They had talked to each other. As neighbors will, you know. Of course she hadn't realized who Angela was at first.

Did she remember seeing a tall, light complected young Black man accompanying Ms. Davis on numerous occasions?, Harris wanted to know.

Yes. Yes. She remembered the young man. Talked to him too. But she had seen him only once or twice.

Did she know the young man's name?, Harris continued.

Well, she hadn't known his name then, but she knew it now. She had seen his picture on television. His name was Jonathan Jackson.

And did she know what had happened to him?, Harris asked.

Yes, Ms. Young said. She knew what had happened to him. He'd gotten killed.

"Do you recall," Harris continued, "observing the young man carrying any items in connection with Ms. Davis moving into the apartment?"

"No," Ms. Young said.

"Well," Harris persisted, "did you see anyone moving anything?"

"All I seen was books," Ms. Young replied. "Angela carried most of the books. What she had, she carried."

We had nothing to ask Ms. Young. She stepped from the witness stand and walked slowly, with some difficulty, towards the exit at the back of the courtroom. And then she paused and turned back to look at Angela. Ms. Young smiled. She said, "Hi," and gave a little wave with her hand, in a neighborly sort of way.

Angela smiled and waved back.

ON JULY 25, 1970, Harris' next witness testified, Angela Davis was again at the Western Surplus store in Los Angeles. She purchased an M-1 carbine, in exchange for the M-68 rifle purchased a month earlier. Ms. Davis said, according to the clerk's recollection, that the M-68 was defective. A proper Firearms Transaction Form was completed, with Ms. Davis providing the necessary identification.

Also on July 25th, another witness testified, Ms. Davis went to a Sears Roebuck store in Los Angeles and purchased a radiator hose and two clamps to fit a 1969 Ford, for $4.92. She wrote a personal check to pay for it.

On July 29, 1970 Ms. Davis cashed a check for $30.00 at the Security Pacific Bank, West Village Branch, located near the campus of the University of California, in Los Angeles. Ms. Davis was accompanied by a young Black man. The teller had no idea who he was.

On July 30th Ms. Davis cashed a $200.00 check at the same bank. She was accompanied by a young Black man. The teller had no idea who he was.

At midnight on the same day, July 30th, Ms. Davis was stopped and questioned by two San Diego police officers at the San Ysidro border station between Mexico and the United States. She was entering the United States. With her was Jonathan Jackson. Ms. Davis told the officers she had gone down to Mexico for the day to do some shopping and pick up a few things.

One of the officers, Jerry Hoover, testified under cross examination that he had filled out the required "Field Interrogation Form," while questioning Ms. Davis. Next to the printed words on the form, "Reason or Charge," he had written, "Communist," he said.

Further down on the same form, Hoover said, he had written: "Subject was stopped by U.S. customs for possession of subversive literature."

Ms. Davis and Jonathan Jackson were questioned for an hour or so, Hoover testified, and then released. There were no charges.

In the very early morning hours of August 1, 1970, a Los Angeles police officer took Jonathan Jackson into custody. The officer testified he saw "the suspect" shortly after midnight, at the corner of 24th and LaSalle Streets, in a stalled car. The lights were off, and "the suspect," according to the officer, seemed to him to be "hot wiring" the car.

Leo Branton objected to the word "suspect." The judge ordered it stricken from the record and instructed the jury to disregard it.

The officer said he took Jonathan Jackson to the police station on suspicion of auto theft. An investigation showed that the car in question was owned by Angela Y. Davis.

Mr. and Mrs. Jackson, Jonathan's parents, came to the police station a few hours later, the officer said, accompanied by Ms, Davis. Ms. Davis informed the police that Jonathan was driving the car with her permission. Jonathan Jackson was released. There were no charges.

On August 2, 1970, Jonathan Jackson was in San Francisco to attend a reception marking the opening of "Soledad House," a new headquarters for the Soledad Brothers Defense Committee, according to Mabel Magers, a friend of Jonathan's, who also attended the affair.

On August 3, 1970 Ms. Davis purchased an airline ticket at the Los Angeles International Airport, from United Airlines, with a personal check. Shortly thereafter she departed on Flight number 536 for San Francisco. Ms. Davis arrived in San Francisco at 8:31 pm, on the 3rd.

On August 4, 1970 Jonathan Jackson was at the home of Ms. Magers in San Jose. Ms. Davis was not present. Jonathan borrowed Ms. Magers' car, a Volkswagen. Ms. Magers testified she did not see her car again until late in August or early in September 1970, when she retrieved it from a parking lot at the San Francisco International Airport. She had to pay a $43.00 parking fee, she said.

On the afternoon of August 4, Jonathan Jackson arrived at the east gate to San Quentin prison. He signed the Visitor's Register, first recording his own name, and then the name of the woman accompanying him, Diane Robinson. However, the guards told him he had come too late in the day to see his brother. Jonathan left.

Madeline Lucas testified she had gone to San Quentin on the afternoon of August 4th to visit her stepson. A middle aged white woman, Ms. Lucas said she departed the east gate of the prison at 2:10 pm.

As she walked down the ramp she noticed a "young Negro couple" walking up the ramp. She recognized the woman because she had seen her picture on television. It was Angela Davis, she said.

Ms. Lucas said she probably would not have noticed them at all, "but as they approached he said something to her and she replied to him, she reached out and touched his arm, and she laughed. And that's when I looked at her and recognized her."

Asked by Harris to identify Ms. Davis in court Ms. Lucas said she didn't know if she could. Finally she asked if Ms. Davis could smile so she could see if there were gaps in her teeth.

Ms. Lucas got off the witness stand and walked over to the defense counsel table. She hesitated and then pointed to Angela Davis. "I think it is this girl here," she said.

Ms. Lucas admitted on cross examination that on that day in August 1970, she had seen the young woman for only a few seconds. She said she didn't notify any law enforcement people about her encounter with Ms. Davis even after she knew that Ms. Davis had been indicted. She had come forward with her story only a week before.

ON AUGUST 5, 1970 Jonathan Jackson returned to San Quentin prison. The records show that he visited with his brother George Jackson from 11:50 am to 2:15 pm. According to the Visitor's

Register he was again accompanied by Diane Robinson. She remained seated in the visitor's waiting room, while Jonathan saw his brother.

Several San Quentin guards testified the young woman at the prison in the company of Jonathan Jackson on August 5th was Angela Davis. All said they had seen the young woman for only a few seconds in passing. All said they had not recognized her at the time, but realized who she was later, after they had seen her picture on television in connection with the August 7th events.

One of the guards, William Twells, stated that a "colored girl" who was "light-complected, about five-foot eight, in her twenties . . . short African hairdo . . ." had accompanied Jonathan Jackson to the prison on August 5th. Twells said the "girl" was Angela Davis.

Twells said he saw her for only a few seconds as he was passing through the visitor's waiting room. She was standing at the foot of the steps leading into the visiting room, waving to George Jackson. He said he told her she couldn't do that and he ordered her to sit down. She did.

Then, Twells said, he continued on his way through the waiting room and on to his next assignment. Asked what that was, Twells said: "I was in the gun rail for segregation feeding." Asked to explain what that meant, Twells said he was guarding the inmates in "B" Section, while they were being fed.

LATE in the afternoon on August 5th, Angela Davis purchased a 12 gauge, single shot, shot-gun at the Eagle Loan Pawn Shop in San Francisco. Ms. Davis filled out the necessary Federal Firearms Transaction Forms, using proper identification. In fact, both clerks had recognized her right away.

The defense was prepared to stipulate to the facts of the purchase, but Harris insisted upon calling both clerks from the pawn shop to testify. Harris should have accepted the defense offer. David Lifson, an older Jewish man, was one of the clerks. His testimony reduced Harris' conspiratorial plot to a farce. Lifson said he had worked in the pawn shop for sixteen years. He told the court how excited he got that day in August when he realized

that a big celebrity was in his shop. He told us the rest of the story:
"I said to Frank [the other clerk], 'You know who you're waiting on?'

"And he said, 'Yeah, I know who I'm waiting on. It's Angela Davis.'

"I said, 'I just thought if you didn't know, I'd tell you . . .'

"It was sort of a whisper," he explained. "It was supposed to be inaudible so she couldn't hear."

Harris continued the direct examination:

Q. Did you have a conversation with the customer after that?

A. Yes, I did.

Q. What was the nature of the conversation . . .?

A. Well, as I remember, I asked her how she thinks she's going to come out with her being dismissed [from the University] and whether she thought she would probably be reinstated—words to that effect— I also asked her—do you want to hear it?

Mr. Harris Yes. Go ahead *(Laughter)*

The Witness Well. I also asked her if she was still on salary. I think she said "Yes," and we sort of had a little rapport, do you know what I mean?

I asked her for her autograph. And she says: "I'll be happy to." And she gave me—wrote her signature "Angela Davis" on our calling card. And what happened to that card I'll never know. I thought I had it in my wallet. but I can't find it. *(Laughter)*

Lifson testified he broke down the shot-gun for her, and put the pieces in a box, so she wouldn't have to carry the gun out into the street. Harris dwelled on the details of how he broke the gun down. Lifson answered for a while. Then he said he really didn't think any of that was very important.

More laughter.

Lifson, said, "Maybe I ought to charge an entertainment fee."

The spectators burst into applause.

Harris said, "I am a little afraid to say anything at this point."

David Lifson said, "A little humor never hurt anybody."

AUGUST 6, 1970. 8:04 am. Jonathan Jackson went to the Hertz

Truck Rental Agency in the Mission District in San Francisco, made a $40.00 deposit and rented a yellow van. The clerk testified Jonathan asked for a later model, but the yellow van was all he had available. Jonathan took it.

10:30 am. A San Quentin guard, Gordon Farrell, testified he saw Jonathan Jackson enter the courtroom in the Marin County Hall of Justice, where the James McClain trial was in progress. Farrell explained he was in court because he was the escort officer for McClain. Jonathan Jackson entered the courtroom carrying some sort of attache case. He stayed only a very few minutes.

10:44 am. Jonathan Jackson placed a collect call to the Hertz Rental Agency in San Francisco. The call was placed from Fleming's Mobil Gas Station, located on North San Pedro Road, just to the south of the Marin Civic Center.

James J. Finnegan, the senior security agent for Pacific Telephone Company in San Francisco, testified that according to the operator's record, the call lasted exactly five minutes and 41½ seconds.

Alden Fleming, a middle-aged, heavy-set, white man, who ran the Mobil Gas Station remembered Jonathan Jackson.

"A colored man and a colored girl," Alden Fleming testified, walked by the gas station about 10 o'clock that morning, and then "they came back and I was working in my office and the colored man came in the service station and told me he had a problem with his car."

Fleming said the girl waited outside.

The man told him, Fleming said, that he had rented a Hertz van, and now it wouldn't start. Fleming suggested he call the Hertz people and find out how much they would pay to get the van started.

The young man called the Hertz people, Fleming continued. They told him they would pay up to $6.00 for repairs. Fleming said the young man didn't seem to know what to do and went outside to consult the woman.

Fleming said he accompanied the young man outside. The man and woman talked to each other. The conversation lasted less than a minute. They decided, Fleming said, to have him try to start the van.

Fleming said he called over his son Peter, and told him to take the tow truck and drive over to the parking lot in the civic center and start the van.

Fleming said his son and the couple left and returned a few minutes later, with the van running. The young man came inside the office and paid him $6.00, and then the couple left.

Fleming said the young man was Jonathan Jackson. He said the young woman was Angela Davis.

Fleming said he did not recognize Ms. Davis at the time, but when he saw her picture on television a week later in connection with the August 7th events he made the connection and realized he had seen her in the station on the 6th. Fleming said he called the sheriff's department.

Sometime later, Fleming continued, an investigator from the attorney general's office came over to see him, and showed him a series of photographs and asked him to identify Angela Davis. He did.

On cross examination it was established that Fleming was shown nine photographs. Four of the nine were pictures of Ms. Davis. In each one she was shown speaking to a large crowd, and standing in front of a microphone.

Of the five other photographs one was too blurred for Fleming to be able to distinguish the features of the individual; three were mug shots of Black women, all with straight hair, and with the names of each subject appearing directly below the picture; and the fifth photograph was of an older Black woman.

Leo Branton asked Fleming if he would agree, that given the fact that four of the nine photographs were of Ms. Angela Davis, and that it was simple to eliminate the other five from consideration, that the investigator had suggested to him just who Angela Davis was?

Fleming agreed and said, "I can't see how it could be any other way."

THREE other people were in the Mobil Gas Station that morning and observed the young couple: Michael Vonada, a local Marin County fireman who was visiting with Alden Fleming in his office when Jonathan walked in; Dennis Bosch, Fleming's mechanic; and Peter Fleming.

All were called to corroborate Fleming's testimony.

Michael Vonada said he happened to stop in to see Alden Fleming that morning because he was in the neighborhood. Vonada said that while Jonathan Jackson was on the telephone to the Hertz people, he stepped outside the office. He saw a "female person" and said "Hi" to her. Vonada said he couldn't remember whether she said anything in response, or just nodded. He said he stood outside about two or three minutes, and then decided to leave and go back to the fire station.

Vonada described her as a "young Black woman, Afro hairdo, about 5'6" to 5'8", light complected . . . good looking lady . . . Her teeth spaced apart. She was smoking a black cigar . . ."

Vonada testified the young woman was Angela Davis. He said he did not recongize her at the time. Later, he said, when he saw her picture in connection with the August 7th events he realized who she was, and called Alden Fleming. Fleming he said, had already called the sheriff's department, so Vonada did not. Later he was contacted by investigators from the attorney general's office.

On cross examination it was determined that Vonada was able to distinguish Angela Davis from other light-complected Black women wearing Afro hairdo's because of the space between her teeth. He said he noticed this on August 6th. He said that's what enabled him to "distinguish her from other photos."

"What was she doing," Leo Branton wanted to know, "standing there with her mouth open so you could see the gaps between her teeth?"

Peter Fleming drove Jonathan Jackson and the young woman to the stalled van. He identified the young woman. It was Angela Davis, he said.

On cross examination Peter admitted that on August 17, 1970, when investigators first showed him a picture of Angela Davis he had no idea whether or not she was the woman he had seen on the 6th.

Leo's cross examination continued:

Q.   And when you testified before the Grand Jury on November the 10th of 1970 and you were shown photographs you were not positive or certain which of the photographs was the photograph of the lady who was in the station on the 6th, were you?

A. No.

Q. As a matter of fact you were shown a photograph of a lady with her mouth open so that her teeth could show, and you said you didn't remember seeing those kind of teeth . . . Isn't that right?

A. I said, I couldn't remember about the teeth.

Dennis Bosch, Fleming's mechanic, testified he "vaguely" remembered seeing the two people come into the service station that morning. He said the young man was in his teens, and he "had on sharp looking clothes . . ." Of the young woman, he said, "She was Black. She was tall. She was almost about 5'8", 5'9", slender, build, fair complexion, Afro hair style. She had a light blouse, mini-skirt. She wore boots."

Bosch said he wasn't sure of the woman's identity. He didn't know who she was.

There were no questions on cross examination.

AUGUST 6th (continued). 11:25 a.m. Jonathan Jackson signed in at San Quentin's East Gate to visit his brother. He was alone.

Louis F. May is white, in his late thirties. He testified that in August of 1970 he was a prisoner at San Quentin. He operated a visitor's tram to deliver people from the parking lot to the prison gate, if they wanted to ride rather than walk, he explained.

On the afternoon of August 6th, May testified, he saw Jonathan Jackson drive a yellow van out of the parking lot. With Jonathan Jackson in the van was a young woman. She was sitting in the front passenger seat. May said the young woman was Angela Davis. He recognized her from all the news media pictures he had seen.

May said he saw Jonathan Jackson and Ms. Davis in the same yellow van the day before, August the 5th. (Previous testimony, of course, had already established that the van wasn't rented until the morning of the 6th.)

On cross examination it was established that May had been in and out of San Quentin since 1961 on various charges ranging from second degree burglary to "lewd and lasvicious conduct and acts upon the body of a child under 14 years of age." In 1966 May was given an indeterminate sentence from one year to life for indecent exposure.

Louis May told Howard Moore he had been paroled from San Quentin on December 1, 1970 — three months after he told investigators he had seen Angela Davis at San Quentin on August 6th.

May said his parole was originally set to end on November 21, 1975.

Instead, he testified, he had already been discharged from parole, as of February 4, 1972 — twenty days before the start of Ms. Davis' trial.

Howard Moore concluded his cross examination of Louis May. A defense investigator had gone to see him. Did he remember that?

Yes, May said. He remembered. She was "some young hippie-type girl."

"And did you tell the defense investigator," Howard asked, "that: 'I'd have sold my mother down the drain to get out of prison'?"

"No," May answered. He had never said that.

SOMETIME after three o'clock in the afternoon on August 6th, Marin County Deputy Sheriff James Layne testified, Jonathan Jackson (again) came into Judge Haley's courtroom to attend the McClain trial. Layne said he told Jonathan Jackson that court had been adjourned for the day. Jonathan left.

Lois M. Leidig, an older white woman from Portland, Oregon was on vacation on August 6, 1970, and had come to San Rafael, California to visit her lifelong friend, Barney Joseph.

Ms. Leidig said that Mr. Joseph had been following the McClain trial, and she went with him on the afternoon of August 6th to attend that trial.

Court was still in session, she said, when a young "Negro male" entered the courtroom. She turned around to look at him because he was carrying a brown paper bag, and the rustling of the paper distracted her. The brown paper bag was filled with clothing.

Ms. Leidig said that McClain turned around several times to look at the young man. Ms. Leidig positively identified the young man as Jonathan Jackson.

Leo Branton conducted the cross examination. He asked Ms. Leidig if she had written a letter on January 11, 1971, to her friend Barney Joseph, which commenced "Dear Barney" and was signed, "As ever, Lois."

Ms. Leidig said she had written the letter.

And in discussing the Angela Davis case in that letter, Leo continued, "I want to ask you if you didn't write this to your dear friend Barney: 'I am hoping for this verdict for all those anarchists involved. Our national courts need a verdict like this. Our former Governor Hatfield, who is too much of a dove, had capital punishment done away with in this state.' Did you write that?"

"Yes," Ms. Leidig replied.

"The truth of the matter is, Ms. Leidig," Leo continued, "you don't remember seeing anything in that courtroom, but you are testifying in this way because of the fact that you want to see this defendant convicted; isn't that a fact?"

"That is not a fact. And I am under oath. And don't you call me a liar!" Ms. Leidig snapped.

AUGUST 6th. 7:45 p.m. Jonathan Jackson checked into the Holland Motel in San Francisco. The innkeeper said he had no independent recollection of the incident. The records showed that Jonathan Jackson took a room for two. The innkeeper said he had no idea who, if anybody, accompanied Jonathan Jackson.

On August the 7th, shortly before 2 p.m. (and after the events at the Marin Civic Center) Angela Davis rushed up to the Instant Service Counter of Pacific Southwest Airlines (PSA) at the San Francisco International Airport, Gate 34, Pier E, according to Marcia Lynn Brewer, the ticket agent on duty that day.

Ms. Davis had no baggage. She bought a ticket for Los Angeles and paid for it with a personal check, using her driver's license for identification.

On cross examination Ms. Brewer explained that PSA operates the Instant Service Counter to provide fast service for late-arriving passengers trying to catch one of PSA's hourly commuter flights to Los Angeles. Ms. Davis acted no differently than other commuter passengers, Ms. Brewer said. And, Ms. Davis had indeed been told that if she hurried she could still catch the two o'clock flight because on August 7th, 1970 that flight was twenty minutes late in its departure for Los Angeles.

HARRIS now turned his attention to the mysterious telephone number found in Jonathan's wallet. The number was 588-9073. There was no area code.

James Finnegan, the man from Pacific Telephone, testified there was such a number in area code 415, the area code for the San Francisco Bay Region. That number, he said, was assigned to a coin operated telephone installed on March 4, 1970, near the American Airlines ticket counter at the San Francisco International Airport.

Harris showed Finnegan a photograph of the telephone booth and asked him to identify it. He did. The picture depicted a telephone booth that seemed to be in an isolated, out-of-the-way spot.

On cross examination Howard Moore showed James Finnegan another photograph of the same telephone booth. Finnegan identified the booth again. The defense photo wasn't cropped. This time the booth was shown to be the very first one nearest the American Airlines ticket counter, in full view of everyone around the counter.

ANTICIPATING Harris' examination of Finnegan, Leo Branton had asked Marcia Brewer a few additional questions. In response to Leo's questions about the location of different airlines at the San Francisco airport, Ms. Brewer testified that American Airlines is located in the new, South Terminal. And, she said, next to American Airlines is Western Airlines. Western Airlines, she continued, does have hourly, commuter flights to Los Angeles. Finally, Leo asked Ms. Brewer if PSA was located in the same terminal building as American Airlines and Western Airlines. No, she said, PSA is located in an entirely different building, in the old, Central Terminal.

Harris' theory was that Angela Davis had been waiting at the telephone booth near American Airlines (in full view of everyone passing by) for five or six hours on the morning of August 7th, waiting for this telephone call from Jonathan Jackson.

From Marcia Brewer's testimony Harris would now have to argue that when the call didn't come through from Jonathan, Ms. Davis panicked. But instead of rushing to Western Airlines (immediately adjacent to American Airlines) to catch a flight to Los

Angeles, she ran all the way to the Central Terminal Building to take PSA.

THROUGH a series of defense-offered stipulations, and a few witnesses, Harris established that Ms. Davis left California on August 15th, arrived in Chicago and went to the home of David Poindexter. In the next several weeks she and Poindexter were in Detroit, Miami and finally New York.

FBI Special Agent Lawrence J. Monroe testified he was in charge of the New York City "fugitive investigation to locate and apprehend Angela Davis."

Monroe said he arrested Ms. Davis and Mr. Poindexter at approximately 6 p.m. on the 13th of October 1970 on the seventh floor of the Howard Johnson's Motor Lodge, in mid-town Manhattan.

Monroe said he immediately escorted Ms. Davis into a room in the hotel and had her finger-printed.

Monroe explained the reasons for this procedure. He said the FBI had received scores of telephone calls from people all over the country, who had claimed to have seen Angela Davis. He said he had personally received many such calls from people identifying "look alikes" to Ms. Davis. Monroe said he had to take the fingerprints to make sure he had apprehended the right woman.

26

Phase two. *Passion (Continued.)* In chambers Albert Harris was extraordinarily blunt. He told the judge, the day after he had suppressed the 18-page diary, that without it his case was in great jeopardy: "Very frankly, we feel, your Honor, that it's very difficult for us to proceed without it."

The importance of the 18-page letter was three-fold, Harris

said. In the first place it was a totally private document, and therefore it truthfully revealed the depth of feeling the defendant had for George Jackson in a way the June 1970 letters did not. "That's the key thing, I think. . . . It's totally private and sincere . . . meant for nobody's eyes except George Jackson."

"The second thing is," Harris continued, "that this letter changed our whole theory of the case. I made that clear in our opening statement. . . ." After the discovery of the diary, and after thinking about it, Harris said, he came to the conclusion that he had been wrong. Angela Davis had not plotted to free the Soledad Brothers for political reasons. On the contrary, Harris said, he realized that, "It was a purely personal enterprise on her part."

Third, Harris said: "I am not unmindful of this case in terms of public attitudes towards the administration of justice. . . ."

"The defendant," he continued, "has been claiming for a year and a half that this is a railroad, it's a frameup and so forth. . . ."

"This case," Harris said, "is important not only to us and to the defendant. It's important to the nation. . . . It's important to the world. . . .

"And I don't think the full truth about this case will ever be known," he concluded, "unless this letter, or at least significant parts of it, are admitted into evidence and it is heard in open court so that the public and the world knows about this event. It's of an importance that I just can't overemphasize. . . ."

"Mr. Harris' remarks are very revealing . . ." Leo responded for the defense. "For a prosecutor to admit that he kept a defendant in jail on a charge of murder for a period of almost a year and had no case against her and did not discover the evidence which was going to make his case against her until August of 1971, more than a year after the crime was committed and more than ten months after she was in custody . . . is a callous and shocking display of unconcern for the rights of human beings . . . I think the only honorable thing would be for the attorney general to dismiss this case. . . ."

Albert Harris wasn't about to dismiss anything. He told the judge he and his assistant would not shirk their responsibilities. They would not cringe before what the judge had described as a Herculean task, he said. They would undertake to edit the 18-page letter. And they would excise those portions of it which the judge had already deemed prejudicial, irrelevant and inadmissible.

The judge said: "If the attorney general wishes to take up that labor and present something to me that I think would be admissible, I'm always happy to have it. . . ."

The session ended.

Two days later another session in chambers was had. Harris presented counsel with a new exhibit, People's 126 A — an edited version of the 18-page letter. It was now seven pages.

Leo Branton said he understood that lawyers were supposed to cooperate with the court and other counsel in determining whether or not evidence was properly admissible. But, speaking for himself, Leo said, he just couldn't participate in this. "We are attempting to pry into the most intimate, the most personal expressions of another human being because the prosecution in this case feels that without doing that he cannot get a conviction. . . ."

Leo left the judge's chambers.

Howard Moore denounced the proceedings as an obscenity.

Harris said he was sorry Mr. Moore found the letter obscene.

Howard said: "It's not the letter I find obscene. It's your pawing over it that's obscene."

HARRIS went through his edited version of the letter, page by page, paragraph by paragraph — which paragraphs he wanted in and which ones could be taken out.

Now, on page eight, for example, Harris said, we feel this paragraph here is very important and should remain in. Harris read from the letter:

> A scene frozen in my mind: I am standing in the little glass cubicle downstairs, standing, waiting, loving, desiring, and then hot cold rage when the chains begin to rattle as you slowly descend the stairs surrounded by the small army of mindless but armed automatons. I, your wife, your comrade who is supposed to love you, fight with you, fight for you. I'm supposed to rip off the chains. I'm supposed to fight your enemies with my body, but I am helpless, powerless. I contain the rage inside. I do nothing. I stand there watching, forced to assume the posture of a disinterested spectator, the whole scene perceived through glass, laboratory-like, mad at them for thrusting this upon me, mad at myself for doing nothing. Mad at myself too because I

could not fail to see how much counter force you were exerting upon yourself, each step, long, hard, unwilling to be restrained by chains and pigs, your entire body with each foot movement in a hard sway. As I re-experience this now, my pulse beats faster, I begin to breathe harder, and I see myself tearing down this steel door, fighting my way to you, ripping down your cell door and letting you go free. I feel as you do, so terrible is this love . . .

"Now the charge in this case," Harris had finished reading the paragraph and resumed his argument, "is that the defendant conspired with others . . . to bring about the freedom of George Jackson through violent means. This is the charge. Here is . . . the admission. . . . The relevance is clear. We think it should go in evidence."

Howard said, "It is disgusting."

Harris said, "Thank you, Mr. Moore. I appreciate that."

Howard said, "Your point of view is disgusting. You are a distorted bigotist. It is disgusting absolutely."

Harris said, "I appreciate those remarks. I am glad the record shows them."

THE ENTIRE letter, Howard Moore again reminded the court, revolved around Ms. Davis' encounter with George Jackson, one year after the events she was charged with plotting. That scene, Howard continued, on page eight, which the prosecution insisted was relevant, that scene frozen in her mind, was the scene on July 8th, 1971, when George Jackson was brought to the Marin County jail to see Ms. Davis.

"It is very clear," Howard continued, "from this letter that what she is responding to is her own predicament. She is in jail. She sees a man she greatly admires and loves. She is describing her own feelings of helplessness. . . . She is helpless to do anything. She is a spectator. She talks about what she is supposed to do, what she should do. She is imagining. . . .

"Judge, you are being asked to put this before the jury as indicative of her state of mind a year earlier. . . . Judge Arnason I just can't see you participating in something that is so atrocious."

Doris Walker said she found her colleague's description of the proceedings as obscene particularly appropriate. For the letter was, she said, more than anything else, what Ms. Davis herself had called it, "a stream of consciousness." And how does one edit a stream of consciousness, Doris asked, without destroying it?

Indeed, Doris continued, that is exactly what the prosecutor had done. He had destroyed it. He had deliberately misrepresented its context, and then he had systematically excised all of Ms. Davis' references to music and philosophy and political theory, all of her descriptions of childhood and people, her experiences in college.

"The law," Doris went on, "recognizes the real foundation for the emotional reactions which have been expressed here today." For the law requires, she said, that "verbal utterances must be taken as a whole, not by fragments or by summary." Editing, she argued, would inevitably result in grave distortions of meaning and context.

Doris maintained that the letter/diary had to be taken as a whole or not at all. And, she said, the judge had already, correctly, ruled it inadmissible. It had no relevance whatsoever to any of the issues in this trial.

The judge said he would take the matter under submission.

TWO WEEKS later Judge Arnason presented counsel with a new, revised version of the 18 page letter/diary, marked for identification as 126 B. The judge himself had edited it. If the prosecution wished to offer 126 B in evidence, the judge said, he would grant the motion.

On Monday morning, May 15th, Harris moved for the admission of 126 B. The defense objected *pro forma*. The judge said he understood that all defense objections previously raised were being reasserted. And they were denied. The diary was in evidence.

Late on the afternoon of May 15th, in a hushed courtroom, Albert Harris read the diary, as edited, into the record. He read in a monotone:

> 7/8. I'm totally intoxicated, overflowing with you wanting you more than ever before. An hour and a half since the last embrace. You're in your cell. I'm in mine . . .
>
> You're still here. I see you. We are one in this indestructible together-

ness they'll never be powerful enough to wrest away from us. I do not
need to say that I feel envious of you now, your powers of expression.
With words effortlessly at my command, like you, I could express the
nuances of all those vast feelings I felt today, feelings which have been
accumulating over centuries, today infinitely magnified, achieving
dimensions of the concrete and now still undiminished in their intensity.

That so much love could exist anywhere, in any two people, even
between us, I never realized. It makes me feel all fluttery and kind of
weak, not though in the sense of succumbing to weakness, for it makes
me feel so much stronger, stronger with your strength without end,
my life-long husband. The most perfect moments of my life, that is
what today was all about, a perfection screaming for more love . . .

As I was pulling myself together then after the court appearance in
Salinas — or better, as I tried futilely to replace the habitual reigns — I
was struck by a similar sense of inexorably succumbing to you, just
you, being absorbed by that huge, beautiful man with whom I had
instantly and unexpectedly fallen in love.

This morning, as I had begun to relate to you, this morning, shortly
after eight-thirty, as I walked the few yards — treading in air, it
seemed — from this cell towards you, towards you, questions, an
incalculable number whizzed through my mind. All the millions of
pieces I had tried to fit together into a picture which would somehow
begin to reflect the reality of the arrangement perhaps different than
the perfection I had already conceived. I knew before that I would be
overwhelmed, that despite all the efforts, all my efforts during our
past, you were going to be something more, surpassing all that I had
managed to discover before — but how?? How??

If you knew what a hard time I'm having tapping out these few words
— my mind wanders into other worlds full of you, my chin in my
hand, reality-fantasies lure me away from this machine and before I
know it the minute-hand on this other machine they've just installed,
has made half a rotation. Today, today, though time seemed short,
eight hours but a moment, it was a moment containing a happy, loving
eternity. Temporarily, I'll say goodby, goodnight. I'm going over to
the other cell, to rejoin you.

Love you, love you with love even more unbounded, even more unconquerable. Your life-long wife.

7/9. I'm just back from the San Francisco court appearance . . .

The last thing I want to do is to have you worrying because you think I am depressed, and there is much, too much to be happy about right now. I am still floating drunk full of you. Do you mind if I indulge myself for a few minutes and recall those things which make me laugh all over? I like your long, unruly hair, and the way it was sticking all up in the front, that child-like mischievous expression on your face when I pushed it down over your forehead . . .

It all adds up to one thing: I love you, George Jackson, every inch on the outside and all the depths and dimensions of your awe-inspiring mind. With this, I will close for now. Please accept this stumbling, sometimes misshapen love I am trying so hard to surrender to you. Good night, George. Your wife sends infinite love.

. . .

Do you know how elated I was when I first discovered that you loved me? I have told you before, but I feel like talking about it once more. I think I was sort of embarrassed when your mother and sisters first told me that you were in love with me. You said something like you fell in love with a picture. I thought then that you had probably fallen upon a picture which made me look better than my actual appearance and that you weren't that serious at all, but then at that time I did not know George Jackson. He was an abstract figure, a brother I had to fight with and for. Even then I felt good each time one of your family said something about how you felt about me, but I didn't know how to respond to something so remote until I saw you and, stunned, I just stared the entire time. All the time I was sort of admonishing myself to stop acting like a young love struck girl experiencing her first great infatuation. Just control yourself. You will soon get over it. That is what I kept telling myself during the trip back, and the next few days in L.A.

During the trip back we took the seaside road through fog and curving mountain ways and green woods and water. I was beside myself with happiness. . . . I must stop now for the day. Loving you and growing ever more impatient.

7/11. I have been trying to wait until the Sunday visitors come and leave.

7/12. When I suggested that thing about our having a more public marriage ceremony, it was conceived only for its publicity value. The first vow was absolute. It fused us for life, and, if we did have a ceremony, we would not be more married than we are now. It would only be an affirmation of what already exists, for the benefit of others. George, I love you. George. George. I love you totally. Your wife.

7/16. Under any circumstances I'll love you to the end. I'm glad we saw each other when we did. It makes me realize that I have not always been as alone as I feel at this moment.

7/23. I hope you are feeling better than I. Send some message today before things deteriorate any further. I love you, George.

Harris walked from the lecturn back to the counsel table. He said, "Your Honor, the People rest their case."

27

Throughout the trial we had been gathering in the lawyers' office at the end of each court day to collectively assess the day's events. These sessions often lasted late into the night or on into the next morning. They were brutally frank. The lawyers did not spare each other, and those of us on the NUCFAD staff who participated in various sessions, didn't spare them either.

Every prosecution witness was important, each cross examination vital. How or why something was or wasn't done by one or another lawyer became the subject of endless debate. The daily ordeals left each of us angry and exhausted. And yet somehow we'd appear in court a few hours later, scrubbed and smiling, seemingly refreshed, calm and united, ready for the next prosecutorial thrust.

Through all the yelling a clear consensus did finally emerge. By the end of the prosecution we were firmly convinced that legally Albert Harris did not have a case.

Harris had told the jury, in his opening statement, that he would prove that there had been a conspiracy, the object of which had been the freedom of the Soledad Brothers.

The only firm testimony he had elicited to suggest any sort of prior agreement between principals in the August 7th events had been McClain's purported question to Jonathan in Judge Haley's courtroom: "Did you bring the tape?"

Everything else suggested the absence of a plan: the confusion in the courtroom, the confusion in the corridor outside the courtroom, the departure through the north arch, walking 200 yards across an open lot, to a brightly colored yellow van, in apparent disrepair.

None of Harris' witnesses could agree on what, if anything, McClain had said as he got into the elevator. It certainly wasn't a serious demand for the freedom of the Soledad Brothers. Harris' star witness, Gary Thomas, couldn't remember hearing anything about the Soledad Brothers. The testimony tended to confirm the defense conjecture that McClain had shouted some sort of a slogan.

It was obvious from the cross examinations, certainly of James Kean and Captain Teague, that several witnesses had testified they had heard mention of the Soledad Brothers in a deliberate attempt to implicate Angela Davis.

THE THEORY that this had been a plot to free the Soledad Brothers seemed transparently absurd. Harris maintained there had been an elaborate plan to force their release and yet, even according to his own witnesses, the demand was apparently made as an afterthought by one of the prisoners (not Jonathan) as he stepped into an elevator, to a reporter who failed to mention it to anyone.

Harris had said he would prove that Angela Davis had had prior knowledge of a conspiracy and had consciously assisted Jonathan in executing it. And yet everything she had done, most of which we had stipulated — cashing checks, shopping in Mexico for the day (which is a common occurrence in southern California), allowing Jonathan to borrow her car, travelling to San Francisco, were routine, everyday activities.

It was clear that Angela and Jonathan had not been living together. It was clear that they had not spent the night of August 6th together at the Holland Motel. It was clear that Angela and Jonathan had been friends; and the incidents at the Mexican border, and with the Los Angeles police, suggested Angela had been protective and concerned.

Spiro Vasos had testified he could discover no fingerprints belonging to Angela on the van, or on any of the weapons, or on any of the boxes of ammunition or on the attache case or on anything else, except a book which obviously belonged to her.

Sherwood Morrill had testified Angela had not signed the Visitor's Register at San Quentin, which tended to support the defense position that she had not been there.

As for the prison guards and the eye witnesses who had allegedly seen Angela on August 4th, 5th, and 6th in the company of Jonathan Jackson, their testimony was virtually worthless. Their racism, bias, motive for testifying were manifest. We thought only two of the witnesses had any credibility at all. One was Michael Vonada, the fireman who testified he saw Angela at Fleming's Mobil Station on August 6th, and the other was Madeline Lucas, who had visited her stepson at San Quentin on August 4th and testified she had seen Angela entering the East Gate of the prison at approximately 2 o'clock that afternoon.

Their credibility was minimal. Even the FBI agents arresting Angela Davis had to take her fingerprints to confirm her identity, and FBI agent Monroe had testified that scores of people had claimed to have seen Angela Davis all over the country. False identifications had been made, and frequently.

Surely the jury would not believe that Angela Davis had walked into a pawn shop in San Francisco and purchased a shot-gun with the knowledge that it was going to be used two days later in an escape attempt, and had not only used proper identification, but had signed her autograph for the clerk!

Harris' theory about the mysterious telephone number in Jonathan's wallet that had Angela standing around the American Airlines ticket counter for five hours on August 7th was ridiculous.

And the notion that Angela had fled the San Francisco Bay Area on August 7th had been all but demolished by the testimony of the PSA ticket agent who confirmed that Angela had been told that if she hurried she could catch the 2 o'clock flight to Los Angeles because there had been a twenty minute delay in its departure that day.

Angela's June letters to George contained nothing incriminating. The letters hardly conveyed a sense of uncontrollable passion. In fact, they contained passages which refuted Harris' case. On June 2nd, for example, she had written:

> We have learned from our revolutionary ancestors that no individual act in response can seize the scepter of the enemy. The slave lashes out against his immediate master. He subdues him. He has escaped, but he has done nothing more than take the first step in the long spiral upwards towards liberation, and often the individual escape is an extension of the real problem. It is only when all the slaves are aroused from their slumber and articulate their goals, choose their leaders, make an unwavering commitment to destroy every single obstacle which might prevent them from transmitting their visions into a new world, onto the soil of the earth, into the flesh and blood of men . . .

The diary contained nothing incriminating. It had been written more than a year *after* the events she was accused of plotting. And even with Harris' monotonal rendition, it had read like a poem.

As the prosecution drew to a close we faced the critical decision: should we put on a defense? From a strictly legal perspective we should not have needed one. A closing argument should have been sufficient to shred the last remnants of Harris' case.

But this was no ordinary criminal proceeding. This was a political trial reeking with chauvinist demagoguery, male supremacist stereotypes and anti-communist melodrama. If the jury was badly infected with any of those assumptions, if they presumed Angela's guilt rather than her innocence, the end could be catastrophic. Without a defense, however minimal, we weren't sure the case could be won.

Doris and Margaret had been preparing the affirmative defense for weeks. They had interviewed scores of prospective witnesses: former prisoners, criminologists, and psychologists, who could testify about the realities of the California prison system and the struggle to change it; Angela's friends and comrades in the Soledad Brothers Defense Committee and the Che-Lumumba Club of the Communist Party; her colleagues in the Philosophy Department at UCLA; her family; others with whom she had been associated in school or in the struggle to free the Soledad Brothers—Professor Herbert Marcuse, Reverend Ralph Abernathy, State Senator Mervyn Dymally, actress Jane Fonda; and the two surviving Soledad Brothers themselves, John Clutchette and Fleeta Drumgo.

If we put on this kind of a broad defense there would be many risks. The more witnesses we presented, the greater the possibility that one or more might become confused or disoriented during what was sure to be a merciless cross-examination. If the jury failed to believe one defense witness, just one, it could jeopardize the entire defense.

After an agonizing debate we finally resolved to present what we called a pin-point defense. We would attack the strongest links in the prosecution's case. We would counter the authenticity of the eyewitness identifications that placed Angela and Jonathan together on August 4th, 5th and 6th, and we would explain Angela's ownership of the guns, Jonathan's access to them, and her purchase of the shot-gun in San Francisco on August 5th. Angela would not testify. The closing argument would provide ample opportunity to expose the racist slurs, sexual innuendos and political essence of the prosecution.

28

The defense presented twelve witnesses in two and a half days. Susan Castro, a young white woman was director of the Model Cities Day Care Program in San Francisco. She had been an active member of the Soledad Brothers Defense Committee in San Francisco.

Shortly after the indictment was returned against George Jackson, John Clutchette and Fleeta Drumgo, she said, she attended several of their pre-trial hearings in Salinas, California.

She saw three Black men brought into the courtroom. "They were chained. Their legs were chained. They had chains around their waists. Their arms were chained to their waists. They had difficulty walking. Some papers were given to them. They could not reach for them because of the restrictions of the chains. I was very moved by it. I was very concerned that it should take place."

Ms. Castro said as a result of that experience she became a member of the Soledad Brothers Defense Committee. She attended the opening of the Soledad House in San Francisco on the Second of August, 1970.

A couple of days later, Ms. Castro recounted, Angela Davis telephoned her. They arranged to meet for lunch the following day at the home of a mutual friend, Juanita Wheeler, where Ms. Davis said she was staying.

Ms. Castro arrived at Ms. Wheeler's home shortly after 12 noon, on Wednesday, August 5th. She and Angela had lunch together. They discussed the work of the Soledad Brothers Defense Committee.

Angela had some criticisms and suggestions concerning the work of the San Francisco Committee. In particular, "she expressed very deep concern about the fact that there were not many Black people . . . participating in the day to day work and that the committee had to broaden itself, had to reach out to the Black community . . .",

After lunch she drove Ms. Davis to the Soledad House. "Angela had never seen it and I wanted to show it to her." They arrived about two thirty in the afternoon. They met Jonathan Jackson at the house.

Ms. Castro said she remained about forty-five minutes and then left to return to work. She had intended to take Angela back to Ms. Wheeler's house, but Jonathan offered to instead.

Ms. Castro also testified about discussions concerning security for the Soledad House, in which she had participated. Jonathan Jackson had been present at some of those meetings. The concern had been "how to carry on the work of the committee and yet protect the contributors and the lists of names and the people who were living in the house from illegal attacks." The use of weapons to protect the house had been contemplated, she said.

On cross examination Harris wanted to know if anyone else was present at Ms. Wheeler's home at the time Ms. Castro said she had met Angela Davis for lunch.

She said no one else was present on that occasion.

Harris asked if anyone "other than Jonathan Jackson, now deceased," was at the Soledad House when she and Ms. Davis arrived there that afternoon.

Ms. Castro said other people were there. She couldn't recall exactly who among the regular staff members was present at that particular time.

"In other words," Harris said, "you can't point to any other single human being whom you can identify who can corroborate the testimony that you have given here today?"

Leo objected and Harris withdrew the question.

JUANITA Wheeler, an older Black woman, said she had known Angela Davis for quite a few years. Ms. Davis had stayed at her home on a number of occasions.

Ms. Wheeler said she had been employed by the *People's World*, a weekly newspaper in San Francisco for 21 years.

On the Friday preceding the opening of the Soledad House, Carl Bloice, the editor of the *People's World*, told her that Angela Davis was coming to San Francisco. He asked if Angela could stay at her home. Ms. Wheeler said she could.

Sometime after the Sunday opening of the Soledad House —Ms. Wheeler said she thought it was on Monday, August 3rd, but she wasn't certain—Angela Davis arrived at her home. Whatever the exact date she arrived late in the evening, around 10:30 or 11 o'clock.

Angela stayed with her for four or five days. She slept at the house each night. She and Angela had breakfast together each morning before she left for work. She left for work around 8 o'clock.

Ms. Wheeler said on the day Ms. Davis was to leave San Francisco, she packed her bag (a small overnight bag) in the morning and put it in the trunk of her car. Carl Bloice borrowed her car sometime later that day and drove Ms. Davis to the airport.

On cross examination Harris' principle concerns were to establish Juanita Wheeler's sponsorship of the Angela Davis Defense Committee in San Francisco, her visits to Angela at the Marin County jail, and her 21 year association with the *People's World* and the Communist Party.

MARVIN Stender, a San Francisco attorney, had served as a legal advisor to the Soledad Brothers Defense Committee. He testified that on Thursday morning, August 6th, at approximately 10 o'clock he received a telephone call at his office from Angela Davis. She was in San Francisco and wanted to talk to him.

Stender said later that morning he met Ms. Davis and drove her to Berkeley. In the car they discussed various problems associated with the Soledad Brothers defense. They arrived in Berkeley about 12 noon. He left Ms. Davis off at a home on Oregon Street in south Berkeley, and continued on his way to the law library at the University of California.

Stender also testified about a police raid on the Soledad House conducted late in the evening on Friday, August 14th, 1970 — one week after the events at the Marin Civic Center. In his capacity as legal advisor to the Soledad House he was called shortly after the raid. Ms. Davis' sister, Fania Jordan, had been taken into custody.

Stender said he went to the police station to see about Ms. Jordan. He entered a large room at the station house. "I saw a young woman seated in a straight back chair in the middle of the room. There were four or five men, all in business suits, around her. They were questioning her. I saw Mr. Harris and several other law enforcement people whom I knew.... I demanded they either arrest Ms. Jordan or release her. They let her go."

Stender said no warrant for Ms. Jordan's arrest had ever been issued. No warrant to enter or search the Soledad House had been issued either, he said.

On cross examination Harris wanted to know if Stender had told the attorney general's office or any other law enforcement agency about "this meeting you say you had with Ms. Davis on August the 6th, 1970."

"No, Mr. Harris," Stender replied. "On the basis of my work with this case I didn't really believe that your office was particularly interested in finding out the truth...."

CARL BLOICE, Black, in his early thirties, was the editor of the *People's World*. He said he had known Ms. Davis for almost three years. They were very good friends.

Bloice testified that late in July 1970 he received a letter from Angela informing him that she would be in San Francisco during the first week in August. He arranged for her to stay with Ms. Wheeler.

He saw Ms. Davis for the first time that week on Tuesday, August 4th, at about 8:30 in the morning. She came to his office at the *People's World*. They met together for approximately two and a half hours. Angela was concerned about coverage of the Soledad Brothers case in the paper, and hoped that a special series of articles could be prepared.

Bloice said he next saw Angela on Wednesday, August the 5th, in the evening. She, Ms. Wheeler, and he, had dinner at the home of a mutual friend in San Francisco.

On Friday August 7th, Ms. Davis arrived at the office of the *People's World* around 8:30 in the morning. She worked there until about 1 o'clock in the afternoon. At that time, Bloice said, he drove her to the San Francisco Airport in Ms. Wheeler's car. At the airport he parked in the press parking lot. They went inside the Central Terminal and to the PSA ticket counter in the main lobby. Ms. Davis, he said, had been intending to take the three o'clock flight to Los Angeles. However, the ticket agent in the main lobby told her if she rushed she could still make the two o'clock flight. She hurriedly left.

Bloice said the next time he saw Ms. Davis she was in the Marin County jail.

Harris' cross examination took a bizarre and unexpected turn. Harris demanded to know if Carl had received a telephone call from Angela Davis sometime in the week or two immediately following August 7th, 1970. Carl said Angela had not called him. Harris insisted she had. Carl denied it. Back and forth it went. Finally Harris got specific:

Q. I want to direct your attention, Mr. Bloice to August the 15th of 1970 — that's eight days after the events at the Marin Civic Center — and I want to ask you if you received a phone call from Angela Davis on that day?

A. No.

Q. Did you receive a telephone call about 9 o'clock in the morning on

August the 15th, 1970, from the Los Angeles International Airport from a Miss Jamala?

A. Not that I recall.

Q. Do you know a Miss Jamala?

A. Yes, I do. She is a friend.

Q. Didn't Ms. Davis use the name Miss Jamala?

A. Never in my presence.

Q. Mr. Bloice, isn't it true that this call, in the name of Miss Jamala made on August the 15th 1970 from the Los Angeles International Airport was in fact a call from Angela Davis just before she left for Chicago?

A. No.

Q. You knew Ms. Davis was going to Chicago; didn't you?

A. No. I had no idea where she was.

Q. Are you a member of the Communist Party, Mr. Bloice?

A. Yes I am.

Q. Isn't it a fact, Mr. Bloice that what you testified to here today is just plain not true? Isn't that a fact?

A. No. That is not true.

Carl was uncomfortable. Harris knew it. Carl had no recollection of this telephone call. Harris obviously had the records from the telephone company which certified that some call from a Miss Jamala had been made that morning. Harris was certain the call had come from Angela. Harris seized upon Carl's reluctance to admit having received it. He had his first defense witness pinned into a corner and he wasn't about to let go.

By the most extraordinary coincidence, Jamala — the real Jamala — was in court that day. It was the only session throughout the entire trial that Jamala, who lived in San Francisco and had a small child, had been able to attend. We were sitting next to each other in the courtroom. She remembered the telephone call very well. It could be easily explained. We passed a note to Leo Branton.

Leo asked Carl a few questions to clear the record:

Q.   You do not remember receiving a call on August the 15th of 1970 from Miss Jamala; is that correct?

A.   I have no recollection of it.

Q.   All right. But you do know a Miss Jamala; don't you?

A.   Yes, I do.

Q.   Is Miss Jamala in the courtroom?

[There was a pause for a minute or two as Carl scanned the spectators section.]

A.   Yes, she is.

Q.   Is it Ms. Angela Davis?

A.   No.

Q.   You don't know any alias or pseudonym or phony name for Ms. Davis, do you?

A.   No.

Q.   Would you point out Miss Jamala, the person who was referred to by Mr. Harris, if she is in the courtroom?

A.   She's right there [*indicating*].

"Miss Jamala," Leo said, "would you stand up, please?"
Jamala stood.
Harris turned to see.
He looked absolutely stunned.

AN EBULLIENT Leo Branton called an unexpected defense witness.

Carola Broadnax testified that because she was Black she had thought it appropriate to adopt an African name. She had chosen Jamala.

She had placed a telephone call to Carl Bloice on the 15th of August 1970 from the Los Angeles International Airport. "That was the day of Jonathan's funeral," she explained, "and several of us, including myself were at the Los Angeles airport to board a plane to come to the funeral, and I made a call to Carl to let him know the time we would be arriving so there would be someone at the San Francisco Airport to pick us up."

VALERIE Mitchell was a young, Black woman who had been active in the Soledad Brothers Defense Committee in Los Angeles. She was a member of the Che-Lumumba Club of the Communist Party. Strikingly beautiful, poised, she began her testimony explaining that she was widely known by another name, which she preferred, an African name, Tamu. It was a Swahili word, she said, and it meant "sweetness."

Tamu said she and Angela Davis were very good friends, and had lived together for several months in 1970. Angela moved from her apartment in July 1970, shortly after Tamu's daughter was born, so the second bedroom could be used for the baby.

Her house had become the center for the Soledad Brothers Defense Committee and the Che-Lumumba Club. Supplies and equipment, including a mimeograph machine, were kept in her home. People were constantly coming and going.

In July and August of 1970 a gun rack was kept in her home in a hall closet. On the rack were several weapons including two carbines, one of which had a collapsible stock. A Browning automatic was kept in a drawer on the lower part of the rack. Ammunition and clips were kept on a shelf in the closet above the rack. The closet was usually kept closed by a sliding door, but it was not locked.

Angela was the registered owner of the weapons. They were occasionally used by members of the Che-Lumumba Club for target practice. The practice was conducted at ranges open to the public for that purpose.

When Angela moved to the new apartment in July 1970 she did not take the weapons with her. They were left in Tamu's house, in the hall closet.

Tamu said she had known Jonathan Jackson well. He frequently came to her home. On Saturday, August 1, 1970, Jonathan came to her house and asked to use the mimeograph machine. He was printing some leaflets for the Soledad Brothers Defense Committee. He worked for some time. Tamu left the apartment to run some errands. When she returned, Jon was gone.

Later that day she and another friend drove to San Francisco. They arrived very late that night. They attended the opening of the Soledad House on Sunday, August 2nd. Tamu returned to her home in Los Angeles very early Monday morning, August 3rd.

A week later, on Saturday, August 8th, Tamu continued, Angela Davis and Franklin Alexander came to her home. They were distressed, deeply upset, They asked whether or not the weapons were still in the gun rack. Tamu had no idea. She had no occasion to go into the closet in more than a week. They looked in the closet. Both carbines were gone. The Browning automatic was gone. The ammunition and clips were gone.

"What, if anything, did Franklin say?" Leo continued the direct examination.

"Do you want me to tell you everything he said?," Tamu asked.

"Yes," Leo replied. "Tell me what he said."

"Franklin said 'Oh shit!' " Tamu recalled, "and Angela said, 'Oh, no!' "

Tamu continued. Angela and Franklin had a newspaper with them containing details of the episode at the Marin Civic Center the day before. They feared that some of the guns Jonathan had used may have been registered in Angela's name. Angela and Franklin asked her when she had last seen Jonathan. Tamu told them of his visit the previous Saturday.

Tamu said Franklin and Angela left her house. The next time she saw Angela she was in the Marin County jail.

ELLEN Broms, a young white woman, lived and worked in Los Angeles. She was employed by the county as a social worker.

Ms. Broms testified she had known Franklin Alexander for over ten years. They were close friends. They had met in the early sixties when both had been students at Los Angeles City College. She saw both Kendra and Franklin socially, and had met some of their friends, including Angela Davis.

Ms. Broms said on Friday evening, August 7th, Franklin and Angela came to her home for dinner. They arrived between 7:30 and 8 o'clock. Kendra was not with them. Both seemed very relaxed through dinner. They had been intending to go to a movie after dinner, but they couldn't agree on what to see. They remained at home instead, listened to records, played scrabble.

At approximately 10:30 Franklin received a telephone call from Kendra. Following her call Franklin turned on both the radio and the television to listen to the news. They heard the 11 o'clock reports.

"There was a description," Ms. Broms said, "of the shoot-out where a judge was killed and two convicts and also a young man who had brought in some weapons."

Angela became terribly upset. "She couldn't believe Jonathan was dead. She kept saying, 'He is so young.' She just couldn't believe it. She started to cry," Ms. Broms said. Angela became so distraught, Ms. Broms continued, that she finally insisted she take a tranquilizer, and that both she and Franklin spend the night.

The next morning, she said, her husband or Franklin, she couldn't remember which one, went out and brought back a newspaper. Angela and Franklin read the details of the Marin episode. There was a picture of Jonathan holding a carbine. Both thought the carbine looked similar to one Angela owned. Then there was reference to a shotgun in the story. Angela said she had given Jonathan a shotgun on Thursday. He was to have brought it to the Soledad House. It was to have been used for security.

Franklin and Angela left to go to Tamu's house.

ROBERT J. Beren, a special agent with the California Department of Justice, attached to the attorney general's office, was the next defense witness. He testified he was in charge of the investigation to ascertain the assignment of the telephone number found in Jonathan Jackson's wallet.

Beren said he knew Jonathan Jackson had resided in Southern California. Nevertheless, he had limited his investigation to the San Francisco Bay Region and checked telephone numbers within the 415 area code only.

James Finnegan, Pacific Telephone's chief security agent, was back on the witness stand, this time for the defense. Finnegan testified that at the instruction of defense counsel he had made the necessary inquiries to determine if the telephone number found in Jonathan Jackson's wallet could have been assigned to a number in the 213 area code, in Southern California.

Finnegan said there was such a number assigned to a private residence, from May 1970 to July 30th 1970, in Huntington, California, a Los Angeles suburb. The number was discontinued after July 30th for non-payment. Given the short duration of its operation it was possible the number had not been listed in the telephone directory.

ROBERT H. Buckhout, an assistant professor of psychology at California State University, Hayward, was qualified as an expert witness and testified about the reliability of eye-witness identification.

Dr. Buckhout's credentials were impeccable. Most of his research had been conducted for the United States Air Force, until his retirement a few years earlier with the rank of captain.

Dr. Buckhout said on the basis of his experience and research it was his opinion that most eye-witness identifications were unreliable because of what he termed the "marginal conditions for observation."

Buckhout described more than a dozen of these conditions and illustrated some with anecdotes based upon his experiences, or cases he had studied.

The insignificance of the event observed, the shortness of time for observation, the physical condition of the observer (vision, color-blindness, lighting, etc.), social conditioning, a desire to follow a leader, to be a part of history, to conform, were all factors influencing the reliability of eye-witness identification.

For example, Buckhout said, he was involved in an experiment at a university. A black bag was place over the head of a student. Additionally, his entire body was covered. It was impossible to detect anything about his actual physical appearance. He walked onto the campus. Many people, interviewed afterwards and asked to describe what they had observed, said they had seen a Black man with a bag over his head. They assumed he had been trying to make some sort of a political statement.

As another example of social conditioning influencing a person's perception of an event, Buckhout told of an experiment which had been conducted in New York. A group of people were shown a filmed sequence for a very few moments. The sequence depicted a simulated attack. A white man wielding a knife was shown attacking an unarmed Black man.

Asked to recall what they had witnessed, the majority of white people interviewed, reversed the attack and said they had seen a Black man wielding a knife against a white man.

Buckhout described another experiment he had conducted. He drew two lines, one obviously shorter than the other, on a blackboard. He paid a group of people to say the shorter line was in fact the longer one.

Then he brought an innocent person into the room, exposed him to the opinions of the paid group, and asked the person to identify the longer line. Invariably the person identified the shorter line as the longer, to conform with the opinion of the other people in the room.

Buckhout said he had been given the transcript of the testimony of several witnesses in this trial who had identified Ms. Davis on one or another occasion prior to August the 7th 1970. Buckhout said in his opinion, based upon his experience and expertise, all the witnesses had been affected by one or more of the factors he had innumerated.

On cross examination Harris asked Buckhout if this conformity pressure he had described could be great enough to cause people to lie. Buckhout said it could cause them to misrepresent what they had seen.

"And this conformity pressure can arise from a lot of different sources, can't it?" Harris continued.

"Yes," Buckhout answered.

"And it can apply and determine or have an influence on a great many decisions; isn't that right?" Harris asked.

Harris got to the point, "Couldn't this pressure to conform within a small group of people who are committed to a common cause bring about a decision to testify and perhaps to testify untruthfully?"

There was an objection. It was sustained.

CHARLOTTE Gluck was the office manager in the administrative office of the philosophy department at the University of California at Los Angeles. Between August 1969 and July 1970, she said, the office was inundated with telephone calls concerning the retention of Ms. Angela Davis by the philosophy department. The calls were "very distressing." In addition the office was inundated with letters commenting upon Ms. Davis, the philosophy department, the department chairman, and related matters.

Leo introduced in evidence several bound volumes of these

letters. They had been sorted by defense counsel and each volume marked according to category: death threats, psychotic, sexual, etc.

Leo read a couple of samples.

Defense Exhibit, 22—J, a letter addressed to Angela Davis:

> We haven't forgotten the old days Big Mouthed Angela Davis. The Ku Klux didn't fool around with Courts and judges. They acted. Then asked questions. Thank God there are still some left in America who love the U.S. enough to stop this type. Our greatest war is not overseas. Where can this Commie go. She has had her day in front of the camera of T.V. She is marked for life./Signed/A true American.

Defense Exhibit 22-L, a letter addressed to Angela Davis:

> Listen you Commie Bitch. Get your burrhead out of UCLA. We con't need your Commie nigger shit talk. Our problems of the day are keeping Black Panthers from raping white women. Robbery—nearly every market held up is held up by two niggers. And selling dope and raping and killing children white under 12 years of age, and stabbing senior citizens in the back and robbing them.

BEFORE the next witness could be brought into court the judge asked that the jury be escorted out.

Fleeta Drumgo was then brought from the basement holding cell. His feet shackled, a chain around his waist, his left arm chained to his waist, he was placed in the witness box.

The jury was returned.

Fleeta Drumgo was asked to raise his (unchained) right hand. The oath was administered.

Fleeta said he resided in San Quentin State Prison. He said he had been involved in a court proceeding with George Jackson and John Clutchette. They had been popularly known as the Soledad Brothers.

Fleeta said he had known James McClain. McClain had been a prisoner in the Adjustment Center at San Quentin and had occupied a cell adjoining his.

Fleeta said he knew of no plot to escape or to seize hostages to procure the freedom of himself, John and George. Neither McClain nor anybody else had ever said anything about it. The first time he heard about a plot to free the Soledad Brothers was when he read it in a newspaper a day or so after the events.

Fleeta moved. A chain scraped the leg of the witness chair. Leo continued:

> *Q.* Mr. Drumgo, I have here a certified copy of an acquittal in the *People of the State of California vs. John W. Clutchette* and *Fleeta Drumgo*. Are you the Fleeta Drumgo named in this document of acquittal?
>
> *A.* Yes.

Harris cross-examined. He wanted to know if Fleeta had been present at the meeting involving George Jackson and Angela Davis in the Men's Mess Hall at the Marin County jail on the 8th of July 1971.

Leo objected. The judge had already ruled inadmissible testimony detailing what took place at that meeting. Harris persisted. He was not interested in what had been said at the meeting. He wanted to know what had been done at the meeting. Specifically he wanted to know what had taken place between Ms. Davis and Mr. Jackson.

The judge sustained the defense objections. The subject was closed. Harris sat down.

Before the witness could be excused the judge asked that the jury be removed. Fleeta, still in chains, was escorted back to the basement holding cell. The jury was returned.

Leo Branton said: "Your Honor, the defense rests."

29

Five thousand people gathered in San Jose on Saturday, May 20th, 1972. It was the last great outpouring of that movement, born eighteen months before in a Black church in south central Los Angeles, that was about to win the freedom of Angela Davis.

A coalition of 120 national and regional organizations representing every conceivable political tendency and social movement in the progressive spectrum, co-sponsored the event. Its theme was freedom, its resolve unity.

We had wanted Angela to speak, but the judge had denied permission, invoking restrictions imposed by the bail order. She was not even to attend the rally, he said.

We had use of a house across the street from the rally site. Angela watched the rally from the attic window.

James Baldwin arrived in San Jose a few days later. He was to be the guest of honor at a few receptions in private homes to raise still needed funds for the defense.

I picked him up at the airport and drove him to our home. Angela came a while later with Victoria, and later other friends and comrades joined us. We all sat around the living room for hours, each of us regaling him with stories of the trial: Jessica Mitford announcing the demise of the prosecution's case; the police officer in distress shouting, free all our brothers in Folsom; Otelia Young's unforgettable wave; Miss Jamala rising from the spectator's section as in a vision.

Baldwin was roaring with laughter. Angela was sitting on the floor, legs crossed in front of her. For the first time in as long as I could remember she was relaxed, laughing, already reminiscing.

Court reconvened on Tuesday, May 30th. Albert Harris presented his rebuttal witnesses. He had two.

Dr. Bruce Spivey was an opthamologist, practicing in San Francisco. He was qualified as an expert witness. He was asked to evaluate the eye-witness identification made by Alden Fleming, who testified he had seen Angela Davis in his Mobil Station on August 6th. Dr. Spivey wasn't very helpful. He confirmed the opinions offered by the defense expert, Dr. Buckhout. Alden Fleming had not been a very reliable witness.

Harris called his second rebuttal witness, Lester Jackson. Mr. Jackson lived in Pasadena, California. He was employed by the United States Postal Service. He was the father of Jonathan and the father of George.

The jury was excused. Mr. Jackson had already informed the judge in chambers, he would not testify. Harris had insisted upon questioning him in open court.

Harris asked his first question:

"Mr. Jackson, did you drive your wife Georgia and your son,

Jonathan to the Los Angeles International Airport on Saturday morning, August 1st, 1970?"

The question and the desired affirmative answer were intended to impeach Tamu's testimony.

"I had only two sons," Mr. Jackson said. "I just don't want to take part in these proceedings."

"Mr. Jackson," the judge's voice seemed very loud, "I order you to answer the question. Do you understand that if you refuse to answer the question I may hold you in contempt of court?"

"Yes, I understand that," Mr. Jackson said.

"Do you understand," the judge continued, "that if you refuse to answer the question I may impose certain sanctions upon you? I can order you confined in the country jail for five days; I can order you placed in the custody of the sheriff's department until this case is concluded; I can order you to pay a fine. Do you understand that, sir?"

Mr. Jackson said he understood. But he had had only two sons and they were dead and he couldn't take part in these proceedings, "Judge, as a father and a family man I hope you can understand my position."

Jack Tenner, a Los Angeles attorney, retained by Mr. Jackson, addressed the judge. He said the entire proceeding was morally outrageous and legally impermissible. He said he wanted the record to be perfectly clear. Mr. Jackson was not refusing to answer a particular question. To Mr. Jackson it didn't matter what questions were asked. He didn't want to take part in the proceedings at all. The judge said he understood.

Tenner continued. He urged that no sanctions be imposed on Lester Jackson. Certainly, he pleaded, Mr. Jackson could not be sent to jail.

There was a brief recess. Fania moved quietly among the spectators in the courtroom. It was possible, she said, that the judge would impose a jail sentence. Our lawyers weren't sure what was going to happen. In any event, it was important that there be no sudden outburst in the courtroom. If Mr. Jackson was taken into custody we were asked to rise in silent tribute.

Court resumed. Leo Branton appealed to the judge to impose no sanctions. He asked the prosecution to join in that request. Harris refused.

"Mr. Jackson," the judge said, "will you answer the question?"
Mr. Jackson said, "No, sir."

The judge said: "Mr. Jackson, I find you in contempt of court. I will now impose sentence. I fine you $100."

Court recessed for the day. Representatives of the press quickly raised a hundred dollars amongst themselves and paid the fine.

We returned to the lawyers' office. Lester Jackson slumped wearily onto the couch in the front office. Angela sat down next to him, took his hands in hers. There was nothing left to say.

30

The defense was scheduled to make its closing argument on Thursday, June 1st. The judge reserved a seat in the courtroom for his son. Albert Harris reserved another for his wife.

People began gathering at the entrance to the courthouse at 3 o'clock that morning. By 7 a.m. a couple of hundred were standing on line. Only a handful were to get inside.

There were no frivolous theatrics attached to our closing argument. The jury had to be told something of the Black experience in America. They had to understand the intensity of Angela's love for George in terms of her commitment to Black people, and his commitment to the struggle. Only in this way could the jurors be made to uphold the presumption of innocence when they began their deliberations, and believe in Angela's innocence when it was over.

Leo Branton said: "I rise to speak to you today on one of the most important days of my life. . . . I rise to address you as an Officer of this Court, a member of a very noble profession. But more importantly, I rise to address you as a Black man, to defend my Black sister, Angela. . . You have to understand what it is about the history of this country which has made an Angela Davis

. . .," he continued, "and you have to understand what it means to be Black."

Leo sketched three hundred years of history from the horrors of the African slave trade to the nightmare of bondage; from the fugitive slave law to John Brown's raid on Harper's Ferry and Frederick Douglass' flight to England to avoid prosecution as a co-conspirator by hysterical Virginia slave masters; from the rape of the African woman to the Dred Scott decision that said a Black man had no rights a white man was bound to respect; from the betrayal of Reconstruction and the Lynch Terror to the killing of Malcolm X and Martin King and Medgar Evers and Fred Hampton and Mark Clark and the four little girls in the Birmingham church.

"And there is something else," he went on. "Angela Davis is not only Black and a militant, she is a Communist. . . . Surely I don't have to remind you what this country has gone through since World War I. . . . Communists have been put on trial for advocating their first amendment rights. . . . Angela Davis was fired from her job at UCLA because she was a Communist."

Angela Davis did not leave California because of a consciousness of guilt, Leo maintained. No Black person in this world would have wondered why Angela Davis finally fled California after the FBI warrant for her arrest was issued. "They would only have wondered why she allowed herself to be caught . . .," he said. "And that is how you must look at this case, through the eyes of Angela Davis."

"No matter what you say about Angela Davis," Leo went on, "no matter what the prosecution might say . . . I think there is one thing we can agree on. She is no fool . . . this woman is a college professor. You have heard her articulate writings enunciated here by the prosecution. You heard her make the opening statement to the jury. Can you believe she is a fool? Well, in order to find her guilty of these offenses . . . you have got to believe that she is a fool . . . do you think this woman would go out and buy a shot-gun to blow a judge's head off and give her own name and sign an autograph? . . ."

Leo reminded the jurors of the circumstantial and speculative trivia which constituted Harris' conspiratorial theory—from

Angela's everyday, routine activities, to the unreliability of the eye-witness identifications, to her specific rejection of an individual act of escape as a viable form of struggle in her June 2nd letter to George Jackson.

"The prosecution has contended," Leo went on, "that the object of this conspiracy was to free the Soledad Brothers. It is a theory that was concocted by the prosecution in this case only when they decided they could tie Angela Davis into the crime. They must find a motive for Angela Davis to be involved. The only thing they can think of is the Soledad Brothers . . ."

But then, Leo continued, one of Harris' witnesses added something else, on his own initiative. He testified that the escaping prisoners not only demanded the freedom of the Soledad Brothers; but they demanded the freedom of all political prisoners; and the authorities were supposed to have had until 12 noon to free all of them; and the demand was made at 11:15 that morning!

"You know what is the significant thing about this whole business?" Leo asked. "It's rubbish. Rubbish . . ." Whatever the intent of those who undertook to escape on August 7th, 1970, Leo insisted, it had nothing whatsoever to do with freeing the Soledad Brothers. That was a theory advanced by the prosecution for one reason, and one reason only: to put Angela Davis in chains.

Leo prepared to move on to the issue of the diary. It was Harris' characterization of it, and of Angela's love for George that formed the lie upon which the presumption of guilt hung. The diary had to be lifted from defilement. It had to be lifted from even the amenities of judicial etiquette with which Judge Arnason had treated it. The jury had to be able to confront Angela's love for George: to comprehend in some small way the beauty of its intensity; and the courage of its passion. They had ultimately to seek identity with it, as they would seek to identify with any other human experience.

"The sorriest thing about this case," Leo began, "is the lengths to which the prosecution has gone to take words in a letter, words of love and affection of one human being to another and transpose them into something criminal . . . It is an obscenity to delve into the most personal, touching aspects of a person's life, and that is what Mr. Harris has done . . . He has taken words out of context and attempted to make something criminal out of them . . ."

Leo continued. He had done something similar. He had taken words out of context also, but in a different sort of a way. With the help of the playwright Dalton Trumbo, Angela's prison diary had been put into poetic form. It was this poem he would read to the jurors.

"We do not know how deeply Angela Davis felt for George Jackson," Leo said. "We only know how deeply she was able to express her feeling . . . She wrote:

> Do you know how elated I was
> When I first discovered you loved me?
> I did not know George Jackson;
> He was an abstract figure,
> A brother I had to fight for;
> I didn't know how to respond
> To something so remote
> Until I saw you
> And, stunned, I stared
> Like a love-struck girl.
>
> After the court appearance in Salinas
> I was struck with a sense of you—of you
> That beautiful man with whom I had
> Instantly and unexpectedly
> Fallen in love.
>
> During the trip back
> (We took the seaside road
> Through fog and curving mountains
> And green woods—and water—)
> I was beside myself with happiness,
> Loving you and growing ever more impatient. .
>
> I love you
> I love you totally
> I love you to the end
> I love you, George.
>
> . . .

I'm intoxicated
Overflowing with you,
Wanting you more than ever.
Since that last embrace
You're still here
I see you
We are one
They'll never wrest away from us
These feelings—
Accumulating over centuries
Today infinitely magnified,
Undiminished in their intensity.

That so much love could exist
Anywhere
In any two people
Even between us
I never realized.

. . .

This morning—this morning—
As I walked the few yards
(treading in air, it seemed)
From this cell toward you—toward you—
The millions of pieces
I had tried to fit together
Into a picture which would reflect
The reality of the man I love
Would be there—those and more—
In an arrangement more perfect
Than the perfection
I had already conceived.
Though time seemed short
Eight hours but a moment
It was a moment containing eternity.

. . .

Goody bye—goodnight
I'm going early to
That other cell
To rejoin you.
I love you
I love you with love
Unbounded
Unconquerable.

"The life of my people, ladies and gentlemen," Leo continued, "has been one of tragedy, oppression, hatred and injustice . . . The life of Angela Davis for the last two years has been one of terror and agony . . . This case has been a sorry stain on the history of justice in this country. But the last chapter has not yet been written.

"We hope that when you twelve people, tried and true, write the final chapter in the case of the *People vs. Angela Davis,* you will say that you were chosen, you served, you considered and you brought back the only verdict that could comport with justice in this case, and that is a verdict of not guilty . . ."

Albert Harris presented his rebuttal.

Mr. Branton, he said, had spoken at great length about the injustices suffered by Black people in the United States. There was no doubt that Mr. Branton had spoken truthfully, and that his words were meaningful. But *People vs. Angela Davis* was a specific case, with a specific set of facts, from which the guilt of the defendant could be clearly and inexorably inferred.

"You have a job to do," Harris told the jurors. "You have to resolve the facts and apply those facts under the law and decide the only time it is ever going to be decided who was responsible for the killing of Judge Harold Haley and for crippling Gary Thomas . . ."

Harris continued. There had been a conspiracy to free the Soledad Brothers. The evidence was clear and forceful. This had been the purpose of August 7th, and it was the reason for the participation of Jonathan Jackson and the participation of Angela Davis.

Harris went through each facet of his conspiratorial theory and each corroborating detail from 104 prosecution witnesses. Each element of her activity was explored in excruciating detail: Angela's arrival in the Bay Area on August 3rd, her visits to San Quentin on the 4th, and 5th, her purchase of the shotgun on the 5th, her supposed visit to the Marin County Civic Center with Jonathan on the 6th, and to San Quentin and then back to the civic center.

Harris said he had to suggest to the jurors that the defense witnesses had lied. They knew each other well, many of them were associated with a Communist publication called the *People's*

World, they shared activities in the Soledad Brothers Defense Commitees. Susan Castro, for example, had been the Bay Area Coordinator at one time for the Soledad Brothers Defense Committee.

"It is Susan Castro's testimony standing alone on August 5th," Harris contended. "That is it. No corroboration, no record, no nothing. Got up there and testified to a luncheon. Three prosecution witnesses testified that Angela Davis was at San Quentin. I have to suggest to you that Susan Castro was lying. There wasn't any luncheon. Angela Davis wasn't at that apartment. She was at San Quentin . . ."

Harris went on, making reference to the diary. "Suppose," he said, "there had been some question about the authenticity of this letter. Apparently there isn't but suppose there had been some questions as to whether Angela Davis wrote the letter . . ."

Harris asked rhetorically: "Couldn't you just hear Leo Branton? How absurd, how ridiculous. Can you believe that Angela Davis is on trial on these serious charges and in the Marin County jail and that she would write a love letter to the man who is supposed to be the object of the conspiracy? Do you think she is a fool? . . ."

Harris said: "I agree. But the fact is she did it. And the fact is she bought the shot-gun. And the fact is she had been to San Quentin with Jonathan Jackson . . . The fact is she was at that service station and at the scene of the crime . . ."

Harris concluded: "Nothing you do, no matter what verdict you bring in, will do anything to restore Judge Haley to life, to his bench, to his robes, nor will it bring Gary Thomas out of the wheel chair. But what you can do is see that justice is done in this case. I want to ask you to look at the evidence fairly, not blinded by emotion. Evaluate it . . . The evidence can lead to only one conclusion: the defendant is guilty of all three offenses as charged."

THE TRIAL drew to a close. Our committee issued a final appeal: "As the jury begins to deliberate it is absolutely crucial that a massive campaign be launched to demand the dismissal of all charges against Angela Davis . . .

"The ultimate verdict," we wrote, "rests with the people."

31

The case went to the jury at 11 o'clock Friday morning, June 2nd.

We gathered on the lawn in front of the courthouse.

Someone scribbled the word "VIGIL" in big letters on a piece of cardboard and leaned it against one of the concrete planters in the square.

Angela went to the lawyers' office.

More people assembled.

Reporters ambled back and forth between the vigil and the newsroom in the basement of the municipal court.

Angela's family gathered. Sallye Davis and Fania, with Eisa in tow; Angela's father, Frank Davis, her brothers Reggie and Ben, Ben's wife Sylvia, their little boy, Benjy.

Friends came with sandwiches and apple cider.

Reggie and Fania started a game of football.

Eisa and Benjy took turns riding a great dane belonging to a fellow-vigiler, while a beaming grandfather snapped one picture after another.

Across the street from the courthouse was a National Guard Armory. A couple of hundred soldiers were inside on standby alert, waiting for the verdict.

I was sitting on the lawn munching a sandwich when I saw Captain Johnson rush from the sheriff's office. He bounded across the square towards the courthouse. I got up to meet him.

Did I know where Angela was, he wanted to know.

I said I thought she was at the lawyers' office.

No, he said. He had just checked. She wasn't there.

What was wrong, I demanded to know.

He couldn't tell me, he said. But we had to find Angela right away. He asked Fania to come with him to see the judge. They disappeared inside the building.

A moment later Carolyn Craven, a reporter from KQED educational television, hurried from the press room. She was frantic. The words tumbled out in rapid succession: "There's been a hijacking. A plane out of Seattle or going to Seattle or something. A couple of Black men are involved, according to the reports. They're demanding half a million dollars and the release of Angela Davis."

Fania came from the judge's chambers with the same news. She said, "They're crazy . . . All these FBI agents and sheriff's deputies are running around in there with the judge . . ."

We found Angela. She was at the Plateau Seven restaurant a couple of blocks from the courthouse having lunch. The judge telephoned her at the restaurant. He told her to wait there. He was sending a car. She was to come to his chambers.

A few moments later Leo Branton, Howard Moore and Doris Walker hurried past us. The judge had called them. The FBI wanted Angela taken into custody.

Someone got a car and parked it in front of the courthouse and turned on the radio. We listened to a minute-by-minute account of the hijacking.

The hijackers were now enroute to San Francisco, aboard the plane they had commandeered. They wanted four parachutes, the newscaster said. And they wanted Angela Davis to be at the end of the runway in a white dress, with the money and the parachutes.

Rob Baker called the courthouse from our San Francisco office. He reached Stephanie Allan, our press director, in the newsroom. The wire services, radio stations, newspapers, were calling our office demanding a statement. They wanted to know if we had had a prior knowledge of this hijacking? And would Angela Davis go to the airport?

We wrote a statement. Stephanie issued it from the courthouse. We didn't know anything about this hijacking. There was no conspiracy. The whole thing was ridiculous. And no, Ms. Davis was not going to the airport.

Doris Walker came outside for a few minutes. She remained in the secured area. Fania and I talked to her through the fence.

The FBI had wanted Angela to be available to go to the San

Francisco airport. Judge Arnason had told them she wasn't going anywhere. She was staying with him. The hijacking was their problem not hers.

Doris said the judge had sent her out to see if members of the family wanted to come inside and wait with Angela, in his chambers, until this thing was over. The whole family went inside.

The tension eased. Doris and I started to kid around.

"Oh, by the way," Doris said, as she turned to go back inside. "Mary Timothy is the jury foreman."

"Mary Timothy!" I exclaimed. "Just a minute! What else is happening?"

Doris said the jurors had asked for and received all of Angela's letters to George, the San Quentin Visitor's Register for August 4th, 5th and 6th, and one volume of the hate mail sent to Angela while she was at UCLA. The jurors had also asked to see the indictment, but the judge had refused to release it because it was not evidence.

THE DAY after the United Sates had resumed the bombing of North Vietnam— it was the third week of the trial—Ms. Timothy had come to court with a peace button pinned to her blouse. We had appreciated the symbolic gesture. Through the last eight weeks of the trial we had watched her every gesture, sigh, grimace and smile. She, Ralph Delange, Rosalie Frederick and Robert Seidel were our strongest jurors. If Mary Timothy had been chosen foreperson, it had to mean the jury was at least in a positive frame of mind.

But they had asked for the Visitor's Register and the letters. That probably meant they were considering the conspiracy charge first. That could be a good thing. If they resolved that issue and voted an acquittal, the case would be over.

On the other hand, the fact that they had asked to see the register and the letters meant they were divided. How badly divided? There was no way to know.

I WALKED back to the vigil. A crowd had gathered around the car. I went over to catch the latest report on the hijacking melodrama.

Someone said, "The whole thing was a hoax."

I said, "What are you talking about?"

"Listen," the person said, motioning toward the radio.

I listened.

It seemed some FBI agent or other in Seattle had invented the hijackers' demand for the release of Angela Davis. And another FBI agent somewhere else had added the "white dress at the end of the runway" routine on his own initiative.

The plane had just landed in San Francisco. Local police officials had talked with the hijackers. The hijackers didn't know anything about any demand for Angela Davis. They didn't want Angela Davis. They wanted $500,000 in cash and four parachutes.

SATURDAY, June 3rd. We resumed the vigil at 9 o'clock in the morning. The jury resumed its deliberations.

We played with Eisa, Hollis, Benjy, Joshua, Eisa. We talked. We played cards. We played frisbee, softball, soccer, football, frisbee.

Fania performed a series of gymnastic feats on the lawn. She had an appreciative, if easily distracted, audience.

Kate Millett, author of *Sexual Politics*, who had come to San Jose to observe the last weeks of the trial, was involved in a discussion, purportedly on the strategy and tactics of women's liberation. She kept coming back to the trial.

Angela, Kendra, Franklin spent most of the day at the lawyers' office or at the apartment complex where the lawyers lived. Periodically they joined the vigil. Each time they arrived we scrambled up, thinking the jury had reached a verdict.

Howard Moore came out to the vigil about 3:30 in the afternoon. He reported that Ms. Timothy had sent a note to the judge requesting permission to adjourn for the day. However, she wanted to know if they could resume deliberations the next morning, even though it was Sunday.

Originally the judge had proposed that the jurors take the day off. Religious services were to be made available, and an afternoon picnic had been arranged.

Howard said the judge had quickly passed a note back to Ms. Timothy. Of course the jury could deliberate on Sunday, if it wished.

A verdict was near. There could be no other reason for Ms. Timothy's request.

As Howard was leaving he turned to me and said: "Ms. Timothy is trying to make history, isn't she?"

SATURDAY night. We were all invited to a barbecue at the home of Andrew Montgomery. Andrew was a pivotal figure in San Jose's Black community—in the church and in the Black caucus. It was he who had guraranteed that press conference with Sheriff Geary and the Reverend C.W. Washington at the Antioch Baptist Church back in January.

It seemed like the whole neighborhood had turned out to see Angela. We parked a few blocks away and walked the rest of the way to Andrew's home.

The street was alive with people.

Ben Davis had organized a football game. He played pro ball as a defensive back for the Cleveland Browns. He had quite a game going.

Ben and Kendra were in this big huddle down the street. Benny was motioning this way and that. They got ready to make the big play. And then we heard Kendra yelling: "No, Benny! No! That's no good! This way! This way!"

We walked on. I saw Margaret. Then I saw Angela.

Angela was wearing a faded polo shirt and shorts.

Angela and Margaret were jumping rope.

Angela hollered: "Hey! Bettina! Do you remember how to jump double dutch?"

A group of children stood across the street watching Angela jump rope. Right in front was a little fellow, maybe five years old. He was wearing a baseball cap about two sizes too big. Angela saw him and flashed a smile. He ran to her, threw his arms around her waist and hugged her. The rest of the children rushed over, jumped up and down and all around and squealed with joy. They wanted her autograph. She laughed and borrowed a pen and signed whatever it was they shoved in front of her—a cap, a shirt, a shoe.

SUNDAY, June 4th. We resumed the vigil at 9 a.m. The jury resumed its deliberations. At 10:30 Franklin strode across the lawn signalling to me and Charlene and Stephanie. Containing his passion. . .

"The jury has reached a verdict," he said. "Start getting the people together."

Excitement bubbled across the square. Small knots of people clustered here and there, waiting for the deputies to open the gates.

Mickie Lima, the chairman of the Party in Northern California, came. I ran over to him with the news that a verdict had been reached. He already knew. I told him we were sure it would be an acquittal. He was very subdued.

"Take it easy," he said. "It may not be."

I stared into his face. I knew he was already planning the next campaign. . .

The Davis family arrived. Sallye Davis said she didn't want to go inside. She would wait outside. We urged her to come in. No, she insisted. Someone could come out and tell her what had happened.

Angela said, "Mamma. You have to come in. . ."

So Mrs. Davis said okay and we walked around to the back of the building and lined up behind the cyclone fence and waited to be processed. Angela meanwhile had gone into the courtroom through the side entrance with the lawyers as she had been required to do throughout the trial.

They opened the gates at 11:30. Only two people could go in at a time. Each person was searched thoroughly, assigned a seat and photographed. This time there were less than thirty seats reserved for the public.

The assistant attorney general had reserved several seats for members of his staff. Steve Sparacino, the bail bondsman, had reserved a seat for himself. Double the number of deputy sheriffs had been assigned to guard the courtroom.

The press corps was brought in a group from the newsroom. Each reporter was searched, assigned a seat and photographed.

We waited. Angela stepped out into the corridor to wait with us. She was trembling.

We started singing, *"Woke up this mornin' with my mind staid on freedom. . ."*

Captain Johnson appeared. He was in full dress uniform. He said we couldn't sing.

At 12:30 we were told to take our seats in the courtroom.

The jury was brought in. I looked at Ms. Timothy. She was ashen. So was Ralph Delange.

The judge came in. He said, "Ms. Timothy, has the jury reached a verdict?"

Ms. Timothy said, "Yes, your Honor. We have."

The judge instructed her to hand the verdicts to the court clerk. She handed the clerk a sheaf of papers. The clerk handed the papers to the judge.

The judge read the verdicts to himself. His face betrayed no emotion. He shuffled the papers, handed them back to the clerk. He told the clerk to read the verdict.

The clerk read in a loud, clear voice: "In the Case of the *People of the State of California vs. Angela Y. Davis*, Case Number 52613 . . . Kidnapping in the first degree . . . The jury finds the Defendant Angela Y. Davis, Not Guilty."

Angela put her head down.

Franklin began to sob.

The clerk continued: ". . . Murder in the first degree . . . The jury finds the Defendant . . . Not Guilty."

A single gasp filled the room; then silence. There was one more count.

The clerk continued the recitation: "In the Case of the People . . . vs. Angela Y. Davis . . . Case Number 52613 . . . Conspiracy. The jury finds the Defendant . . . Not Guilty."

A great triumphant roar surged across the room.

Fania leaped up in ecstasy, crying.

Angela and Kendra were holding onto each other laughing and sobbing.

There was another roar.

The judge banged his gavel demanding order and silence. There were a few moments. The judge thanked the jurors, and he thanked the lawyers, and the lawyers thanked the judge. And then the judge said: "The defendant is discharged and her bail is exonerated. This trial stands adjourned."

The jury was being escorted out. They were smiling now and some of them were crying. We didn't know what to do. Howard stood up, raised both fists and shouted, "All Power to the Jury!" We started to applaud, louder and louder.

Angela vaulted over the divider into the spectators section and reached for Sallye.

We left the courtroom. Angela stood in the corridor. She could not go on. Leaning against a few of us, her head flung back, her face momentarily twisted in anguish, she wept uncontrollably.

We walked outside. A great crowd swirled around us stomping, shouting, swaying, singing, whistling, laughing, crying.

The jurors came out. They were still on the other side of the cyclone fence. The crowd surged toward them cheering and waving. The jurors smiled and waved back.

Margaret leaned her head against Sallye Davis' shoulder and sobbed.

Leo stood on the courthouse steps and shouted: "It's your victory . . . It's Angela's day!"

"Oh, God!" a woman cried. "This has got to be . . ." Her voice trailed off. Someone hugged her.

"If Albert Harris comes out here," a young man bantered, "I'm gonna make a citizen's arrest!"

Joshua was perched on Jack's shoulders waving his arms frantically, "Mommy! Mommy! Angela's Free!"

I heard Angela's voice: "This is the happiest day of my life . . . People all across the country and the world who worked for my freedom see this as an example of things to come. From this day forward we must work to free every political prisoner and oppressed people everywhere."

NEWS of the verdict was broadcast around the world. Within minutes our offices and homes were inundated with an unending stream of telegrams and phone calls.

They interrupted the Giants baseball game at Candlestick Park to announce the verdict. The San Francisco crowd whooped and hollered as if their team had just scored the winning run.

In Los Angeles members of the Angela Davis Defense Committee ran through the neighborhood with bull horns announcing the victory. Traffic stopped. People rushed from their homes.

A few miles away, in Watts, presidential hopeful George McGovern addressed an election rally of several thousand. The news swept the crowd. A chant started way in the back and rolled on like a mighty wave, "POWER OF THE PEOPLE SET ANGELA FREE!"

EPILOGUE

1

Ruchell Magee, the sole surviving prisoner of the August 7th events, was tried for first degree murder and aggravated kidnapping in San Francisco.

The trial began on November 27th, 1972. The presiding judge was Morton Colvin. The defense counsel was Robert Carrow, court-appointed and serving over Magee's continued objections. Ruchell wanted to represent himself. The prosecutor was Albert Harris.

Harris had to change his theory of the crime again because in order to prove aggravated kidnapping he had to prove that hostages had been taken for purposes of extortion.

In Angela's trial the extortion plot was supposed to have been the freedom of the Soledad Brothers. But Angela had been acquitted. So Harris threw out the conspiracy charge against Ruchell altogether. Then he altered the definition of extortion.

The extortion, he said now, consisted of Ruchell Magee holding a gun on San Quentin guards and sheriff's deputies "extorting" them from executing their official duty to stop the escape.

Ruchell Magee's trial lasted twenty weeks. He was flown from San Quentin to the San Francisco Hall of Justice every morning in

277

an army helicopter. He was brought into court bound in chains.

SOMETIME in December, 1972, Ruchell's mother, Elmar Magee, died in Louisiana. San Quentin authorities finally got around to telling him about it. When Ruchell got to court that Monday morning he asked if there could be a one-day recess.

The judge denied the request. Ruchell protested. The judge ordered Ruchell removed from the courtroom. Ruchell was put in a holding cell. The trial proceeded.

Former President Truman died on December 25, 1972. President Nixon declared Thursday, December 28th, a day of national mourning. Judge Colvin recessed the Magee trial for two days.

A MONTH into the trial Judge Colvin told the lawyers they were taking too much time in picking the jury. He said he had reviewed the transcript and decided that both sides had been repetitious and unduly time-consuming in their questioning of prospective jurors. He told the lawyers that from now on they would have only twenty minutes in which to question each person. And if that didn't expedite matters, the judge continued, he would lay down further guidelines. A jury was selected.

RAMSEY Clark, the former United States Attorney General under President Lyndon Johnson, petitioned the court on behalf of the defendant Magee. Clark asked permission to join in the proceedings as a defense counsel.

Judge Colvin denied the request. He said Mr. Clark had not been admitted to the California Bar and therefore could not practice law in the State of California without special permission from the presiding judge. Judge Colvin said he couldn't grant that special permission because he was not personally familiar with Mr. Clark's qualifications.

Defense attorney Robert Carrow appealed Judge Colvin's decision to the California State Supreme Court. The Supreme Court stopped the trial, reviewed the appeal and granted the defense motion. Ramsey Clark was made co-counsel. The trial proceeded.

ALBERT Harris' key witness was Gary Thomas. On August 5th, 1972—two days before the second anniversary of the Marin events—California Governor Ronald Reagan had appointed the former district attorney to a Municipal Court Judgeship in Marin County.

Judge Thomas testified: "I turned my head and looked at Judge Haley. I saw his face, then an instant later I saw his face dissolve. I saw the flesh move away from the right side of his face as if in slow motion . . . There was a sawed-off shotgun. It was held by Ruchell Magee . . . All I know is that it was in his hand and it went off. . . ."

Ruchell Magee testified in his own defense. The judge ordered his shackles and handcuffs removed. But he said Magee could not testify from the witness stand "due to his performance" in the courtroom. He was ordered to remain seated behind the defense table.

Ruchell said he had made a bid for freedom on August 7th, 1970 to save his own life. "At the time," he explained, "there was a plot to systematically murder me by San Quentin officials, judicial officials, the attorney general and judges. . ."

Ruchell continued: "They wanted to murder me to hide their own crimes . . . They're illegally holding me in prison on a known, fraudulent conviction . . . The state cannot show any legal cause for me to be held in prison. . ."

Ruchell explained the circumstances of his 1963 conviction, the details of his 1965 re-trial on the same charges before the same judge, the false pleas entered by court-appointed defense counsel over his strenuous objections, the doctored trial transcripts, the countless petitions he had filed in every conceivable state and federal court to obtain his freedom.

Ruchell said: "Something kept telling me that [if] I was going to get out of prison, I was going to have to break out. And something else said, 'keep on filing petitions' . . ."

Ruchell emphasized that he had joined the escape attempt "only to take my freedom." He had no intent to hurt anyone or kidnap anyone.

"I did not shoot Judge Haley," he said. "I did not see his face blown away. His face was not like these pictures when I observed him last . . . Judge Haley was waving out of the front window of the van and shouting 'Don't shoot!' Then he waved out of the back window, saying 'Don't shoot!' Shooting was going on when he was waving. . ."

Ruchell insisted that all the shooting was done from outside the van. "I didn't do any shooting. I was trying to hug the floor myself. I was down on the floor when I was hit . . . ," he said.

IN HIS summation Albert Harris told the jurors: "I think it is up to you to decide which of the stories is credible. Either you believe Judge Gary Thomas when he said he saw Magee pull the trigger, or you believe the defense's version that Judge Haley was killed by someone else. Judge Thomas saw the wound inflicted by Magee."

JUDGE Colvin delivered his instructions to the jury. Ruchell made one last appeal for justice. Still in chains, he ripped open his shirt exposing the gunshot wounds he had suffered on August 7th. He shouted: "You are the kidnappers! I was wounded trying to escape to freedom!"

Ruchell Magee asked the judge to read the 13th amendment to the United Sates Constitution abolishing chattel slavery, to the jurors. The judge refused.

The jury began its deliberations. On several occasions the jurors returned to court to ask the judge for further instructions. Then the foreman informed the judge that the jury was deadlocked.

The judge ordered the jurors to continue their deliberations. Enough time and money had already been spent on this trial, he said. The jurors were to resolve the conflict and render a decision.

The jury deliberated thirteen days. On April 3rd, 1973 the foreman told the judge that the jurors had done the best they could. They were deadlocked. They could render a partial verdict, he explained, but they were unable to agree on all of the possible lesser charges.

The judge didn't want to hear the partial verdict. If there was disagreement only on the lesser charges it meant there had been unanimity for acquittal on the primary verdict. He declared a mistrial, dismissed the jury, and ordered that a second trial be held forthwith.

Defying the judge, the lone Black juror on the panel, Moses

Sheppard, and several of his fellow-veniremen, publicly revealed the details of the jury's deliberations. Later they signed affidavits affirming the truth of their account for defense counsel. The overwhelming majority of the jurors had not believed the main thrust of the prosecution.

The jury they said, had hung eleven to one for acquittal on the murder charge. The jury had found Ruchell Magee not guilty of aggravated kidnapping altogether, and had hung eleven to one for conviction on a lesser charge of simple kidnapping (forcibly taking a person from one place to another, but without intent to commit extortion).

It was an impressive verdict. It reflected the growing public concern about the prison system. It revealed the impact the mass movement for Angela's freedom had made. It was a testament to the uncompromising, heroic resistance of Ruchell Magee.

The State of California responded accordingly. On April 24th, 1973, California Attorney General Evelle Younger announced that Ruchell Magee would not be retried on the murder charge.

The reason, Younger explained, was that "the absence of the death penalty in California creates the absurd situation in which a murder conviction carries a lesser penalty than the aggravated kidnapping charge. . ."

Younger said Ruchell Magee would be retried for aggravated kidnapping instead, so the maximum penalty could be exacted, the jury's (unrecorded) verdict of acquittal notwithstanding.

On May 2nd, 1973 Ruchell's court-appointed lawyer, Robert Carrow, was sentenced to ten days in jail and a $1,000 fine for contempt of court by Judge Colvin.

As he imposed sentence the judge recalled that on February 22nd, Mr. Carrow had said, "Your Honor, I submit this trial is becoming a joke."

Judge Colvin said: "This goes beyond the bounds of advocacy . . . This was a willful, deliberate and calculated act to disrupt the orderly judicial process. . ."

The sentence was stayed ten days pending appeal.

ON MAY 7th, 1973 Ruchell Magee was flown from San Quentin to the San Francisco Hall of Justice in an army helicopter. He was brought to court bound in chains. He appeared before Judge

John Ertola, the Presiding Judge of the Superior Court of San Francisco. A new trial date was to be set.

Ruchell presented the judge a handwritten motion requesting a change of venue for his second trial. The judge retired to his chambers to consider the motion.

Newsmen reported hearing muffled laughter coming from the recesses of the inner sanctum.

Judge Ertola returned to the courtroom in five minutes. He granted Ruchell Magee's motion. The judge said he would announce the new trial site on May 15th. It was the first time in Ruchell's ten year struggle of filing appeals, writs, petitions and mandates that any judge had ever granted one of his motions.

2

The long hot summer of 1973 began in San Jose, California on Friday night, May 11th.

Henry Dillard was Black. He was thirty years old. He worked in a rubber factory. He was the father of five children. He was at home on Friday night, May 11th. The neighbors weren't sure who summoned the police to his home or why they came.

The police did come. They sealed off all the streets within a square mile of Henry Dillard's home. Then they surrounded his home. Henry had a rifle. The neighbors weren't sure whether Henry fired at the policemen. But the policeman fired at him. The living room walls were pock marked with bullets.

Henry was wounded in the initial barrage. He hid in an alcove near the front door. The policemen burst through the front door. They went careening into the back bedroom. Henry slipped out the front door. The neighbors helped him. They got him to a car. They tried to get him to a hospital. They didn't make it.

There was a police roadblock. Henry staggered from the car.

He was still holding the rifle. He fell onto the front lawn of somebody's house, spread-eagled on his back. As he fell the rifle flew out of his hand. It landed on the sidewalk about ten feet away. A policeman came up and stood over him and laid his chest open with two loads of buckshot.

A couple of weeks after Henry's killing we went to the San Jose City Council. Community groups that had struggled for justice in the murder of John Henry Smith pleaded with the city council to take some action. This was the seventh police killing of a Black or Brown person in San Jose in less than three years.

Jessie Dillard, Henry's father, addressed the council. He said he had been a construction worker in San Jose since 1946. "I built this town," he said, "and I ain't goin' to run away from it. . ."

Mr. Dillard continued. He'd been an active member of his union, the Laborer's Union, Local 270, and he was a member of the Community Alert Patrol, and he'd been a part of the Angela Davis Defense Committee.

Jessie Dillard told the council to take some action. Fire the officer who had killed his son. Bring the man to trial for murder.

The councilmen explained to Mr. Dillard that they couldn't take any action until all the facts were in.

Roberta Allen, Henry's widow, told the council about their son. He was three years old. He had already told her he was going to kill those policemen who had killed his daddy.

"What am I going to tell him?" she said. "What am I going to tell that boy? . . .

"I'm tired. I am tired. . .

"This time justice is going to be done."

3

Four days after the murder of Henry Dillard, the Ruchell Magee trial was ordered moved to San Jose.

"I had a strange feeling from the start we were going to wind up with this case," Sheriff Geary told reporters at a news conference at the main jail. "It's like coming full circle from the Angela Davis case," he said.

Sheriff Geary explained that Ruchell Magee would be housed in a third-floor maximum security cell in the main jail in San Jose—the same cell originally intended for Ms. Davis. Geary said he expected Magee to be ordered moved from San Quentin within a week. He also said that the Magee trial would probably take place in the same security-equipped courtroom used for the Davis trial.

Those who had been working to avenge the murder of Henry Dillard joined forces with those committed to winning the freedom of Ruchell Magee, and the two struggles converged . . .

This story does not yet have an end. It only has a beginning. The beginning is slavery. The end will be the day of freedom. The day of freedom is socialism. The events I have described here took place sometime toward the beginning of the end.

AFTERWORD TO THE
CORNELL PAPERBACKS EDITION

In June 1973, I went to see Ruchell Magee at the San Jose jail. He was dressed in an all-white prison uniform. His feet were shackled, and the chains ran up under his crotch and around his waist. One hand was chained to his waist; the other was free. Ruchell was of small stature. I found him soft-spoken. He was also sorrowful, desperately frustrated, cynical, and given to expressions of paranoia. These things seemed to me consistent with the conditions under which he existed. I spent much of the summer working on his case, and I continued to see Ruchell until December, when he refused a visit from me without explanation. I contacted many of the people in the San Jose and San Francisco communities who had worked on Angela's defense. We succeeded in securing an interview for him with a reporter from the *San Jose Mercury*. The story was sympathetic and prominently featured.

On May 10, 1974, Ruchell Magee pleaded guilty to aggravated kidnapping. On May 13, he asked the judge if he could withdraw the plea. Judge Ingram said Ruchell would have to prove that he "did not freely plead guilty." Ruchell said he made the plea under "conditions of harassment and intimidation." He was allowed to withdraw the plea. On August 14, 1974, after months of further delays, motions, and countermotions, Ruchell once again pleaded guilty to the kidnapping charge. On January 24, 1975, he was sentenced to life imprisonment. Ruchell Magee has been in prison now for a total of forty-two years. He is fifty-nine years old.

SOLEDAD BROTHER Fleeta Drumgo was among those who became known as the "San Quentin Six," accused of killing three guards and two inmates at San Quentin on the day George Jackson was killed. Others indicted by the Marin County grand jury were Hugo Pinell, John Larry Spain, Luis Talamantez, David Johnson, and Willie Tate. George Jackson was also indicted, posthumously. All were either African American or Latino. David Johnson and Willie Tate were among those brothers in B section who had signed the original affidavit exposing the guards' murder of Fred Billingslea back in February 1970. All were imprisoned in San Quentin's "Adjustment Center."

On December 11, 1974, Fleeta wrote to me:

> Comrade Bettina:
>   Revolutionary greetings, love and solidarity is extended to you and all the righteous from the brothers and myself here in triple max!
>   I was talking to FDJ [Fania Davis] yesterday and I told her that I wanted to write to you because I felt that by having a regular exchange [it] would help me counter the agony of this concrete and steel casket. . . .

Fleeta and I wrote to each other until his release.

Awaiting trial, the San Quentin Six filed a lawsuit in San Francisco's Federal District Court alleging that their confinement in San Quentin's Adjustment Center violated their human and constitutional rights. In mid-December 1975, while their trial was in progress, U.S. District Court Judge Alfonso Zirpoli ruled that confinement in San Quentin's Adjustment Center and the use of chains constituted "cruel and unusual punishment." Having personally toured the prison, Judge Zirpoli wrote in his decision that

> plaintiffs live in an atmosphere of fear and apprehension and are confined . . . without affirmative programs . . . and without possible rewards and incentives from the state which will give them some semblance of hope for transfer out of the Adjustment Center.
>   The continuous segregation of plaintiffs 24 hours a day except for meager out-of-cell movements . . . ; the unwarranted use of tear gas to remove plaintiffs from their cells; and the abhorrent and shocking use of excessive restraints in the combined form of hand manacles, waist belt, leg irons and neck chains for all of their out-of-cell movements constitutes cruel and unusual punishment in violation of the Eighth and Fourteenth amendments. . . .

Judge Zirpoli ordered the defendants in the suit—the previous director of corrections, Raymond K. Procunier; the present director, J. J. Enomoto; and the warden of San Quentin, R. M. Rees— to accord due process to the plaintiffs through a hearing to be held within fifteen days or to release the men into the main line of the prison population. San Quentin authorities refused to acknowledge or comply with Judge Zirpoli's order. Before their intransigence could be legally challenged, the trial of the San Quentin Six came to its dramatic conclusion.

The trial, conducted in Marin County, began in April 1975. It lasted sixteen months—the longest trial in California history to date. Before it began, authorities had been forced to release Willie Tate. He had completed his original indeterminate sentence of six months to ten years. He was released on $100,000 bail pending the San Quentin Six trial. The jury returned its verdict on August 13, 1976. Luis Talamantez, Fleeta Drumgo, and Willie Tate were found not guilty on all (forty-six) counts. David Johnson was convicted on a single count of simple assault. John L. Spain was convicted of first-degree murder. Hugo Pinell was convicted of felony assault.

Luis Talamantez was freed August 20, 1976, after eleven years in prison.

Fleeta Drumgo was freed on August 25, 1976, after nine years in prison.

David Johnson was released on probation August 31, 1976.

Fleeta took up residence in the Bay Area and began to pull his life together. It was not easy. Three years after his release, Fleeta Drumgo was shot to death on an Oakland street. His killer was never apprehended.

Johnny Spain was released from custody in the mid-1980s. Hugo Pinell remains in San Quentin.

THE ATTORNEYS in the Davis case resumed their respective practices. Leo Branton returned to Los Angeles, where he is in semi-retirement. Howard Moore, Jane Bond Moore (his wife, also an attorney), and their children left their family home in Atlanta and took up permanent residence in Berkeley. Doris Brin Walker continued in her law practice in San Francisco and in her active role in the National Lawyers Guild. Margaret Burnham returned to the East Coast. She became the executive director of the National Conference of Black Lawyers. Later relocating to Boston, Margaret was appointed a municipal court judge by Massachusetts' governor, Michael Dukakis. She served in this capacity from 1977 to 1983. She was the first African American woman ever appointed to the Boston courts. Margaret eventually went into private practice, specializing in civil rights law. She also teaches constitutional law at MIT.

FANIA DAVIS settled in Oakland after the trial and attended the University of California law school at Boalt Hall. She graduated with highest honors and established a law practice specializing in civil liberties, civil rights, and labor law. She also handles all of Angela's legal affairs. In 1997–98, Fania concluded negotiations with the City of Birmingham to designate the Davis family home a historical site. It is to become a Black women's community center. In September 1998 Fania Davis closed her law practice in order to devote her full time to pursuit of a doctorate at the California Institute of Integral Studies. Her dissertation is titled "African Spirituality and Social Transformation."

Mrs. Sallye Davis, widowed in 1982, maintained her residence in Birmingham for some years. After her retirement she spent several months of each year living with each of her four children and their respective families. She now lives with Angela.

VICTORIA MERCADO moved from Watsonville to the Bay Area and took up residence in Oakland. She remained close friends with Angela, Fania, Kendra, and Franklin. She worked in a warehouse, joined the International Longshoremen and Warehousemen's Union (ILWU), and became an activist in this most progressive of independent unions on the West Coast. Victoria was particularly committed to winning parity for women workers in this male-dominated industry, in job classifications, wages, and working conditions. She lived with her lover, an African American woman. In May 1982, Victoria was shot and killed by a man who ostensibly had come to purchase her car. Her lover was critically wounded. She and her lover were unarmed. No motive for the attack was ever established.

Victoria's funeral was held at St. Patrick's Church in Watson-ville, where she had grown up. Kendra was beside herself with grief. We embraced on the steps of the church. "I told her to let the stupid car go! I told her," she wept, rasping the words be-tween sobs. Angela leaned heavily on Franklin as she walked down the center aisle of the church, her tear-stained face ashen. Later we gathered at the Mercado family home. "She always wanted all of us to come home with her," Kendra said. "She al-ways wanted us to all be together with her, and meet her family."

MARY TIMOTHY, foreperson of Angela's jury, wrote to me after the trial. She asked if my husband and I would join her and her husband, Art, for dinner. Jack and I were delighted to accept her invitation. From this initial meeting, Mary and I became close friends. For several weeks after the trial we saw each other often, and she questioned me intensely about many aspects of the case. I was already working on this book and shared all my materials and the trial transcript with her.

Mary eventually wrote a book about her experiences on the An-gela Davis jury. It is called *Jury Woman*. The first edition was self-published; then the Reverend A. Cecil Williams of Glide Memo-rial Church in San Francisco issued a second edition under Glide's imprint. The book is still available in some libraries. Mary gave a detailed account of her view of the prosecution's case and of the jury's deliberations. Most revealing was the fact that at no time did anyone on the jury vote Angela guilty of any of the charges. One juror had voted "undecided" on the conspiracy charge in the first straw poll the jury took. *Jury Woman* is written in a clear, accessible style, as direct and candid as Mary herself always was.

Eleven years before the trial Mary Timothy had been diagnosed with breast cancer. She'd had one radical mastectomy, and then another four years later. Toward the end of the trial she was pretty sure the cancer had recurred. She said nothing about it. She felt the outcome of the trial, "with Angela's life in the balance," as she put it afterward, was too important to risk her removal from the jury. The verdict coincided with Mary's fiftieth birthday. Within a few weeks she was in surgery. The cancer had metasta-sized. With her skills as a research assistant at Stanford University's medical center, Mary innovated a combination of Western and alternative therapies. The cancer went into remission. She was able to go back to work. She lived for six more years.

Mary used to say that I was the first Communist she'd ever known. I used to say she was the first non-Communist (or Party ally) with whom I had had a committed relationship. Her friendship was a pivotal one in my life. She introduced me to football, P. G. Wodehouse, and Adrienne Rich. Feminism was new to both of us and we learned about it together. She often said: "I wish I'd known this stuff twenty years ago!" eyeing me pointedly. Mary encouraged me to write. She explained to me that there was nothing wrong with being a lesbian.

In the weeks before her death she systematically put her life in order, said good-bye to friends and co-workers by phone or in person. She gathered her immediate family around her. She included me in it. I was with her when she died on the afternoon of January 10, 1978, six months shy of her fifty-seventh birthday.

KENDRA AND FRANKLIN ALEXANDER stayed on in the Bay Area after Angela's trial, and eventually bought a home. It was in Berkeley, on 62nd Street above Telegraph Avenue. Kendra always said she wanted to live in Oakland, where there was a large Black community. She was chagrined that her address was in Berkeley. Actually, their home was on the Oakland border and became the community center Kendra had envisioned. A constant flow of family and friends were always welcomed. Kendra and Franklin raised a son, Jordan Winston Alexander. She used to say he "is the light in my eye."

After the trial, Kendra joined the staff of the Communist Party in Northern California and eventually became chair of the district. I attended countless meetings with her. She was an effective and tireless organizer. She was beloved in the Party and in her community, especially among the Black children who, as they put it, "hung out with Mrs. Alexander." Sometimes Kendra and I also hung out together, and she came to Pacific Grove, on the central California coast, where I lived with my lover and our three children. I had left the Party, but our friendship was not circumscribed by Party affiliation.

Franklin became a warehouseman at a major plant in Oakland and lent his considerable organizing talents and charisma to the ILWU. He remained a catalyst within the Black community, sparking a national campaign against apartheid in South Africa which preceded the U.S. student movement for "divestment" by a decade. (The divestment movement was a largely successful student campaign in the 1980s to force the universities to divest their funds from U.S. corporations with large investments in South Africa.)

In June 1992, Angela threw a big party at her home to celebrate Kendra and Franklin's twenty-fifth wedding anniversary.

A year later, in May 1993, Kendra organized a tribute to my father. It was to celebrate the fiftieth anniversary of the publication of his book *American Negro Slave Revolts*. It was held at the First Congregational Church in Oakland. Five days later, at home in Pacific Grove, I received a frantic telephone call late at night from my former husband, Jack Kurzweil. He was now living in Berkeley, too.

Jack said, "Kendra is dead." I couldn't believe it.

"What are you talking about?" I whispered into the phone.

Kendra was dead. She had burned to death in a fire in the family home. Franklin had gotten out, and their son, Jordan, had not been at home. Angela got on the line. She told me she had been driving nearby and seen the fire engines roaring up 62nd Street. She had never imagined it was Kendra and Franklin's home. Angela could hardly speak. She said: "For a long time we thought she must've gotten out. We thought maybe she was dazed or hurt, wandering in the neighborhood. We searched and searched."

All I could say was "Oh, my God!" over and over again, while my lover and my daughter hovered nearby.

A week later we attended the first of two memorial services. We were back at the same church in Oakland where Father's celebration had been held two weeks before. There in the front row were Kendra's mother, Mrs. Harris; her sister, Patti; her son, Jordan; and her husband, Franklin. And there were Angela and Fania, and Charlene Mitchell, who had flown in from New York. Hundreds of people had gathered in the church. Patti spoke tenderly of her sister. A childhood friend from L.A. spoke. Fania offered a testimonial. I read a poem. Angela delivered the eulogy. Franklin kissed and embraced each of us as we came forward and again as we left the podium. He pulled himself together to speak. A group sang of freedom. At the front of the church there was a giant photograph of Kendra. She was smiling and beautiful, her face all lit up with life.

Swamped with grief, Franklin and Jordan staggered back into their lives. Jordan graduated from high school two weeks after his mother's death. Franklin went back to work; talked about rebuilding the house; met with an architect and contractor. Aided by Angela and Fania and many, many other comrades and friends, Franklin still could not bear his grief. On the first anniversary of Kendra's death he took his own life.

A YEAR AFTER her acquittal Angela Davis attended the founding convention of the National Alliance Against Racist and Political Repression. We met in Chicago. It was June 1973. Several hundred people came, many of whom had been at the center of Angela's defense in their local communities. Angela was elected cochair with Carl Braden, a long-term white civil rights activist from Kentucky who headed the Southern Conference Educational Fund, and Burt Corona, a well-known Chicano activist from Los Angeles. The Reverend Ben Chavis, an African American civil rights activist from North Carolina, was elected vice chair and treasurer. Representatives from the American Indian Movement, the Puerto Rican Socialist Party, and the Asian American community served on its board of directors. Charlene Mitchell became its executive director. Angela, in concert with Charlene, Burt, Carl, and Ben, coordinated national campaigns to free specific prisoners, support in-prison movements, and stop police violence. The alliance was funded through private donations and by the honoraria Angela received for her speaking engagements. We celebrated the twenty-fifth anniversary of its founding in 1998.

Angela traveled the world in the first months of her freedom. Festooned with flowers, feted and honored, she assumed an unparalleled position as unofficial representative of oppressed peoples everywhere. I traveled with her on occasion in the United States. Audiences abounded with love for her, and Angela returned every gesture with patience and warmth. She inspired countless young African American women and men to get up in the morning, pull their lives together, do meaningful work, go to college, join the movement. I know this from dozens of personal stories that people have shared with me. She helped hundreds of individuals of all hues and persuasions, in very personal ways, responding to their letters, telephone calls, and encounters after her talks. Angela published her autobiography, *With My Mind on Freedom* (1974), and picked up the threads of her life personally and intellectually. She remained committed to the Communist Party until it became embroiled in a hopeless split after the collapse of the Soviet Union. She helped launch "Committees of Correspondence" with others in the Party as a vehicle to sustain a revolutionary presence on the American left.

Settling in the Bay Area, Angela joined the faculty at San Francisco State University, where she taught courses in African American studies, women's studies, and philosophy. She published two books that focused on developing a race and class consciousness within the women's movement: *Women, Race, and Class* (1982) and *Women, Race, and Culture* (1987). In 1990 she became a professor in the History of Consciousness program at the University of California, Santa Cruz. Her appointment caused considerable consternation in the governor's mansion, but the UCSC chancellor and the UC president held firm to principles of academic freedom, and the Santa Cruz community welcomed her with near unanimity. It is a sweet coincidence that Angela and I should find ourselves teaching on the same campus. Angela is the center of intellectual life for many of the graduate students of color, both in the History of Consciousness program and more generally on campus. When in 1995 she was awarded a President's fellowship by UC to fund research on women of color, the governor's office and the Regents again registered acute distress. Attempts to prevent her from receiving the award, however, were defeated.

Angela's most recent book, *Blues Legacies and Black Feminism* (1997), is the first sustained examination of the blues singers Gertrude "Ma" Rainey, Bessie Smith, and Billie Holiday. In reproducing their lyrics and providing historical context and critical analysis, Angela shows the combination of feminist and race consciousness that was particular to working-class Black women early in the twentieth century.

Angela continues to work for the freedom of political prisoners and to undo the racism of the criminal justice and prison systems. She was a primary organizer for a national conference at UC Berkeley in September 1998. Titled "Critical Resistance," it brought together three thousand scholars, activists, and former inmates to scrutinize the prison-industrial complex and propose initiatives for action.

I TEACH a seminar on African American women's history. In the winter of 1997 I invited Angela to come and participate in our discussion. Students had read her 1970 essay "The Black Women's Role in the Community of Slaves." She wrote it while she was in the Marin County jail and dedicated it to George Jackson. I assigned this essay because it is exemplary of African American women's history in its very origins and production, and because it signals the beginning of scholarly studies of Black women. Several minutes into the class, after introductions and a few comments from Angela, a student leaned across the table and said, "If it's not too personal a question, could you tell us why you were in prison?" Angela laughed with that distinctive giggle of hers. And then she told them the story in a gentle, quiet, easy manner.

Later, after Angela had left us, one of the students said: "It's really amazing to be in the presence of someone who has done so much with her life."

CPSIA information can be obtained
at www.ICGtesting.com
Printed in the USA
FFOW03n1802190215
11180FF